Foolproof
Card Tricks

FOR THE
AMATEUR MAGICIAN

KARL FULVES

Illustrations by
Joseph K. Schmidt

Dover Publications, Inc.
Mineola, New York

Bibliographical Note

This Dover edition, first published in 2009, is an unabridged repub-
lication in one volume of two previously published Dover books, *New
Self-Working Card Tricks* and *More Self-Working Card Tricks*, originally published in 2001 and 1984, respectively.

Library of Congress Cataloging-in-Publication Data

Fulves, Karl.
  Foolproof card tricks for the amateur magician / Karl Fulves. —
Dover ed.
      p. cm.
  ISBN-13: 978-0-486-47270-6
  ISBN-10: 0-486-47270-1
    1. Card tricks. I. Title.

GV1549.F825 2009
793.8'5—dc22

2009017594

Manufactured in the United States by RR Donnelley
47270105   2016
www.doverpublications.com

New
Self-Working
Card Tricks

INTRODUCTION

This collection of card tricks exemplifies the best in streamlined, easy-to-do modern tricks with playing cards. The reader who masters this material will have on hand a repertoire of tricks that can be accomplished under a variety of performing circumstances for audiences of all kinds.

Although the tricks are easy to do, there are a number of rules the reader should observe when using this material. If the magician has to stop and think about what comes next, he destroys the mystery he is trying to create. The rule that should guide all performance of magic tricks is that they should be practiced until they become second nature.

Some tricks are designed to be repeated, but they are few in number and are constructed in special ways to conceal their working. It is best to follow the rule that you should not repeat a trick for the same audience, even if asked. If the audience is insistent, switch to a similar trick that is done by a different method.

Tricks are designed to create a magical atmosphere. The method or secret behind the trick is a kind of nuts-and-bolts series of decidedly unmagical steps meant to always be concealed from audience view. Audiences don't really want to know how special effects are created to produce the wonders they see on the movie screen. In the same way, it is unwise to expose the secret to any trick. The best plan is to keep all magical secrets to yourself.

Patter and presentation suggestions are given for a number of tricks in this book, but each reader should decide what manner of presentation is best suited to his individual style. Choose different kinds of tricks to use in the same performance—for example, a card location, a poker deal and a mind-reading effect. As with patter stories, the more diverse the material, the more interest you generate.

For their assistance in compiling the material that has gone into this collection, I would like to thank Mel Bennett, Martin Gardner, Sam Schwartz and Joseph K. Schmidt. Finally, I would like to dedicate this book to my long-time editor, James T. Spero.

KARL FULVES

TABLE OF CONTENTS

IMPROMPTU CARD TRICKS

Impromptu tricks are an important category in the field of magic. The magician who has a repertoire of impromptu trickery can perform any time with borrowed objects. The tricks in this chapter are among the best that can be done with a borrowed deck of cards.

1. Silver Trap

Mike Rogers invented a visual method of revealing a chosen card. Besides the deck of cards, the magician uses two coins. One coin is placed on top of the deck, the other on the bottom. When the deck is thrown from hand to hand, a previously chosen card ends up trapped between the coins. The following routine is adapted from his original trick.

Method: Place the deck on the table. Grip it from above by the ends with the right hand. The right thumb releases the bottom card. Insert the first coin into the break, Figure 1.

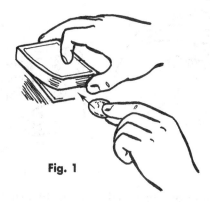

Fig. 1

Release about half the deck off the thumb. Insert the other coin into the break. Take the right hand away from the deck. At this point there is a coin about half way down in the deck and

1

another coin one card up from the bottom. The right hand now lifts off the top ten or twelve cards. Ask the spectator to mix them, note the top card and then replace the packet on top of the deck.

Say, "You've heard of metal detectors. These two coins contain a metal that is sensitive to the ink in playing cards." As you speak, lift up all the cards above the upper coin and place this packet on the table. Put the balance of the deck on top of it. Use care in handling the cards so that the coins stay in place. Take the coin off the top of the deck. Show it on both sides and place it on the table.

Say, "One coin is positive and one negative." Lift off all the cards above the other coin and place this packet on the table. Put the remainder of the deck on top of all. Take the coin that is now on top of the deck, show it on both sides and place it on the table.

Place the deck in the left hand while saying, "It's important that your card isn't on top of the deck." Remove the top card, show it and place it in the middle of the deck, and add, "Or the bottom." Remove the bottom card, show it and place it in the middle of the deck.

Say, "The reason it's important is that I'm going to place a coin on top . . ." Put one of the coins on top of the deck. Place the right middle finger on the coin. Put the thumb on the bottom of the deck, Figure 2.

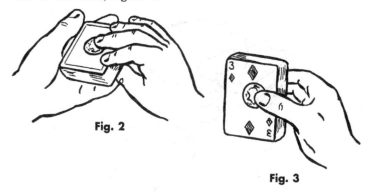

Fig. 2

Fig. 3

The right hand now turns palm-up. In the process, the deck turns face-up. Pick up the other coin with the left hand. Slide it under the right thumb as in Figure 3, while saying, ". . . and the other coin on the bottom."

Say, "We're ready for the coins to find your card." The crucial move now takes place. Contact the back card of the deck with the right first and third finger. Gently toss the deck from the right hand on the left hand. The back card of the deck is retained by the first and third fingers. The result is that this card, the chosen card, ends up trapped between the two coins, Figure 4.

Practice the trick with coins of various denominations. You may find, for example, that it is easier to do the trick with quarters than with dimes. Whichever coins works best for you, stay with that choice.

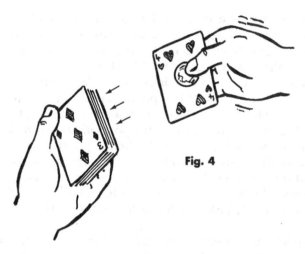

Fig. 4

2. Future Vision

The spectator shuffles face-up and face-down cards together. The cards are dealt off in pairs. If both cards are face-up, they go in one pile; if both are face-down, they go into a separate pile; all other pairs go into a discard pile. A prediction written before any cards have been dealt is opened. It correctly predicts that the spectator will have dealt four more face-down cards than face-up.

The trick is based on ideas of Stewart James and Bob Hummer.

Method: On a slip of paper write, "You will have four more face-down cards than face-up cards." Fold the slip of paper. Place it in a drinking glass for safekeeping.

Ask someone to shuffle the deck. When he is satisfied that the cards are well mixed, take back the deck. Hold the face-down deck in the left hand. Push cards into the right hand in twos and threes, apparently at random. Silently count the cards. When you have counted twenty-four cards, say, "I'll put the prediction in the middle of the deck for safekeeping." Place the prediction paper on top of the larger packet. Put the twenty-four card packet on top of all.

Your work has now been done. The rest of the trick takes place with the cards out of your hands. Ask the spectator to cut off about a third of the deck, turn it face-up and place it on the table.

When he has done this, ask him to cut off about half the remainder of the deck and place it face-down on top of the face-up packet. The number of cards is not important as long as the prediction slip is in this portion of the deck.

Ask him to pick up the remainder of the deck, turn it face-up and place it on top of all. At this point there is a face-up portion of the deck on top, then a face-down portion containing the prediction, than a face-up portion at the bottom. Ask the spectator to lift off all the cards above the prediction paper.

He places the prediction aside. Then he turns the cut portion over and riffle shuffles this packet into the balance of the deck. He may give the deck a few straight cuts and one more shuffle for good measure, just as long as he doesn't turn any cards over.

The spectator is asked to deal cards off in pairs. If a pair contains two face-up cards, he deals them into a heap on the left. If the pair contains two face-down cards, he deals them into a heap on the right. If the pair contains one face-up and one face-down card, he deals them into a discard heap off to one side.

He continues in this way until he has dealt through the deck. Have him count the cards in the face-up heap. Then have him read the prediction. Finally have him count the cards in the face-down heap to verify that your prediction was correct.

3. Three-Way Match

This effect, a card trick without cards, smacks of genuine mind-reading ability, but it is easy to do.

Method: A spectator is asked to think of a card. The magician thinks a bit and pretends to write down the name of a card on a piece of paper. Really he writes "AS," the abbreviation for the ♠A. "I'll label this paper with the number one," he says, but really he writes the number three. The paper is folded and dropped into a glass.

The first spectator tells the audience his card. Let us say he names the ♦5. The magician asks a second spectator to think of a card, any card except the ♦5. On a second slip of paper the magician pretends to write the second spectator's thoughts. In fact, he writes the first person's card, the ♦5. He says he will label this as paper number two, but really he writes the number one. The paper is folded and dropped into the glass.

The second spectator tells the audience his card. Let us say he names the ♣K. The magician says, "Now it's my turn to think of a card different from the other two. I'll write it down and ask *you* to guess my card." On a third slip of paper, the magician writes the second spectator's card, in this case the ♣K. He says he will label the paper number three but really he writes two. The paper is folded and dropped into the glass.

Say, "I've recorded my card, so I can't change my mind. I'll give you a hint and say I thought of an ace. Sir, would you care to guess which ace I have in mind?" Ask two or three people to guess. Almost always someone will name the ♠A.

Say, "I've done this mind-reading test many times, but this has been the most successful demonstration to date." Dump out the three papers and unfold them. They look like Figure 5. Hand paper number one to the first spectator. He verifies that you correctly guessed he would pick the ♦5. Give paper number two to the second spectator. He verifies that you were correct when you guessed he would pick the ♣K. Show the remaining paper to the audience as you say, "And you can give yourselves a round of applause for correctly guessing that I would pick the ace of spades."

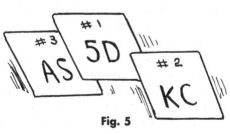

Fig. 5

It will happen sometimes that one of the two spectators will pick the ♠A. Stop the test right there and have the prediction verified on the spot.

4. Lucky Seven

Roy Walton invented a clever location of a chosen card using the number seven. The trick may be done with any borrowed deck.

Method: With the faces of the cards toward you, spread the cards from left to right between the hands. As you do, state that you are looking for a magic card that will help you with the trick. Beginning with the face card, silently count ten cards. Place this packet face-down on the table. Count ten more cards and place this packet on top of the tabled cards. Continue spreading cards between the hands until you come to the first seven-spot. Let's say this card is the ♠7.

Place the ♠7 face-up onto the tabled packet. Place the balance of the deck on top of all. The ♠7 is face-up and twenty-first from the face or bottom of the deck. Invite a spectator to lift off about eight or ten cards from the top of the deck, shuffle them and place them in front of him. We shall call this packet A. Lift off about two-thirds of the remainder of the deck. The number of cards is not important as long as this packet contains the reversed seven-spot.

There is still a small packet of cards in front of you, which we shall call packet B. Ask the spectator to lift off about half of the cards in packet B, shuffle them, note the bottom card and place this group of cards on top of packet A. Point out that the chosen card is between two shuffled groups of cards.

You are holding a packet that contains the reversed ♠7. Drop this packet on top of the small group of cards in front of you. This small group is what remains of packet B. Now place this combined packet on top of the cards in front of the spectator. The deck has been reassembled. Both the chosen card and the reversed ♠7 are at unknown locations in the deck.

Pick up the deck. Spread it between the hands until you get to the reversed ♠7. Cut this card on the top of the deck. Say, "I will use the power of seven to find your card." Flip the ♠7 face-down on top of the deck. Push over seven cards, counting aloud as you do so. Place the seventh card face-down on the table.

Push over seven more cards, counting aloud as before. Put the seventh card face-down on top of the tabled card. Count seven more cards off the top and put the seventh card on top of the tabled cards. By this process you have removed the seventh, fourteenth, and twenty-first cards from the top of the deck. Place the deck to one side. Pick up the tabled group of three cards. Unknown to the audience, the chosen card is on top of this packet. Say, "I'll really test the power of my lucky number now by counting to the seventh card." Count aloud as you transfer six cards from the top to the bottom of the packet. When you get to the number seven, place that card on the table. Ask the spectator to name his chosen card. Turn over the tabled card to reveal that the power of the number seven enabled you to find the spectator's card.

5. Heavyweight

Gamblers are reputed to be able to cut any desired number of cards. It can be done by counting, but there is a quicker way. The secret is to gauge the number of cards by weight. The magician offers to demonstrate how it's done. Given two packets of unequal size, he discards cards from the heavier packet until he thinks the packets are of equal weight. When the two packets are checked, they are exactly equal.

Of the many variations of this popular trick in circulation, this one, by Nick Trost and Mike Rogers, is one of the best.

Method: Make sure the borrowed deck contains exactly fifty-two cards. Without calling attention to the number of cards dealt, push off ten cards and place this packet on the table. Then push off nine cards and place this packet next to the first. Finally, push off eight cards and place this packet alongside the other two.

Say, "Gamblers can always cut off an exact number of cards because they know how much the cards weigh. You try it. These three packets are unequal in weight. Pick up two of them and try to guess which is heavier." Even if he is successful, the spectator will realize that it is not easy to detect the difference in weight between two packets of nearly equal size.

Now comes the secret to the trick. While the spectator tries his hand at guessing which is the heavier packet, secretly glimpse the bottom card of the portion of the deck you still hold in your hand. Let us say this card is the ♦4. Drop this packet on top of the ten-card packet, then this combined packet on top of the nine-card packet, then this on top of the eight-card packet. Pick up the assembled deck and place it in the left hand.

Invite the spectator to cut off about a third of the deck. The number is not important just as long as it is less than twenty-five cards. When he has done this, say, "If we wanted to know how many cards you cut off, I could count your cards, or I could count my cards and subtract from fifty-two. I don't want you to think I would resort to a method like that, so I'm going to use about half the deck."

Count twenty-five cards into a heap on the table. Put the rest of the deck to one side as it will not be used. Place the twenty-five card packet face-up in your left hand. Have the spectator place the other packet face-up in your right hand. Pretend your hands are a balance scale. Lower your right hand and simultaneously raise your left hand as if weighing the cards. Then raise your right hand and lower your left.

Say, "Too many cards over here." Thumb off one or two cards on the left. Let them fall to the table. Repeat the balance scale bit. Shake your head and say, "Still too many." Thumb off one or two more cards from the larger packet. Continue doing this until you see your key card, the ♦4 in our example. Thumb off this card from the larger packet. Move your hands up and down as before, and smile and say, "Now they're balanced."

Give the spectator one packet. You and he deal simultaneously from your respective packets to the table, matching each other card for card. You will each deal exactly the same number of cards.

6. Double Find

This trick is based on an idea of Walt Rollins. Two packets of cards are placed on the table. One spectator looks at a card in one packet. Another spectator looks at a card from the second packet. Each person cuts his packet several times. The magician does not know either card, nor does he know their locations, but he adjusts each packet so that when cards are dealt simultaneously off the top, the two chosen cards show up at the same time.

Method: Without calling attention to the number of cards you use, push off ten cards and hand them to a spectator to shuffle. Push off another group of ten cards and hand them to a second spectator to shuffle.

Take back the first group. As you place it in your left hand, glance at the bottom card and remember this card as your first key. Take the second group, remember the bottom card as your second key, and place this group on top of the first.

Hand the combined packet to the first spectator. Ask him to give it several straight cuts. When he has done this, take back the packet. Push off ten cards without reversing their order. Give this packet to the first spectator. Give the remaining group of ten cards to the second spectator.

Each person is invited to look at and remember the top card of his packet. Then each person gives his packet several straight cuts. Take the first spectator's packet. Remark that you will look through it and try to get an impression of his chosen card. Spread the cards so you can see the faces. Locate the key card and cut it to the top of this packet. Put the packet on the table.

Take the packet from the second spectator. Spot the key card in this packet and cut it to the top. Put the packet on the table alongside the first. Ask each person to name his card. Say, "I've adjusted the cards so that your two cards will show up at the same time." Deal cards off the tops of the two packets simultaneously. The chosen cards will show up at the same time.

7. A Card Moves Up

This is an excellent opening trick to use when performing with a borrowed deck of cards. After the deck has been shuffled by a spectator, the magician takes it behind his back "to better focus on the cards." He then says, "I'm going to focus on a particular card, a card with mysterious powers, the two of diamonds. Right now it's—let's see—it's twentieth from the top of the deck."

He brings the deck into view and gives it a shake. "By shaking the deck a certain way, the two of diamonds moves up. Now it's fifteenth from the top." The deck is shaken back and forth two or three more times. "Now it's twelfth, eighth, sixth. I'll stop right here. If I tap the deck like this, the two should turn over.

Let's see how well it followed instructions." The magician counts down to the sixth card. It is the ♦2 and it is face-up.

Method: When the shuffled deck is handed to you, grip it at about the midpoint as shown in Figure 6, so that about half of the face card is exposed. State that you will do the trick blindfolded. Close your eyes and put your right hand over your eyes, but not so tightly that you can't see straight down. The audience thinks your eyes are closed, but really you have focused your gaze in the vicinity of your left hip. Do not move your head as you shift your gaze downward.

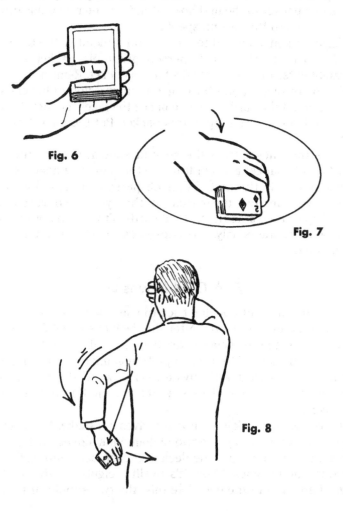

Fig. 6

Fig. 7

Fig. 8

You are going to put the deck behind your back. As the left hand swings down to the left hip, the hand will naturally turn to a palm-down condition, Figure 7. If you look between the left arm and the body, Figure 8, you will clearly see the face card of the deck.

Practice this maneuver so that the left hand does not have to pause as it swings to the side and then behind the back. This devious method of secretly glimpsing a card was devised by Bob Ostin. Properly done, it cannot be detected.

As you patter about the ♦2 (or whatever the face card happens to be), secretly turn it face-up and place it on top of the deck. Then transfer five more cards from the bottom to the top of the deck. The reversed ♦2 is now sixth from the top. Bring the deck into view.

Shake the deck to start the ♦2 on its journey. Remark that the ♦2 is twentieth from the top, now fifteenth, twelfth, eighth, and finally sixth. Tap the deck to turn the magic card face-up. Then count to the sixth card (or have the spectator do it) to reveal that the ♦2 is indeed sixth from the top and also face-up.

PREPARED MAGIC

Some tricks require a small investment in time to prepare the apparatus. Such tricks can't be done on the spur of the moment, but the advantage gained is that the magician has a head start on the audience. These tricks are strong in effect and have well-concealed methods.

8. Odd or Even?

This is a clever twist on a classic prediction. Three heaps of cards are placed on the table. The magician says, "One of these heaps is even. The other two are odd. In a moment I'm going to ask you to choose one of these heaps. First I want to show you this sealed envelope. Inside is some writing that predicts which heap will be chosen." The spectator chooses any heap. No matter which heap is chosen, the prediction is shown to be correct.

Method: Cut a piece of paper to a size that just fits the inside of the envelope you are going to use. On the paper write, "You will pick the seven group." The prediction is shown in Figure 9.

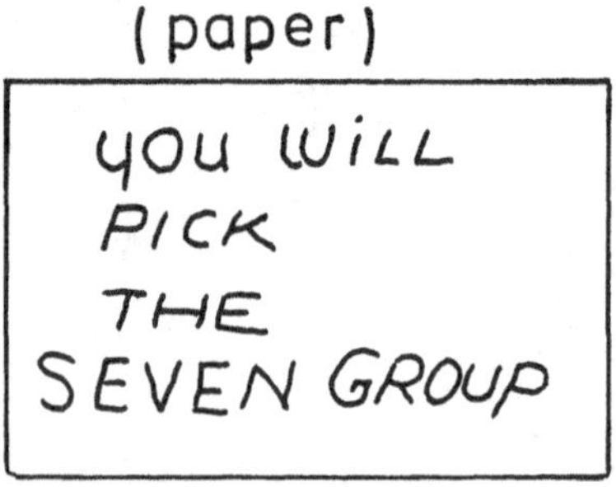

(paper)

you will
pick
the
seven group

Fig. 9

It is important that the "S" in "Seven" be to the left of the other words as shown in the diagram. The reason will become clear in a moment. Place the sealed envelope containing the prediction in your pocket. Place three sevens on top of the deck. This completes the preparation.

To present the trick, place the deck below the level of the tabletop. Push off the top three cards. You don't want the audience to see exactly how many cards you use to form each packet, so make sure the packet is carefully squared before placing it face-down on the table.

Push off a group of four cards. Square the packet and place it on the table alongside the first packet. Finally, push off a group of seven cards. Place this packet on the table. The three packets are shown in Figure 10. They are shown with the cards

Fig. 10

spread so the reader can see the arrangement. In performance, each group would be carefully squared.

After you have placed the three groups of cards on the table, remark that one group is even and the other two odd. Display the prediction and place it in plain view.

Ask the spectator to choose a group of cards. Emphasize that he can change his mind. The procedure you will follow depends on the packet the spectator chooses. If he chooses the group of seven cards, count each of the other two groups without showing their faces. Then put these cards on top of the deck.

Count the cards in the chosen group. There will be seven cards. Cut open the right end of the envelope, Figure 11, remove the prediction and show it to be correct.

If he picks the group with the three sevens, pick up the other two groups, putting one on top of the other. Spread them face-up to show eleven random cards. Put these cards on top of the deck. Turn over the cards in the chosen group, revealing three sevens. Cut open the envelope as shown in Figure 11, remove the prediction and show it to be correct.

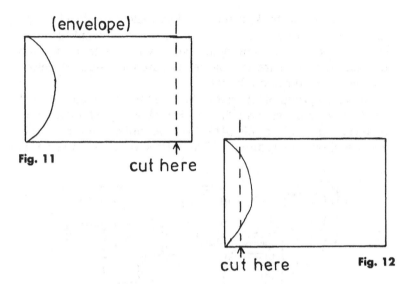

Fig. 11   cut here

cut here   **Fig. 12**

If he picks the group containing four cards, you would appear to be in trouble. This is where the twist comes into play. It is based on an idea of Richard Himber's. Deal each of the other groups face-down, showing two packets with an odd number of cards. Then count the chosen packet, showing an even number of cards.

Fig. 13

you will pick the even group

Cut open the envelope from the opposite side, Figure 12, cutting between the "S" and the "e" in the word "Seven." Drop the cut-off end of the envelope into the pocket. Show the prediction, Figure 13. It correctly states that the spectator would pick the even group.

9. Lies, All Lies

The premise of this trick is offbeat and entertaining. It is an adaptation of a principle devised by Stewart James.

Method: Place nine playing cards in a heap on the table. Put any ten-spot on top of the heap. We will assume this card is the ♣10. Fold a one-dollar bill in quarters and place it on top of the ♣10. Place the rest of the deck on top of all. Case the deck until the time of performance.

To do the trick, remove the deck from the card case and place it face-down on the table. Lift off the top half, shuffle it and hand it to the spectator. Ask him to think of a number between one and ten, fan the cards so he can see the faces, and remove any card of the chosen value. If he thinks of the number two, for example, he would remove any two-spot. Ask him to remember it and place it on top of the heap. Take the heap from him. Pick up the other half of the deck (the packet containing the dollar bill) and place this packet on top of all.

As you say, "George Washington is a hero of mine. I carry his picture wherever I go," spread the cards between the hands until you get to the folded dollar bill. Cut the deck and complete the cut so the dollar bill is on top of the deck. Unfold the bill. Point to the picture of Washington while saying, "George Washington couldn't tell a lie. In this trick I'm required to tell two." Place the dollar bill to one side.

Push off the top ten cards without reversing their order. Place this packet on the table. Put the rest of the deck on the table near the spectator. Turn your head to one side and say, "While I look away, deal a group of cards off the top of the deck equal to the value of your card. In other words, if you picked a three, deal a heap of three cards to the table."

When the spectator has done this, turn and face him. Pick up his dealt packet and place it on top of your ten-card packet. "The first lie is that you picked a ten." As you speak, deal ten cards off the top of the packet into a heap on the table. Drop the balance on top. "I'm required to say it again. You picked a ten." Deal ten cards off the top of the packet.

"Two negatives always produce a positive. Here's the positive." Tap the packet you just dealt. "I said ten, and it is a ten." Turn up the top card of the tabled packet. It will be a ten.

Holding a small group of cards in your hand say, "Truth has a

way of rising to the top. What card did you pick?" The spectator names his card. Turn up the top card of the packet in hand.
It will be the chosen card.

On occasion, the spectator will in fact have picked a ten-spot
even though you asked him to choose a number *between* one
and ten. You will know this because the top card of the dealt
packet is not a ten. In this case, say, "Not a ten. The ten is here."
Turn the packet over to show a ten at the face. Then say,
"George Washington must have intervened so I would not be
required to lie. You did pick a ten after all." Turn over the top
card of the packet in hand to reveal the chosen card.

10. Mental Math

Three spectators are needed to perform this puzzling excursion
into higher mathematics. They freely concoct three numbers,
each of three digits. The numbers are added to produce a four-
digit total. The magician causes four cards to invisibly jump
from the deck into the card case. When the four cards are
shown, their values exactly match the numbers in the total.

Method: Place an ace, a three and a pair of sevens in the card
case. Close the flap and drop the case into your pocket. If no
card case is available, you can seal these four cards in an envelope or carry them in your wallet.

When ready to perform "Mental Math," have the deck shuffled. Then remove an ace and place it face-down on the table.
Remove a two and place it face-down on the ace. In like manner,
remove any three through nine in mixed suits, one card at a
time and in numerical order, and place each card in turn onto
the tabled cards. The order of the cards from the top down is
9-8-7-6-5-4-3-2-A. Do not show the faces of the cards as you deal
them into a tabled heap.

As you remove the cards, remark that you want to try an
experiment in higher mathematics: "Let's mix the cards up a
bit." Hold the packet in the left hand. Push off the top two cards
without disturbing their order. Place them on the table.

Do the same thing with each of the next three pairs. Finally,
place the remaining single card on top of all. The order of the
cards from the top down is A-3-2-5-4-7-6-9-8. Pick up the packet.
Deal three heaps of cards, dealing from left to right a card at a
time. You will have three heaps of three cards each.

The first heap contains the A-5-6. Give these cards to spectator A. The next heap contains the 3-4-9. Give these cards to spectator B. The last heap contains the 2-7-8. Give these three cards to spectator C.

Ask each spectator to mix his cards and select one. Ask A to name the value of his card, keeping in mind that the ace has a value of one. Say he picked the 5. Write it on a piece of paper. Ask B to name the value of the card he picked. Let's say he picked the 3. Write 3 on the pad to the right of the 5. Let's say that spectator C picked the 8. Write 8 on the pad to the right of the other two numbers. In this way you have formed the number 538.

Have A, B and C each pick a card from the two remaining cards that each person holds. Say this new number is 192. Write it under the first number. Finally, have each person call out the value of their final card. In our example this number would be 647. Write it under the other two. Draw a line below the numbers and add them. The result is 1377 as shown in Figure 14.

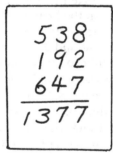

Fig. 14

Remove the card case from your pocket. Remark that there is a new type of computer that gets answers by teleportation. Squeeze the sides of the card case as you shake it from side to side. Nothing appears to have happened. Slowly release pressure. A rattling sound will be heard from inside the card case. Open the card case and withdraw the cards one at a time. Arrange them in a row to show that they match the total of 1377.

11. Two by Two

This trick was devised by the author. While showing six pairs of cards, the magician remarks, "It is said that Noah of ark fame collected animals two by two. At first, things were a bit disorganized." The cards in each pair are random cards. No two cards match. The magic word is spoken. The cards are again dealt out two at a time. Now each pair consists of matching cards.

Method: Arrange twelve cards in mixed suits in the following order from top to bottom: 6-10-3-K-5-6-2-3-K-5-10-2. Hold this packet face-down in the left hand. Push the top two cards off with the left thumb. Without reversing their order, take them with the right hand, turn them face-up to show two cards that don't match, then turn them face-down and place them on the table to the left.

Push over the next two cards. Take them with the right hand. Show the faces and drop them into a heap on the right. Push over the next two cards. Take them with the right hand. Show the faces and drop them on the heap that is to the left.

Show the next pair of cards and drop them onto the heap on the right. Show the next pair and drop them on the heap to the left. Show the last pair and drop them on the heap to the right. Place the right-hand heap on top of the left.

As you show the cards remark, "When the animals were gathered and taken aboard the ark, there was a certain amount of confusion, but Noah put things right very easily." Openly transfer the bottom card of the packet to the top. Snap the fingers. Then deal pairs face-up off the top to show that the cards suddenly match.

12. The Card Castle

Sometimes the introduction of an offbeat or unusual piece of apparatus will add to the novelty of a card trick. In this trick, an adaptation of a brilliant trick invented by Al Leech, the magic occurs inside a card castle.

Method: The castle is constructed by placing four cards in a row on the table and connecting them with tape, Figure 15. Fold the apparatus to form a box, Figure 16. Use tape to connect the

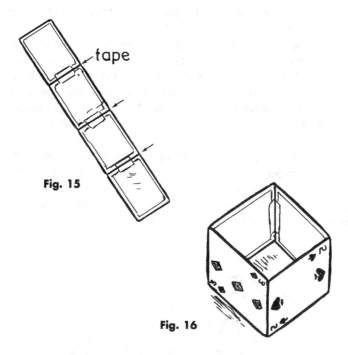

Fig. 15

Fig. 16

first and fourth cards together. This completes the assembly. The apparatus folds flat and may be carried in your pocket.

You will also need a deck of cards and two jokers. To present the trick, say, "This is a story about an ancient castle and the royalty that called the castle home. Every castle had its court jester. This one had two." Remove the two jokers and place them to one side for the moment. "And here's the royalty." Remove the kings and queens from the deck.

"The court jesters liked to hide in unexpected places." Pick up the deck with one hand and the two jokers with the other. Place this apparatus behind the back or below the near edge of the table. When the cards are out of sight of the audience, place one joker face-up under the top card of the deck. Put the other joker face-up on the bottom of the deck. Bring the deck back into view, but take care to keep the cards squared so as not to reveal the whereabouts of the two reversed cards.

Say, "Two members of the royal family wanted to sneak away for the day. Pick a king and queen to represent the couple." Let us say the spectator chooses the ♣K and ♥Q. Place these two cards face-down on the table in a squared packet. Drop the deck on top of them.

Turn the deck face-up, taking care not to expose the reversed jokers. Hold the deck by the ends. Slide the back card away from the deck, Figure 17, and say, "We'll use this card to indicate where the deck is to be cut." Hand this card to the spectator. Ask him to slide it into the middle of the deck at right angles, Figure 18. While he does this, hold the deck to keep the cards square.

Place the deck on the table. Lift off the cards above the right-angle card, Figure 19, and place this packet on the table. Complete the cut by placing the balance of the cards on top of all. Carefully square the deck and turn it face-down. The cards chosen by the spectator are now in the middle of the deck.

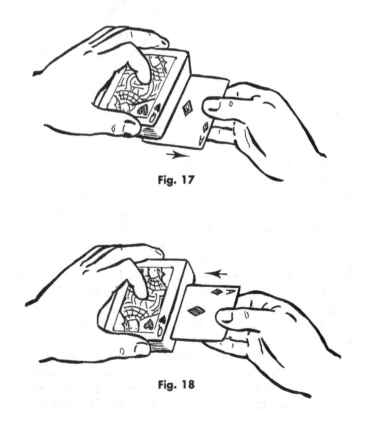

Fig. 17

Fig. 18

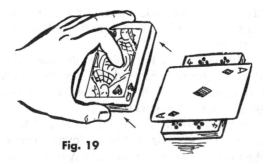

Fig. 19

"The royal couple hid out in the castle. Rents being what they are these days, I don't have a real castle, but I did bring along this architect's rendition." Remove the card castle from your pocket. Open it out (see Figure 16 above), lower it over the deck and say, "The royal couple didn't count on the fact that the jesters were lurking about. It took about ten seconds for them to find the couple."

Snap the fingers. Lift off the card castle and place it aside. Spread the deck face-down on the table. The two jokers are face-up in the middle and there are two cards between them. Remove all four cards. Turn them over in a spread or fanned condition to reveal that the jokers caught the royal couple.

See also the trick called "Paradox" in the next chapter (see p. 29) for another use of the principle behind this trick.

13. The Card Detective

Removing the ♣8 from the deck, the magician remarks that this card represents a detective. "The card detective always gets his man. Let me show you how."

A spectator picks two cards by a random process. Let us say that one card is a five and the other a diamond. "This means that the detective is going to be on the lookout for the five of diamonds." The spectator cuts the detective card into the deck. When the deck is examined, the detective card is right next to the ♦5.

Method: To prepare, remove the ♣8 and place it aside for the moment. Cut the ♦5 to the bottom of the deck. Place any other five-spot eighth from the top of the deck, and any diamond ninth from the top. To complete the preparation, place the ♣8 on the bottom of the deck. Before doing the trick, check that all the cards are in place: There is a five-spot eighth from the top, any diamond ninth, the ♦5 second from the bottom of the deck, and the ♣8 on the bottom.

To present the card detective, hold the deck face-down in the left hand. Remove the bottom card and say, "Sherlock Holmes was a famous detective. His calling card was the eight of clubs." Place the ♣8 in front of the spectator.

Put the deck face-down on the table. Cut off the top two-thirds. Hold this packet in the left hand. Invite the spectator to insert the ♣8 into the packet about halfway down from the top, Figure 20. Allow the detective card to protrude from the front of the packet for about half its length.

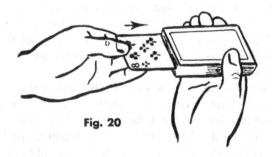

Fig. 20

Say, "This card is an eight, so we'll count eight cards." Count eight cards off the top one at a time into a heap on the table. Call this packet A. Deal each of the remaining cards down to the ♣8 into a separate heap alongside the first, counting them aloud as you deal. Call this packet B. The situation is shown in Figure 21.

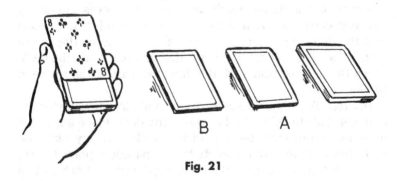

Fig. 21

While saying, "Sherlock was out of town when the crime occurred," place the face-up ♣8 on top of the other half of the deck (the packet that was the original bottom half of the deck, the far right packet in Figure 21). Cut this packet and complete the cut. Then place the cards in hand on top of the packet that contains the ♣8. Give this large packet a cut and complete the cut.

Say, "The culprit was identified by a composite sketch," and turn up the top card of packet A. "He was a five-spot." Turn packet B over so it is face-up. Point to the face card and say, "And a diamond. Sherlock was informed that he should be on the lookout for the five of diamonds."

Snap the fingers. Spread the large packet face-down on the table. The ♣8 will be face-up. Remove it and the card that is face-to-face with it. Turn that card over to reveal the ♦5 as you say, "Sherlock always gets his man."

14. Fooling the Experts

William Alstrand fooled a number of card experts with a trick based on a simple but well-concealed bit of subterfuge.

Method: To perform this version, secretly put a pencil dot or other small mark at diagonally opposite corners of a card, Figure 22. Let us say this card is the ♦7. Place it anywhere in the deck.

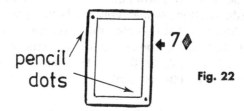

pencil
dots

Fig. 22

The preparation will not interfere with the performance of other card tricks. When ready to perform this trick, cut the ♦7 to a position fourth from the top of the deck. Place the deck on the table in front of the spectator and say, "I don't want to touch the deck. Please cut it into two heaps." When the spectator has done this, say, "Would you select either heap? You have an absolutely unrestricted choice. There is no sleight of hand. The heap you take is the one you keep."

The deceptiveness of this trick lies in your opening remarks. When the deck has been cut into two heaps, if he takes the top half of the deck, ask him to cut the other half into three heaps. If he picks the bottom half of the deck, ask him to cut that half into three heaps.

When the spectator has done this, say, "Deal one card from the packet you hold onto the top of each of the three heaps." When this has been done, say, "Now look at the top card of your packet. Remember this card. Place it on top of the center heap. Place one of the end heaps on top of the center heap, and one below." When this has been done, say, "To make sure your card really is lost in the pack, shuffle the two halves of the deck into one another."

After this has been done, the audience must agree that no one could know the location of the chosen card. This is true, but you are about to make it seem that its location is a foregone conclusion. Take the deck from the spectator and say, "All things come in threes, and that is the case with this trick. If we want to find your card, we deal three heaps like this." Deal a heap of eight or nine cards, then a second heap of eight or nine cards. Be on the lookout for the pencil-dotted card. If it hasn't shown up yet, deal a third heap and continue dealing until the marked card shows up. Stop the deal at that point. Ask the spectator to name his card. Turn up the pencil-dotted card and it will be the chosen card.

If the marked card shows up before you start the third heap, stop the deal at this point and put the balance of the deck aside. Pick up the heap that contains the chosen card on top. Deal it into three heaps. Ask the spectator to name his card. Pick up the packet that contains the marked card and turn over that card to reveal the chosen card.

15. Cloned Thoughts

A pencil-dotted card is used in this trick also, so one may use this one as a follow-up to "Fooling the Experts." The pencil-dotted card can be anywhere in the deck at the start. We will assume it is the ♦7.

Method: Ask the spectator to give the deck a shuffle. When he has done this, spread the cards face-down on the table saying, "While I turn my head aside, I'd like you to remove four or five cards like this." Slide four or five cards out of the deck. Make sure that one of them is the pencil-dotted card.

Say, "Then I'd like you to mix them like this," and give the packet a quick shuffle. "And then I'd like you to pick one card out of the group, look at it and put it back anywhere." As you speak, remove the pencil-dotted card. Don't look at it. Just drop it on top of the packet.

"Finally, I'd like you to shuffle the packet so even you don't know where your card is." Pantomime an overhand shuffle, but don't actually mix the cards. Drop the packet on top of the deck. The pencil-dotted card is now the top card of the deck. Turn your head aside while the spectator removes some cards, chooses one and shuffles it back into the packet. Turn and face the audience again. Ask him to drop his packet on top of the deck. He then gives the deck two or three straight cuts.

Say, "Now I'm going to pick a card, but I don't want to pick the same card you did. Take the deck and cut your card to the bottom of the pack." After the spectator does this, direct him to place the deck face-down on the table. Remove the top card of the deck and place it in your left hand. Remove the next card and the next, placing each card on top of the cards in the left hand. Continue doing this until the pencil-dotted card shows up. Because of the above handling, the pencil-dotted card will show up within the first five cards you deal. Place this card on top of the packet in the left hand.

"That should be enough cards to choose from." Spread the packet face-down between the hands. "With the cards face-down like this, any card can represent any other card. I think I'll pick the one in the middle." Tap the back of the middle card but don't remove it from the packet. Square up the packet and drop it on top of the deck. Give the deck a straight cut.

"Now comes the hard part. I'll look at the *faces* of the cards and pick out the card I just chose from the *back*." Turn the deck face-up. Spread the cards from left to right between the hands so you alone can see the faces. Find the ♦7. The card just to the left of this card is the card chosen by the spectator. Remove it and put the rest of the deck aside.

Remark, "You chose your card by looking at the face. I chose my card by looking at the back. What card did you pick?" The spectator names his card. Turn your card over as you reply, "So did I."

TESTS FOR ESP

Many of the people who believe in extrasensory perception suspect that they too have similar skills. The tricks in this chapter appear to test a spectator's psychic abilities.

16. Brainchild

This trick was devised by the author.

Method: Using any borrowed deck of cards, remove the ace through six in mixed suits and arrange them in this order from the top down: A-6-5-2-4-3. Do not let the spectator see the arrangement. Simply remove the cards from the deck in the above order and place them in a face-down heap on the table. Remove a second group of six cards in mixed suits, but arrange them in this order: 6-2-3-5-4-A.

Place one group on top of the other. Hand the packet of twelve cards to the spectator. Look through the deck and find either of the remaining four-spots. Let's say this card is the ♣4. Remove it and place it face-down on the table without showing the face. The rest of the deck is placed to one side.

Ask the spectator to put his initials on the back of the ♣4. Explain that a signed card can't be switched or tampered with, and say, "Now for the test. I'd like you to put the packet behind your back so I can't have any clues as to the order of the cards. Please cut the packet and complete the cut. Good. Now cut it once more and complete the cut. And finally, give it one more cut and complete the cut.

"Each cut may appear to be random, but sometimes we are guided by design and purpose. Take the top card off the packet and place it sight unseen on top of the deck. Now take the signed card and place it on top of the packet. In this way we replace a random card with a signed card.

"There is just one more instruction. Once again I'm going to ask you to give the packet three complete cuts."

26

When this has been done, the spectator brings the packet into view. Take it from him. Deal the top six cards in a face-down row on the table. Then deal the remaining six cards in a row below the first row and say, "If you cut one card above or one card below the point you chose for the cut, then the order of the cards would be shifted forward or back. But this is the order you chose. Let's see the result." Turn up all the cards in place except the signed card. The result may look like Figure 23.

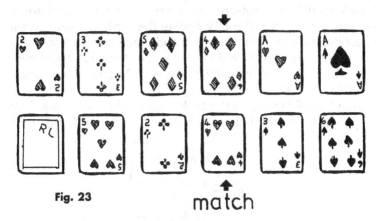

Fig. 23   **↑ match**

Point out that two cards (and only two) are in the same position in each row, i.e., the four in the upper row is in a position corresponding to the four in the lower row. Remark, "I wonder if this was by chance or design. Please turn over the signed prediction card." The spectator does and it is a matching four. On occasion, the spectator may exchange the signed card for one of the fours. Point up the amazing coincidence.

17. Do You Have ESP?

This is a modified version of an innovative trick invented by Norman Houghton. Removing a small packet of cards from an envelope, the magician says, "Psychic investigators use a group of cards like these to test a person's ESP ability. One of these cards is different from the others." The cards are spread face-up. The spectator picks one card. It can be any card in the packet. There is no force. Let's say the spectator picks the ♠6.

Say, "Good. I said that one card stands out from the rest. Let's see if you picked the right one." The remaining cards in the packet are turned over. They are all shown to be red-backed. The chosen ♠6 is turned over. It is the only blue-backed card in the packet.

Method: Remove five cards of mixed suits from a red-backed deck and five from a blue-backed deck. Make sure that all ten cards are different from one another. Arrange them so the colors alternate. Place them in the envelope.

At the time of performance, slide the cards out of the envelope with the faces toward the audience. Invite a spectator to engage in a test of ESP ability. Spread the cards face-up. Ask the spectator to look over the cards and name one that seems to stand out. Whichever card is named, cut the packet and complete the cut so that the named card is at the face of the packet. Say this is the ♠6.

Deal the ♠6 face-up to the table. Square the packet and hold it face-up in the left hand. Push over the face card, Figure 24.

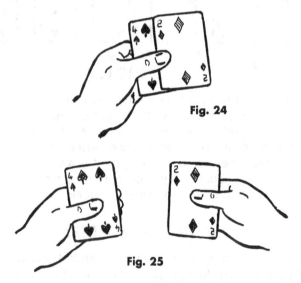

Fig. 24

Fig. 25

Take this card in the right hand, Figure 25. Now turn both hands palm down, Figure 26. This shows the backs of the cards. Say the backs are red. Turn the hands palm-up again. You are back to Figure 25. Take the face card of the left-hand packet onto the card in the right hand, Figure 27. Hold them in a squared condition and place this pair of cards face-up on the table.

Repeat this same sequence with three more pairs of cards.

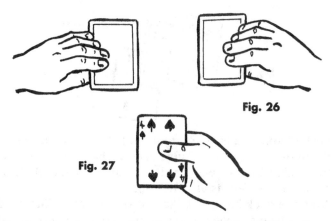

Fig. 26

Fig. 27

The illusion that is created by the above display is that all cards are red-backed. There will be eight cards on the table in a squared packet and one card in the hand. Turn over the card in hand to show the back. Turn this card face-up and drop it onto the tabled packet. Then turn the squared packet face-down. You have shown eight cards, all of which apparently have red backs.

While saying, "What makes your card different is this," pick up the chosen card and turn it over to reveal that it has a blue back. This comes as quite a surprise. Return the cards to the envelope before the audience asks to see them.

18. Paradox

"Paradox" is based on a clever trick invented by Al Leech. The spectator places a face-down card between two face-up cards. Then he picks a card, let's say the ♣3 and returns it to the deck. The card between the face-up cards is turned over. It is the ♣3.

Method: Remove the red fours and place them face-up on the table. Invite the spectator to shuffle the remainder of the deck and give it a straight cut.

Say, "I'd like you to try your hand at predicting a card. Remove any card from the deck. Don't look at it. We're going to place it between the fours for the moment." Whatever face-down card the spectator picks, slide it between the fours as shown in Figure 28.

Square up the three cards. Place them on top of the deck and say, "I'm going to cut them into the deck for safekeeping, but I don't want anyone to see where." Place the deck below the edge

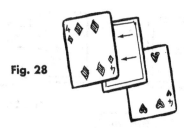

Fig. 28

of the tabletop so it is out of sight. Transfer the top face-up card to the bottom of the deck. There is now a face-down card on top of the deck, with a face-up card concealed beneath it. The bottom card of the deck is also face-up.

Bring the deck into view. Place it on the table. Cut the deck into three heaps. Keep the cards squared so you do not reveal the whereabouts of the face-up cards. Pick up the center heap and invite the spectator to pick a card from it. Let's say he picks the ♣3. Gather the deck so that the cards are back in order. In other words, the original top third goes onto the middle third, and these onto the bottom third of the deck.

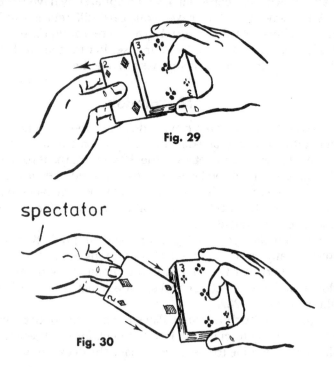

Fig. 29

spectator

Fig. 30

Place the spectator's card face-down on the table. Drop the deck onto this card. Turn the deck face-up. Take care not to expose the face-up cards. Grasp the deck by the ends with the right hand as shown in Figure 29. "We're going to cut the deck but I'd like you to indicate the cut point." The left fingers draw the back card of the deck out as shown in Figure 29. Give this card to the spectator.

Hold the deck steady while the spectator inserts the card into the deck from the side as shown in Figure 30. Cut the deck at that point and complete the cut and say, "Your card is the three of clubs, a black three. If you recall, before we started you put a card between the face-up fours. If that card is also a black three, you correctly foretold the card you yourself would later choose, proof you have psychic powers."

Turn the deck face-down. Spread it across the table. The face-up fours will be in the middle with a face-down card between them. Remove this group of three cards. Turn over the middle card. Not only is it a black three, it is the same black three chosen by the spectator. Congratulate the spectator and say, "You can't do much better than that."

19. Thoughts in Color

A spectator chooses a random card from a packet. The cards are given to another spectator. This person knows nothing about the chosen card, yet is able to pick it out without fail.

Method: Remove ten pairs of cards from the deck and place them in a heap on the table. The top card of each pair is red, the bottom card black. As the cards are removed, do not show the faces to the audience. The explanation you give is that you don't want anyone's choice to be subconsciously influenced later on.

The rest of the deck is placed aside. Ask a spectator to give the packet of twenty cards one or two straight cuts. Pick up the packet and hold it in the left hand. Push over the top two cards without disturbing their order. Say, "I'd like you to tell me to stop as I deal cards to the table." Take the pair with the right hand. Drop it to the table. Do the same with the next pair and the next, and so on until the spectator calls stop.

Take the top single card of the packet into the right hand.

Show it to the spectator. Ask him to remember it, but caution him not to tell anyone which card he picked. Drop this single card onto the tabled cards. Push the next pair of cards off the packet. Take it with the right hand and drop it onto the tabled cards. Continue doing this until you have one card remaining in the left hand. Take this card with the right hand. Use it as a scoop by sliding it under the tabled cards as you scoop up the cards and again take them in the left hand. The card used as a scoop stays on the bottom of the packet.

Deal the top card of the packet onto the table to the left. Deal the next card on the table to the right. Deal the next card onto the left-hand card. Deal the next card onto the right-hand card. Continue dealing this way until you have dealt all twenty cards into two heaps.

Pick up the top two cards of the right-hand heap and say, "Cards come in two colors, red and black." Show the faces of the two cards. One will be red and one black. Replace them on the right-hand packet.

"Please tell us the color of the card you chose." The spectator might say that he chose a red card. Pick up the left-hand packet and give it to another spectator. "Sir, please look over the faces of these cards and pick out a red card. Don't show us the card you picked."

This person will be surprised when he looks at the faces of the cards in the packet handed to him because nine cards will be black and only one red. Further, the red card is the card chosen by the first spectator. When he has removed a card, take the rest of the packet from him. Shuffle it into the other packet and return these cards to the deck.

Turn attention to the first spectator. "For the first time, please tell us the name of the card you chose." The spectator might name the ♦A. Ask the second spectator to turn over his card. It is the ♦A.

The secret to this trick is simple, so you may want to set it up in advance with a friend who will not let on how simple it really is. The friend can do a little acting and pretend he is having a tough time picking out one card from so many. When it is revealed that he picked the correct card, credit him with great psychic ability.

20. Prediction Supreme

The performer writes an "X" on a piece of paper and says, "This is my prediction. It could be the letter X or the Roman numeral for the number ten, or it could mean that X marks the spot." He deals nine cards off the top of the deck. A spectator cuts the packet as often as he likes and then deals the cards into three heaps, dealing a card to each heap in turn until all nine cards have been dealt out.

The spectator is told he can take the top card of each heap, or the middle card of each, or the bottom card of each, or he can take all three cards from one heap. Let's say the spectator elects to take the top card of each heap. He adds together their values and arrives, say, at a total of 15. The deck is turned face-up. The spectator counts to the fifteenth card. This card may be the ♠9. Clearly, this card does not match the prediction. But then the card is turned over. There on the back is a large "X."

Method: Beforehand, arrange nine cards in mixed suits in this order from top to bottom: 6-7-2-A-5-9-8-3-4. Place this packet on top of the deck. Turn the deck face-up. Take the bottom card, draw a large "X" on the back with a marking pen, and place this card fifteenth from the face of the deck. You may wish to mark the back of the joker so that the other fifty-two cards can be used for later tricks.

To present the trick, write a large "X" on a piece of paper, remarking that this is your prediction: "This is the card I dreamed you would pick." Deal three cards off the top of the deck into a heap on the table. Deal another heap of three to the right of it, and another group of three to the right of that.

Ask the spectator to pick the top card of each heap, the middle card of each, or the bottom card of each. Alternately, he can take all three cards from the same heap. When he has made his choice, ask him to total the values of the three cards he picked. While he does this, pick up the other two heaps, give them a shuffle and drop them on top of the deck.

The spectator will arrive at a total of 15. Turn the deck face-up. Ask him to count to the fifteenth card. When he arrives at the card, act puzzled that it does not match the prediction. Then turn the card over to reveal the "X" on the back.

21. Double Think

A popular theme in card magic is the color guessing trick, i.e., the trick where the spectator correctly guesses whether the cards are red or black. Roy Walton invented a clever twist on the premise.

Method: Preparation consists in having ten red cards on top of the deck, ten black cards just below them, and the ♦10 twenty-sixth from the top. When ready to present the trick, hold the deck face-up in the left hand. Spread the cards from left to right. As you do, remark that there is a ten-spot in the deck that has special properties. When spreading the cards between the hands, take care not to spread beyond the ♦10 or the audience will see the stack of reds and blacks. But make sure the audience sees the cards up to the ♦10 as you spread them because you want to create the illusion that the deck is well mixed.

When you get to the ♦10, say, "Here it is, a card with two unusual features." Toss the ♦10 face-up to the table. Square the deck. Turn it face-down and place it on the table. Cut off about a third of the deck, anywhere between fifteen and twenty cards. Put the rest of the deck aside as it will not be used. Explain that you would like the spectator to deal the cards randomly into two heaps, "like this." Deal cards into two heaps, dealing one or two into a heap on the left, two or three into a heap on the right, then a couple of cards to the heap on the left, and so on. Count silently as you deal. Stop dealing when you have dealt ten cards.

Fig. 31

Pick up either of the dealt heaps. Place it on top of the other tabled heap. Place the face-up ♦10 onto the tabled heap. Finally, place the cards in hand on top of all. Hand the cards to the spectator. Ask him to deal haphazardly into two heaps. It does not matter where the ♦10 lands. He deals all of the cards into the two tabled heaps.

When he has finished dealing, say, "That should guarantee

they are well mixed." Pick up the heap that contains the ♦10 and hold it in the left hand. "Now we'll cut them like this." Lift off all the cards above the ♦10 and place this cut-off group on the table to the right. Place the ♦10 on the table between the two heaps, Figure 31. Scoop up the heap on the far left and place it on top of the cards in hand. Then scoop up the heap on the far right and place it on top of all.

Tap the ♦10 and say, "Locked into this card are two important pieces of information. First, and most obvious, the ten of diamonds is a ten." Deal ten cards off the top of the packet onto the ♦10. Say, "Second, it is a red ten," and snap the fingers. "And that produces ten reds." Turn over the cards you just dealt. The audience is surprised to discover that all ten cards are red.

"If we turn the ten over, it works its magic the opposite way." Turn the ♦10 face-down, tap it against the cards in hand and say, "In the world of playing cards, the opposite of red is black." Toss the ♦10 to the table. Turn over the cards in hand and spread them to show all black cards.

22. Psychic Aura

This is a handling of a perplexing trick invented by Nick Trost. The magician explains that sometimes playing cards radiate an invisible aura that can be detected only by certain people. Two rows of six cards each are dealt to the table. The spectator is asked to move his hands over the cards until he feels an impulse to stop. Then he brings his hands down so his fingers contact three adjacent cards in each row. He might choose the cards shown in Figure 32.

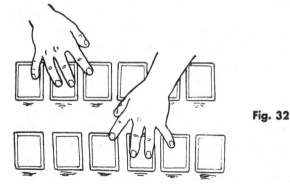

Fig. 32

The cards not chosen in the two rows are removed and placed on the deck. Then the cards from one row are dropped on top of the deck and the deck is given a cut. "You could have chosen any cards, but something compelled you to pick certain cards."

The spectator is asked to place both hands on top of the deck to transfer the aura to the deck. The deck is spread face-down on the table. There are now three face-up cards in the middle of the deck. When the spectator looks at the three cards on the table, they match the reversed cards.

Method: Remove three each of the sevens, nines and jacks from the deck. Arrange them in the order 7-9-J-7-9-J-7-9-J. Place this packet on top of the deck. Deal off the top three cards, turn them face-up and place them on the bottom of the deck. This completes the preparation.

To present the trick, remark that all objects give off auras. Deal the top six cards into a face-down row on the table. Deal the next six cards into a row below the first row. Take care not to expose the reversed cards on the bottom of the deck.

Say, "The aura can even exist in playing cards. Let's see if we can detect the aura. Pass your hands over the two rows. Stop on impulse and drop each hand on a different row so that your fingers contact three cards that are next to one another." You can demonstrate this to the spectator. Then have him do it. He might pick the cards shown in Figure 32.

Remove the six cards he didn't touch. Give them a quick shuffle and drop them on top of the deck. Unknown to the spectator, the cards left in the upper row are a seven, nine and jack. The three cards in the lower row are random cards. Ask the spectator to indicate one or the other group. If he picks the cards in the upper row, say, "Good, we'll use those." Gather the cards in the lower row and drop them on top of the deck. If he indicates the cards in the lower row, say, "Good, we will put those cards on top of the deck with the others." No matter which row he picks, interpret it in such a way that the three cards left on the table are the seven, nine and jack.

When the three random cards have been placed on top of the deck, give the deck a cut. Complete the cut and say, "Let's see if the aura is working. Cover the deck with both hands. This transfers the aura from the cards on the table to the cards in the deck." Spread the deck face-down on the table. There are three face-up cards in the middle. Invite the spectator to turn over the three cards on the table. The values will match the values of the reversed cards in the deck.

23. Number, Please

This computer age we live in is a world controlled by numbers. In this feat, the magician produces a spectator's lucky card, and then goes on to reveal his telephone number in a surprising manner. This handling of a classic trick was suggested by Sam Schwartz.

Method: A fifty-two-card deck is required. You must secretly find out the spectator's telephone number. Let us say it is 423-7568. To prepare the trick, stack the following cards from top to bottom: ♦9-8-6-5-7-3-2-4. The first card (♦9) is the lucky card you are going to predict. The other seven cards in mixed suits are the spectator's telephone number. Drop the deck on top of the packet and you are ready to perform the trick.

Remark that numbers control our lives more and more. On a piece of paper write, "Your lucky card is the nine of diamonds." Fold the paper and place it on the table. Place the deck face-down in front of the spectator. Ask him to lift off the top half, shuffle it and replace it on the balance of the deck. Explain that for this trick the picture cards will each have a value of ten. All other cards have their face value.

Ask the spectator to deal the top four cards into a face-up row. Let's say he deals an 8, a 6, a 9 and a 7. Take the deck from the spectator. Explain that you want to bring the value of each card in the row to ten. The first card is an 8, so you deal two cards onto the 8 (because 8 plus 2 equals 10). The next card is a 6, so you deal four cards onto the 6. The next card is a 9; deal one card onto the 9. The last card is a 7; deal three cards onto the 7.

Then say, "That normalizes the deck. Now we can deal directly with the values themselves." The first card is an 8. Deal eight cards off the top of the deck into a heap and drop the deck on top of the dealt heap. The next card is a 6. Deal six cards off the top into a heap and drop the deck on top of this heap. The third card is a 9; deal nine cards off the top of the deck into a heap and drop the deck onto this heap. The last card is a 7; deal seven cards off the top of the deck into a heap and drop the deck on top.

Say, "Now we arrive at a card that might bring you luck," and deal the top card of the deck onto your prediction. "Finally, we will deal some cards that should have personal meaning for you." Deal the top seven cards into a face-up row on the table. The cards will show up in the order 8-6-5-7-3-2-4, the reverse of the spectator's telephone number. Say, "Do these numbers have meaning to you?" The spectator shakes his head. "They don't ring a bell?" The spectator still says no.

"We might have better luck with your lucky card. This is the card I predicted would be your lucky card." Open the prediction, showing that you wrote down "Nine of diamonds." Turn over the card you placed near the prediction. It is indeed the ♦9. "Maybe we should take a look at these other numbers again." Now read them off in reverse order, i.e., 4-2-3-7-5-6-8. The spectator will be surprised to realize that he has arrived at his own telephone number.

When the spectator deals four cards in a face-up row at the start of the trick, remember that all tens and picture cards count as 10. If a picture card is dealt, you do not deal any cards onto it to bring its value up to 10 because it already has a value of 10.

ROYAL ROUND-UP

In a deck of cards, royalty is represented by the jacks, queens and kings. Court cards figure prominently in each of the tricks in this chapter.

24. King Quartet

The spectator finds a selected card while the cards are in his own hands. There is a surprise ending when the four kings show up unexpectedly. This is a handling of a trick favored by Frank Garcia.

Method: Secretly place the four kings on the bottom of the deck. That is the only preparation.

Put the deck on the table. Ask the spectator to cut off the top half, packet A in Figure 33. Direct him to shuffle this packet and place it on the table. Place the other half of the deck on top, but at right angles as shown in Figure 34.

Invite the spectator to look at the top card of the upper packet (packet B in the drawing). He then replaces it on top of packet B, picks up packet B and gives this packet a straight cut to bury the chosen card in the packet. Place packet A on top of all.

Say, "Let's see if I can find your card." Look through the deck as if looking for the chosen card. Really, find the kings and cut them to the top of the deck. When you have done this, hold the

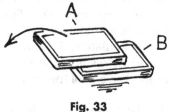

Fig. 33

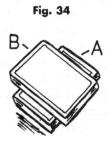

Fig. 34

deck face-down in the left hand and say, "This is going to be tougher than I thought." Deal the top five cards off the deck into a heap on the table. Unknown to the audience, the top card of this packet is the chosen card. Under it are the four kings.

"For some reason I think that royalty is involved here. I'd like you to spell 'king' and transfer a card one at a time for each letter from the top to the bottom of the packet, like this." Spell k-i-n-g, dealing a card for each letter from top to bottom. Hand the packet to the spectator. He follows your direction, spelling k-i-n-g and dealing a card from the top to the bottom for each letter. When he has done this, direct him to deal the top card of the packet to the table.

Tap the tabled card, shake your head and say, "No, that's not it." The spectator repeats the deal/spell again, after which he deals the top card of the packet to the table. Again shake your head. "Nope, that's not it either." The spectator repeats the process two more times, after which there will be four cards on the table and one in his hand.

Say, "What card did you pick?" Whatever card he names, have him turn over the card in hand. It will be the chosen card. It seems as if the trick is over; but then say, "I'll tell you why I thought royalty was involved." Turn up the four tabled cards to reveal the four kings.

25. Royal Rescue

This is a different way of performing "King Quartet." The spectator places about a third of the deck aside. He takes another third of the deck for himself, shuffles it and picks a card. The magician deals the remaining third of the deck into four heaps.

The top card of each heap is given to the spectator. He mixes his chosen card in with the other four cards. The magician takes the five cards and glances at them. He says, "You didn't pick a king, did you?" The spectator says no.

"That makes my job much easier." Immediately, the magician removes one card from the packet and shows it to the spectator. It is the chosen card. This looks like the end of the trick, but there is a twist.

"When you said you didn't pick a king, I pretty much knew what card you must have taken." So saying, the magician turns over the other four cards. They are all kings.

Method: Before the trick begins, secretly leave the four kings in your pocket. Perform several tricks with the deck. Put the deck in your pocket, making sure the deck goes on top of the kings. Then pretend to remember one more trick you wanted to perform. Remove the deck with the four kings secretly added to the bottom.

Place the deck on the table. Ask the spectator to cut off about a third of the deck and place it aside. He then cuts off about half the remainder, shuffles it and removes one card as his chosen card. While he does this, pick up the bottom third of the deck and deal it into four heaps, dealing a card at a time to each heap in turn. Then take the top card of each heap. Don't show the faces of the cards. Hand these four cards to the spectator. Ask him to add his chosen card to the four cards, mix them and hand them back to you.

Fan the cards so you can see the faces and say, "You didn't pick a king, did you?" The spectator says no, and you reply, "Good. Then this must be your card." Remove the chosen card from the packet (it is the card that is *not* a king) and show it to the spectator. Then say, "When you told me you didn't pick a king, you made my job much easier." Deal the other four cards into a face-up row to show they are all kings.

26. Witch Hunt

In this trick, devised by the author, the four queens symbolize witches.

Say, "Witches live in secrecy. Even their next-door neighbors don't suspect. That makes it difficult for witches to contact one another for a get-together. Nowadays, computer programs make it easy." As you speak, remove four random cards from the deck and place them face-down on the table. Remove two queens and put them on the tabled cards. Remove four more cards and put them on top of the tabled packet. Remove the other two queens and put them on top of all. Don't show the faces of the cards you remove from the deck because you don't want the set-up to be known to the audience.

Remove any ace, two and three from the deck. Place these three cards face-up in front of the spectator. Put the rest of the deck to one side. Pick up the twelve-card packet. Turn it face-up and spread the cards in bunches while saying, "The witches were scattered about. It was the job of the computer to bring them together."

Turn the packet face-down and hold it in the left hand. Point to the three cards in front of the spectator and say, "That's the computer software. All we have to do is put the program in the right order. Please arrange those three cards in any order you like. Witch Hazel will guide you in your choice." The spectator arranges the three cards in any order. Let us assume the order is 2-A-3.

"The first number is two, so we deal two heaps." Deal the packet into two heaps, dealing a card at a time from left to right. When all twelve cards have been dealt, place the left heap on top of the right. "The next card is the ace, or one. We deal one heap." Deal the cards into a single heap on the table.

"Finally, we have the three. This directs us to deal three heaps." Deal three heaps, dealing a card at a time from left to right until you have dealt all twelve cards. Pick up the heap on the left and place it on the center heap. Place this combined heap on top of the far right heap.

Deal the top four cards into a face-up row on the table. These will always be the four queens. As you deal, say, "And that brings together the Wicked Witch of the North, the Wicked Witch of the East, the Wicked Witch of the South and the Wicked Witch of the West."

27. Jack Finds Your Card

Method: "In movies, Ace Ventura is a detective who finds missing pets. In a deck of playing cards, Jack O'Diamonds finds missing cards." As you deliver this line, spread the cards between your hands with the faces of the cards toward you. Find the ♦J and remove it from the deck. In the process of looking for this card, secretly memorize the top and bottom card of the deck. Let us say that one of these is the ♠3 and the other the ♥2.

Place the deck on the table. Ask a spectator to cut the deck into three heaps. Keep track of the location of the bottom third of the deck. After the three packets have been formed, slide the middle heap to one side as you say, "We will use these cards in a moment.

"Jack O'Diamonds will try to find a card you are about to choose. First he has to know how many cards are in one of these heaps." Pick up the bottom third of the deck. Count aloud as you deal them into a heap on the table. It does not matter how many cards there are, though you do not let on. What you really want to do is reverse the order of the cards in this heap.

After the deal, say, "Hmm, eighteen cards (or however many you counted). That is an important piece of information." Place the two heaps alongside one another on the table. Invite the spectator to riffle shuffle them together.

Turn your head to one side as he does this. Invite the spectator to look at and remember the top card of the combined heap he just shuffled. Unknown to him, this card can only be one of the cards you remembered at the beginning of the trick, in our example either the ♠3 or ♥2. Ask him to slide the chosen card into the middle heap (the one placed aside earlier).

Face the audience. Push the middle packet toward the spectator as you say, "You hold on to this for the moment." Spread the other packet face-up on the table and remark, "Jack O'Diamonds is talented at finding missing cards. Let's see if he can figure out which card is missing from this portion of the deck." As you speak, look over the cards until you find either the ♠3 or the ♥2. The card not found is the chosen card, but don't reveal this information just yet. Instead, pick up the ♦J and slide it along the face-up spread. Do this two or three times, then hold the ♦J up to your ear. Pretend to listen to what he has to say, then go on to reveal the chosen card.

28. Bluebeard

In a little-known sleuthing episode, Scotland Yard tracked down the infamous Bluebeard. This trick explains how they did it.

You will use a red-backed deck of cards and a blue-backed ♣K. Place the ♣K in your left jacket pocket so the back of the card is close to the body. This is the only preparation. The deck itself is unprepared and may be used for other tricks.

When ready to perform Bluebeard, have the spectator shuffle the red-backed deck. Take back the deck and remove the aces, kings, queens and jacks. As you do, remark that Scotland Yard was aware that a member of royalty had been suspected of committing numerous crimes, but they didn't know the culprit's true identity. The aces, kings, queens and jacks are the royalty in a deck of cards, so they will represent the suspects.

Take back the balance of the deck and place it in your pocket so that the bottom card of the deck is face-to-face with the ♣K. Ask the spectator to mix the packet of sixteen cards. He then cuts off a small bunch and places them face-down on the table. Ask him to press his thumb on the top card of the small packet so as to leave a thumb print.

Remove the deck from your pocket. Keep the deck face-down so the audience doesn't see the reversed ♣K on the bottom. Place the deck on top of the small packet. Carefully square the deck. Place it behind your back as you remark, "The detectives had just one clue, Bluebeard's thumb print. I'll try to locate the card with the thumb print, but I won't look at any cards."

With the cards out of sight behind your back, turn the deck face-up. Silently count sixteen cards off the face without reversing their order. At this point you hold two face-up packets behind your back, one in each hand. Place the larger packet onto the face of the sixteen-card packet. Turn the deck face-down and bring it into view as you say, "I turned one card face-up. The location of this card depends on the number of cards you have over here." As you say "over here," tap the packet of cards in front of the spectator.

Deal cards off the top of the deck. Direct the spectator to simultaneously deal cards off the top of his packet. He matches you card for card. When he has dealt his last card, you will deal the face-up ♣K as you say, "We suspected all along you knew where he was hiding. And we knew he was Bluebeard because blue is the key to the mystery." Turn the ♣K over to show that this card has a blue back.

29. Kings Can Count

Remark, "You've heard the old nursery rhyme that the kings were in the counting house. It comes from the fact that in a deck of cards, the kings are the accountants. I'll show you how fast they can count."

From a shuffled deck, the performer removes the four kings and puts them on the table. The aid of two spectators is then enlisted. We shall refer to them as Al and Bob. The deck is given to Al. He deals a number of cards off into a heap. It can be any number up to half the deck. This heap is given to Bob. Al keeps the remainder of the deck.

The performer taps the kings against one heap, then against the other. "They've gotten all the information they need." The performer holds the kings up to his ear. He nods and writes on a slip of paper, "Al will have four more than Bob." The slip of paper is folded and placed in full view.

One of the spectators takes two of the kings. For the sake of example he might pick the ♣K and ♦K. Since he chose these two suits, he counts the number of clubs and diamonds in his packet. The other spectator gets the ♠K and ♥K. Therefore, he counts the number of spades and hearts in his packet.

When the numbers are compared, it is found that Al has exactly four more clubs and diamonds than Bob has spades and hearts. Any borrowed deck of fifty-two cards may be used. There is no prior preparation. The presentation of this classic trick was devised by Sam Schwartz and the author.

Method: Make sure the deck contains fifty-two cards. Remove the four kings and place them face-up on the table.

Ask Al to deal any number of cards up to half the deck into a heap on the table. Remember that the kings have been removed, so the deck contains only forty-eight cards. Half that number is twenty-four, so the spectator can't deal more than twenty-four cards off the top. Silently count the number of cards he dealt. Whatever that number, subtract it from twenty-four. Write this on a piece of paper. For example, if Al deals a packet of twenty cards, subtract twenty from twenty-four to get four. Write, "Al will have four more than Bob" on the paper. Fold the paper and place it on the table. The dealt packet is given to Bob. Al keeps the remainder of the cards.

Each person gets two kings. Each counts suits according to the procedure given above. Thus, if Al gets the ♣K and ♥K, he would count the number of clubs and hearts in his packet. If Bob gets the ♠K and ♦K, he would count the number of spades and diamonds in his packet. Each person announces his number. The prediction paper is then unfolded and read aloud. The prophecy is always correct.

On occasion the spectator will deal exactly twenty-four cards to the table. In this case the number of cards in the first spectator's two suits would equal the number of cards in the second spectator's two suits. The prediction would then be worded to read, "You each have the same number!"

DIE-CEPTIONS WITH CARDS

Tricks that combine cards and dice in logical ways suggest presentations based on gambling themes. Dice can be found in board games and may be purchased in department stores. Should you want to perform a card trick using dice, but no dice are at hand, there are tricks in this chapter which make use of invisible dice.

30. Fate in Numbers

If cards and dice are in tune with one another, the results can be fortuitous. This trick and the one following it were designed to be used in conjunction with one another. Both were devised by the author.

Method: There is a simple set-up. From the top down arrange the top nine cards in the order X-X-A-5-3-6-2-X-4. The letter "X" indicates an indifferent card. When ready to perform the trick, toss a die onto the table. Remark that you want to do a trick with dice and cards, but first you want to test that the circumstances are right for such a demonstration. Ask the spectator to roll the die and call out the top number. He then turns the die over and calls out that number.

If he calls out 1 and 6 (or 6 and 1), spell o-n-e, dealing a card for each letter into a heap. Then spell s-i-x, dealing a card for each letter into a separate heap. Turn up the top card of the "six" heap, revealing a 6. Turn up the top card of the "one" heap, revealing a 1 (ace).

If he calls out 2 and 5 (or 5 and 2), spell f-i-v-e first, then t-w-o, each time dealing a card for each letter, and forming a separate heap for each number. Turn up the top card of each heap to reveal a 5 and a 2.

If he calls out 3 and 4 (or 4 and 3), spell t-h-r-e-e first, then spell f-o-u-r, forming two heaps as described above. Turn up the top card of each heap to reveal a 3 and a 4.

31. Making the Point

Method: Give the deck a good shuffle. As you mix the cards, say, "In dice games, the person throwing the dice has to make his point before losing his turn. Other bettors decide whether or not he is going to succeed. It helps to be able to know before the game which point is going to be thrown." As you speak, spread the cards between the hands so you alone can see the faces. Silently note the card that lies seventh from the top and the card that is eighth from the top of the deck. Let's say the seventh card is the ♥2. Find the mate of this card and place it on the table. "Mate" means the card of the same value and color. In this case you would place the ♦2 face-down on the table.

Note the eighth card from the top. If it is the ♣3, find the mate of this card, the ♠3, and place it face-down on the table. Put the balance of the deck face-down in front of the spectator. Hand him two dice. He rolls the dice and adds together the topmost faces. Let's say he rolls a 6 and a 5. He adds the numbers together, getting 11, and counts eleven cards off the top of the deck into a heap on the table.

Either die is covered with a coin or a poker chip. The spectator then turns over the other die, bringing a new number to the top. Say this number is 2. He deals that number of cards off the top of the deck onto the tabled heap. The deck is placed aside.

The coin is lifted from the die. In our example the number on that die shows a 6. The spectator deals six cards off the tabled heap, forming a second heap. The top card of one heap is turned over. It is a red deuce. "That is your point. Here's the number I bet on." Turn up the matching red deuce.

"Here's your second point." Turn up the top card of the other heap. It is a black three. Turn over your other card, revealing a matching black three. As you turn this card over, say, "If you're going to bet, it pays to know the outcome before the game begins."

32. The Phantom Die

The magician gives the card case a shake. Something is heard to rattle around inside. "That," he says, "is a special die." He pretends to throw the die on the table. "Call out the number you think came up."

As he speaks, the magician deals a row of six cards on the table. The spectator might say the number rolled on the invisible die was 5. The fifth card in the row is counted to and turned face-up. It might be a 7. "We arrive at a seven. That's our value card. Now let's try for suit."

The six cards are pushed to one side and a new row of six cards is dealt out. The magician gives the card box another shake and pretends to throw the die to the table. "What number was rolled this time?" The spectator might say 3. The third card in the row is turned up. It is a diamond. So the magician says, "Now we have a value, seven, and a suit, diamonds, so our card is the seven of diamonds."

He gives the card box another shake. The sound from within stops. "Here's why the die is special. It can turn into any card, even the card we just made up." The card box is opened. There is no die inside but there is a playing card. When removed and turned face-up, it proves to be the ♦7. This trick was devised by the author.

Method: Beforehand, place the ♦7 in the card box and close the flap. Twelve cards are stacked as follows from the top down: X-♥7-X-♣7-X-♠7-X-♦8-X-♦J-X-♦3. The letter "X" indicates an indifferent card which should be any suit except diamonds. The first six cards in this stack are used to force a card with a value of 7. The second group of six cards is used to force the diamond suit.

When ready to present the trick, make sure the spectator is sitting across the table, facing you. Grasp the card box at the sides. Hold it loosely and shake it back and forth. Something is heard rattling around inside. Remark that you have a special die in the box. Place the card box on the table. Deal a row of six face-down cards, dealing from left to right, a card at a time, off the top of the deck. Place the balance of the deck aside.

Pick up the card box, give it a shake and pretend to throw the die to the table. Ask the spectator which number was thrown. If he calls 1, 3 or 6, ask him to count to that number from his left. If he calls 2, 4, or 5, count to it from your left. With this strategy, you must arrive at a 7. Turn it face-up. Show the card on either side of it in the row to be of random value. Leave the face-up 7 on the table. Gather the other five cards and place them on the bottom of the deck.

Deal out another row of six cards. Pretend to drop the invisible die back into the card box. Give the box a shake and pretend to toss the invisible die to the table. Ask the spectator to tell you the number that was thrown. As before, if he names an odd number, he counts to it from his left. If he names an even number, count to it from your left. Turn the card face-up. It will be a diamond. Turn up the card on either side of the chosen card to show other suits. Leave the chosen diamond on the table. Gather the other five cards and place them on the bottom of the deck.

The cards arrived at are a 7 and a diamond, indicating that the chosen card will be the ♦7. Pick up the card box. Hold it loosely by the sides, Figure 35. Shake the card box back and

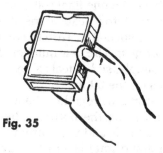

Fig. 35

forth. Tighten your grip until the card stops moving. As you perform these actions, remark that the special die is special because it can change into any card, even a randomly made-up card like the ♦7.

Open the card box. Remove the card so that the back of the card is to the audience. Then turn the card around to show that it is indeed the ♦7.

33. Futurism

Three cards are chosen by the roll of a pair of dice. It if found that the magician has correctly predicted the identity of each of the three cards.

Method: For this trick, invented by H. A. Adams, you will need two dice and a deck of cards. The cards may be borrowed and the trick done on the spot. With the faces of the cards toward you, run through the deck, saying that you are looking for a particular card on which to record a series of predictions. As you run the cards from hand to hand, memorize the card at the top of the deck, the card that lies fourteenth from the top, and the card that is twenty-eighth from the top. Let's say these are the ♠A, ♦2, and ♣3.

Continue going through the cards until you get near the bottom of the deck. Then pull out any low-value card like a deuce or a four, because these cards have a lot of white space on which you can write. Place the deck face-down on the table. Record your predictions on the card you removed from the deck. In our example, you would write the ♠A, ♦2, and ♣3, in a column. Place the prediction card face-down on the table.

The dice are handed to the first spectator. Ask him to roll them a few times to satisfy himself that they are not loaded. Then have him give them one final roll. Let's say he rolls an 8.

He deals eight cards into a heap on the table. The deck is then passed to the second spectator. Turn the dice over so the opposite faces are uppermost. The new number showing on the dice will be 6 in this example, so he deals a heap of six cards. There are now two heaps on the table.

The third spectator adds together the numbers on top of the dice and the numbers on the bottom. The two numbers now showing have a total of 6, and the bottom two numbers have a total of 8, so the grand total is 14 (it is always 14). The third spectator deals a heap of fourteen cards on the table.

Turn attention to the first spectator and say, "I'd like to check the count again." Pick up the first heap and count it to the table. This serves to reverse the order of the cards and is all you need to make the trick work. Turn up the top card of each heap. One card will be the ♠A, the next the ♦2, and the third the ♣3. Someone turns up your prediction card to verify that you were correct in all three cases.

34. Four on a Die

If you have a moment to set the cards, the previous trick can be used to produce four of a kind. Beforehand, arrange the deck so the four aces are at positions one, fourteen, twenty-eight and twenty-nine from the top. When you are ready to do the trick, call attention to the fact that cards and dice are the apparatus used in many popular games of luck and skill, but that they are seldom used in combination with one another. You then offer to demonstrate a game called two-dice poker.

Method: Place the deck on the table. Ask the first spectator to roll the dice two or three times and then give them a final roll. Say he rolls a 10. He deals ten cards off the top of the deck into a heap on the table.

The deck is passed to a second spectator. Turn the two dice over. The new number will be 4. He deals a heap of four cards in front of himself.

The deck goes to the third spectator. He totals the numbers showing on the top faces of the dice, and adds to this the total of the numbers on the bottom faces of the dice. In our example, he would add 4 and 10 to arrive at 14. He deals a heap of fourteen cards to the table.

The remainder of the deck is then placed on the table. There are three heaps of counted cards plus the remainder of the deck, a total of four heaps. Remarking that in poker one is dealt five cards, the magician picks up the first spectator's heap and deals it into two heaps, alternating a card to each as he deals.

Then he says, "Let's see what happens when cards and dice are combined in one game." The top card of each of the five heaps is turned face-up. Congratulate the spectators on giving themselves the four aces.

35. Mental Dice

By the throw of an invisible die, the spectator finds his own chosen card. This trick is adapted from an effect invented by the mentalist Joseph Dunninger.

Method: Hand the deck of cards to a spectator. Turn your head to one side as you ask him to pretend to throw an invisible die and note the number that comes up. "Whatever your number, deal a heap of cards onto the table containing a number of cards equal to the number you threw. If, for instance, you rolled a five, you would deal a heap of five cards."

The spectator deals cards onto the table equal to the number he has in mind. Say, "Good. And just so we have enough cards to work with, deal a second heap containing the same number of cards." Now there are two heaps on the table. Ask the spectator to pick up either heap and place it in his pocket. Then ask him to shuffle the deck and note the top card. When he has done this, have him pick up the small dealt heap from the table and place it on top of the deck.

Take the deck from him and say, "Roll that invisible die again

and tell me the number you rolled." Whatever the number, deal
that many cards off the top into a heap on the table. We will
assume the number is 4.

Ask him to roll the die a second time and call out the number.
He may say he rolled a 2. Deal two cards off the top of the deck
onto the tabled heap, and then say, "Once more for good luck."
The spectator rolls the invisible die a third time and tells you he
rolled a 5. Deal five cards off the top of the deck onto the tabled
heap. The total of the numbers called out by the spectator must
be at least 7. In this example, he arrives at a total of 11, more
than enough to guarantee that the trick will work.

"Four, two, five. Let's see if these are our lucky numbers."
Place the dealt heap back onto the top of the deck. Pretend to
notice the deck is short a few cards. "Do you still have some
cards in your pocket?" Direct the spectator to add them to the
top of the deck.

Now have the spectator deal out the same three numbers he
just rolled. In our example, he would deal four cards, then two,
then five. Tell him to turn up the last card dealt. It will be the
chosen card.

36. Triple Enigma

While the performer turns his head to one side, the spectator
rolls two invisible dice. Whatever number is rolled, he counts
that many cards off the top of the deck into a heap on the table,
notes the top card of the heap and drops the rest of the deck on
top to bury the chosen card. The deck is given to the magician
behind his back.

The magician brings the deck into view and announces that
the number rolled on the invisible dice was, for example, 8. He
is correct. Then he causes another card to magically turn face-
up in the middle of the deck. This card may be a 3. Counting
three cards, the next card is turned face-up and it is the card
chosen by the spectator.

This triple mystery is based on ideas of Oscar Weigle and
Tony Bartolotta. The small amount of secret preparation is
more than paid off by the series of magical effects that is
created.

Method: Arrange the ♠A through ♠9 in numerical order with
the ace at the face, the two next, and so on. The ♠9 is the top

card of the packet. Drop the balance of the deck on top of the packet and you are ready to begin. (It is a good idea to perform some other trick which makes use of the top half of the deck and won't disturb the set-up. Many of the tricks in this chapter can be used for the purpose.)

When ready to perform "Triple Enigma," place the deck on the table. Invite the spectator to lift off the top half, shuffle it and replace it on the balance of the deck. Explain that you are about to have him choose a card and you want to be sure his card will be a random selection.

Turn your head to one side. Invite him to roll a pair of invisible dice. Explain that he can roll any number *between* 1 and 12. Let's say he rolls 8. He silently deals eight cards off the top of the deck into a heap on the table, notes the top card of the heap and drops the balance of the deck on top.

The cards are handed to you behind your back. Turn and face the audience. With the cards out of sight, turn the deck face-up. Silently push over eleven cards off the face into the right hand without disturbing their order. Turn this packet face-down in the right hand. Use the left hand to aid in turning the top card of this packet face-up on top of the packet. Turn the rest of the deck face-down and drop it on top of all. Finally, cut the deck and complete the cut to bring the reversed card to the center.

Bring the deck into view. Hold it face-down in the left hand. You are about to pick up a small but vital clue that guarantees the success of the trick. Pretend to be studying the number thrown on the invisible dice. As you do, riffle the left side of the deck with your thumb. You will spot the reversed card as the riffle is made, Figure 36. To conceal the presence of the reversed card from the audience, you may wish to keep the right hand

Fig. 36

over the deck, fingers in front, thumb in back, as if you are holding the cards steady while they are being riffled.

Remember the value of the reversed card and subtract this
number from 11 (it is always 11). In Figure 36, the reversed card
is a 3. Subtract 3 from 11 to get 8. Announce that the number the
spectator rolled with the invisible dice was 8.

Say, "Now it's my turn to roll the dice." Pretend to pick up the
two dice and give them a roll. "I rolled a three." Here you name
the value of the reversed card. Tap the deck against the table,
then spread the cards between the hands to reveal the face-up
3. Cut the deck at that point and complete the cut so the 3 is
face-up on top.

"Since this card is a three, we count three cards." Beginning
with the face-up 3, deal three cards off the top into a heap on
the table. Ask the spectator for the name of his card. Turn up
the top card of the deck and it will be his card.

If the spectator rolls 10 with the invisible dice, the ♠A will be
the face-up card. In this case, remark that you will roll *one* die.
Pantomime rolling a single die, then state that you rolled a 1.
Finish the trick as written.

On occasion, when the left thumb riffles the deck, a card will
be face-up but it will not be one of the spades in the stack. This
tells you the spectator rolled 11. In this case, the face-up card is
the chosen card. Reveal that the number rolled by the spectator was a 5 and a 6 for a total of 11; then reveal the name of the
chosen card and spread the deck face-up on the table to show
the chosen card face-up in the deck.

37. Die Version

Two numbers are chosen by the throw of a die. Two cards are
then arrived at from a shuffled deck. It turns out that the first
card indicates the second number thrown on the die, while the
second card indicates the first number. For a bonus, when the
two numbers are added together, they find a card previously
chosen by the spectator. This startling trick is based on a card
effect originated by Stewart James.

Method: Arrange a packet of cards in the order X-6-5-4-X-3-2-A
from the top down. The letter "X" indicates any random card.
Conceal this packet in your back pocket.

To perform the trick, ask the spectator to shuffle the deck.

Spread the cards between the hands and have the spectator pick one. Ask him not to look at the face of the card. Hand him a pen or pencil and have him sign the back.

State that you will put the card in a particular location in the deck. Pick up the signed card with one hand, the deck with the other. Place both behind the back. When the apparatus is out of sight, place the signed card face-up on top of the deck. Secretly remove the packet from the back pocket and place it on top of the deck. Bring the deck into view.

Hand the spectator a die. Ask him to roll it several times to satisfy himself that it isn't loaded. Then ask him to roll a low number (1, 2, 3). Say he rolls a 2. Deal two cards off the top of the deck into a heap on the table, counting aloud as you deal. Place the next card on the table to the left of the dealt heap. Pick up the dealt heap and put it on top of the deck. Turn the die over. A 5 will show. Deal five cards into a heap on the table. Deal the next card to the right of this heap. Pick up the dealt heap and place it on top of the deck.

Point to the card on the left and say, "Over here we dealt two cards and we have a five." Turn the card over to reveal a five-spot. Now call attention to the card on the right. "Over here we dealt five cards and we have a two." As you say this, turn up the card on the right to reveal a two-spot.

Say, "Five plus two is seven," and deal seven cards off the top of the deck into a heap on the table. The next card is face-up. "I wonder what this means." Turn the card over to reveal the spectator's signature.

MORE IMPROMPTU CARD TRICKS

Each of the card tricks described in this chapter is performed at the table, when you are sitting with friends and wish to entertain them with a few tricks using borrowed cards. Some are card locations, some are mind-reading tricks, and at least one trick in this chapter allows you to produce four of a kind from a borrowed, shuffled deck.

38. The Psychic Number

Card expert John Scarne developed this routine from an idea of Herb Runge's. It is a trick with a double ending. The magician correctly predicts the number of cards the spectator had concealed in his pocket, and then predicts the identity of a card at a random position in the deck.

Method: Spread the deck face-up between the hands and say, "Fortune-tellers see the importance of numbers in our everyday lives. A deck of cards represents all kinds of numerical combinations. Let's see if we can concoct a couple of numbers that might have special meaning." As you speak, do the following. Silently count to the eleventh card from the top of the deck and remember this card. Let's say it is the ♠A.

Place the deck face-down on the table and say, "I'd like you to think of a number between one and ten." Pick up a piece of paper. Pretend to concentrate. Nod your head as if you have gotten a mental clue as to the identity of the spectator's number. On the piece of paper write the number 11 (it is always 11). Fold the paper and place it on the table. Then turn your head to one side and say, "Whatever number you are thinking of, please count that many cards off the top of the deck and place them in your pocket."

When the spectator has done this, take the deck behind your back. "We have a number. Now I'm going to read the deck to see which card I should pick." Once again, pretend to concentrate.

In fact, bend one corner of the top card downwards slightly, and replace this card on top of the deck. On a fresh piece of paper write the name of the first card you remembered, the ♠A. Fold the paper and place it on the table.

Direct the spectator to remove the cards from his pocket and place them back on top of the deck. "We are now back where we started, with a full deck of fifty-two cards. The only difference is that we have each chosen a significant number."

Open the first piece of paper. It contains the number 11. Count eleven cards off the top of the deck. As you count, silently keep track of when the bent corner card shows up. It may show up eighth in the count. The number of cards the spectator had in his pocket is always one less, in this case seven.

Say, "My number was chosen on the basis of the theory of numerology. I chose eleven because it is the reciprocal of seven. Did you think of seven?" The spectator acknowledges. "Seven from eleven is four, and in numerology, the card in the fourth configuration is the ace of spades." Tap the top card of the dealt packet. Turn it up to reveal the ♠A. To finish, have the spectator open the second piece of paper. It correctly indicates that the ♠A would show up.

39. Bet a Million

One of the characters in gambling lore is Bet-a-Million Gates, a gambler who would bet on almost anything. His name is invoked in a betting scheme that looks impossible to win. Needless to say, Gates made sure he bet on sure things. The bet is an adaptation of a swindle devised by Walter Gibson. The only requirement is a full deck of fifty-two cards.

Method: When ready to perform, spread the cards between the hands. Remove all twelve picture cards and put them aside. As you do, say, "This is an amazing bet, but it only works with spot cards." Now run through the deck again and openly remove any ace through ten in mixed suits, one card of each value. Place the deck on the table.

Hand the ten-card packet to the spectator and remark, "Bet-a-Million Gates claims that this bet is an infallible money winner for him. Let's test that theory. Please shuffle those ten cards. Then pick one for me and one for you. Don't show me your card."

Let's say the spectator takes a 7 for himself and hands you a 5. At this point you don't know the value of his card. After he has drawn two cards, put the rest of the packet aside as it will not be used. Then turn your card face-up to show that it is a five-spot. Here is where you do the only work in the trick. Silently subtract the value of your card from 30 and remember the result. In this example, 30 − 5 = 25, so you would remember the number 25.

On the table is your card, the spectator's card and the balance of the deck. Say, "Here's the bet," and tap the deck. "I'm willing to bet that the deck contains enough cards to equal your number, plus enough again to equal my number, plus enough again to bring your number to twenty-five. I'm not saying approximately twenty-five. I'm saying *exactly* twenty-five." Of course, the number you name is the number you arrived at when subtracting your number from 30.

Direct the spectator to turn his card face-up. It is a seven-spot. Deal seven cards off the top of the deck. Then point to your card. It is a five-spot. Deal five cards off the top of the deck. Tap the spectator's card again. "I made the claim that there would be enough cards left over to bring your number to twenty-five. Let's see if I'm right."

The spectator's card is a 7, so you begin your count with 8. As you count aloud, deal cards off the top of the packet. You will have exactly enough to bring his total to 25.

Here's another example. The spectator takes an 8 for himself and gives you a 3. Subtract 3 from 30, getting 27. Say, "I'm willing to bet that the deck contains as many cards as your number, plus as many as my number, plus enough again to bring your number to 27." Follow the procedure with cards in hand and you will have won the bet.

40. The Piano Card Trick

Ellis Stanyon called this "one of the best table tricks I have had the pleasure of finding. It is good because of its simplicity. It is better still because sleight of hand is suspected. The performer will do well always to keep up this misdirection essential for telling results."

The "Piano Card Trick" is a classic effect that illustrates the importance of presentation. In recent years, a repeat version has come to light. We will describe the original trick first.

Method: Remark that you would like to try an experiment in sleight of hand. "But this time your hands will help perform the sleights. Please place your hands on the table as if you are playing the piano." When the spectator has done this, take the top two cards from the pack. "Two cards, an even number." Place them in the space between the little finger and third finger of the spectator's left hand.

Take two more cards from the top of the pack. "Two cards, an even number." Place them in the space between the third finger and middle finger of the spectator's left hand. Two more cards are placed between the spectator's middle finger and first finger, and two more between his left first finger and thumb. Each time say, "Two cards, always an even number."

The spaces between the fingers of the spectator's right hand are filled with pairs of cards in similar fashion, but with one exception. When he has only one space to fill—the space between the right first finger and thumb—slide a single card into that space. As you do, say, "One card, odd."

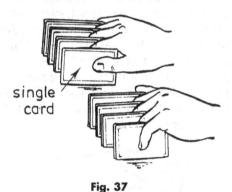

single
card

Fig. 37

The situation is shown in Figure 37, an unusual start for a card trick and one that is guaranteed to get the attention of the audience.

Now take the first pair of cards and say, "Two cards, an even number." Hold one card in each hand and place them on the table to form two heaps. Take each of the next six pairs, separate the cards in each pair and drop them onto the heaps. Each time say, "Two cards, an even number." When there is one card left, say, "Two even heaps, but now we will change the situation."

Display the single card and say, "Which heap should we put the odd card in?" The spectator indicates one of the heaps. Drop the single card onto that heap. Point to that heap and say, "Now this heap is odd. Watch closely for the sleight of hand." Place your hands over the packets, cross your hands quickly, then straighten them. "Did you see it? The odd card has passed from here to there."

Pick up the heap that had the odd card added to it. Deal the cards off in pairs. As you do, say, "Even, even, even, even." Pick up the other heap. Deal cards off in pairs. As you do, say, "Even, even, even." Pause here. Snap the remaining card as you say, "And odd."

41. Player Piano

In recent years another version of the "Piano Card Trick" has come to light, a version favored by Walter Gibson. Keep it in reserve for those occasions when you are asked to repeat the trick. Instead of repeating the original, switch to this version.

Method: Deal sixteen cards off the top of the deck into a heap on the table, counting aloud as you deal. "There can be no doubt that sixteen is an even number." Have the spectator place his hands on the table as if he is playing the piano. This time, place a pair of cards in each of the spaces between the spectator's fingers. The situation is shown in Figure 38. Say, "Even," as each pair of cards is put in place.

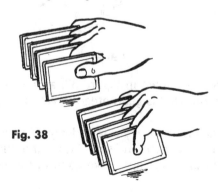

Fig. 38

Take a pair of cards from between the spectator's fingers. Hold one card in each hand. Say, "Two cards, even." Drop them into separate heaps on the table. Do the same thing with each of the next six pairs of cards. When you have one pair left, say to the spectator, "Which pile should I place these two cards on?" Whichever he chooses, drop the pair onto that heap. Say, "Two cards, all even." Ask the spectator to cover this heap with his hand.

Take the top card of the deck and say, "For the first time in this experiment I will introduce an odd card. Watch." Drop the odd card onto the other heap. Press down on that heap, lift your hand and wave it over the spectator's hand.

"It is done." Pick up your heap. Count the cards in pairs as you say, "Even, even, even, even, eight cards, an even number." Now take the cards from under the spectator's hand. Deal them in pairs to the table as you say, "Even, even, even, even, and one odd, nine cards. The odd card has flown to this packet."

42. Zodiac Spell

Using a borrowed deck, the performer finds a chosen card merely by spelling the word "Zodiac."

Method: Remark that every day we make decisions that have an impact on future events. As you speak, spread the deck face-up. "A deck of playing cards represents a random assortment of information. To some, however, the cards tell a story. Tell me, what sign were you born under?" Whatever the spectator says, nod as if it has importance. The real reason for spreading the deck is that you want to secretly note the card that is fourth from the face of the deck. Say this card is the ♦8, Figure 39.

Fig. 39

Square the deck and place it face-down on the table. The spectator cuts the deck into three heaps, Figure 40. Keep track of which heap is the top heap (that is, the heap which was originally on top of the deck) and also the bottom heap. The top heap should be on the spectator's right, the bottom heap on his left. Turn your head to one side. Instruct the spectator to hold his hands out in front of him. He then lowers them so they contact two of the packets, Figure 41.

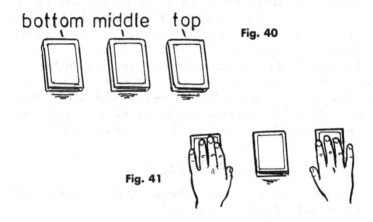

bottom middle   top   **Fig. 40**

Fig. 41

Ask him to pick up the heap under his right hand, shuffle it, note the top card and return the heap to its original position. You don't know which heap contains the chosen card, but the procedure is always the same. Turn and face the audience. Take the top card of the "top" heap and place it on top of the middle heap. Then take the top card of the "bottom" heap and place it on top of the middle heap. Take the top card of the "top" heap and place it on top of the middle heap. Put the "bottom" heap on top of the middle heap, and then place the other heap on top of all. These actions should be done at a steady, even pace, as if you are trying to pick up psychic vibrations from the cards.

Deal cards off the top of the deck until you turn up the previously noted card, in this example the ♦8. Remark that you will spell "Zodiac" and the spectator's card will turn up. Ask for the name of the chosen card, then spell z-o-d-i-a-c, dealing a card for each letter of the top of the deck into a face-up heap. If his chosen card doesn't show up on the last letter, pause, then turn over the next card. It will be his card.

43. Breath Test

Remark, "Science is getting so advanced, it is now possible to identify someone by their breath." The spectator picks a card, breathes on it and returns it to the deck. He then breathes on another card for comparison purposes. This card succeeds in finding the person's selected card. The basis for this trick is a mystery invented by Howard Wurst and Bill Pawson.

Method: Turn your back. Ask a spectator to deal a packet of cards to the table. The packet can contain any number of cards between one and ten. When he has done this, ask him to deal a second packet containing the same number of cards. For the sake of example, he might have dealt two packets of eight cards each.

With your back still turned, have him choose one of the packets, look at the bottom card of this packet and breathe on this card. He then drops the packet on top of the other packet.

Fig. 42

Turn and face the audience. Place the packet face-down in the left hand. Grasp the packet from above with the right hand. The left hand then draws the top and bottom card off simultaneously as shown in Figure 42. This pair of cards is dropped on top of the deck. In a similar way draw off the next pair and drop it on top of the deck. Continue in this fashion with the remaining cards in the packet.

Grasp the deck from above with the right hand. Remove the bottom card. Have the spectator breathe on this card for comparison purposes. "This allows us to match up the DNA." Take back the card and drop it face-up on top of the deck.

Ask the spectator to place the deck behind his back, so you can't influence the cards. He is to give the deck a random cut. After he has done this, have him give it a second cut and then a third cut. The deck is then spread face-down on the table. There will be a reversed card in the middle. The card that is back-to-back with this card will be the chosen card.

44. Encore Breath Test

If you want to repeat "Breath Test," this trick is a good follow-up.

Method: Remove any picture card, say the ♦J. "One card in the deck has the instincts of a bloodhound. I'm going to place him in a secret location in the deck." Hold the deck in one hand, the ♦J in the other. Place both hands behind the back. Turn the ♦J face-up and place it on the bottom of the deck. Bring the deck into view and say, "Choose a number from one to ten." The spectator might choose five. Deal two heaps of five cards each. Turn your head to one side. "Pick either heap. Shuffle it and look at the bottom card."

When the spectator has done this, say, "Good. Now breathe on the card so the bloodhound will have something to go on." The chosen card is still on the bottom of the chosen packet. Direct the spectator to drop the packet on top of the deck. Then drop the deck on the other packet. Lift the deck from above with the right hand. Remove the bottom card and say, "This is the five of diamonds." Ask the spectator to breathe on this card so the bloodhound has a solid clue. Place this card face-up on the table.

Draw the top and bottom card off the deck as in Figure 42 of the previous trick. Drop this pair of cards on the table. Continue

Fig. 43

drawing pairs of cards off in this manner until the bloodhound card (♦J) shows up.

Place this pair of cards on the table near the other face-up card, the ♦J to the left, the face-down card in the middle, the ♦5 to the right, as indicated in Figure 43. Ask the spectator to name his chosen card. "Let's see if the bloodhound card is as good as they say he is." Turn up the card in the middle. It is the chosen card.

45. Dialing the Future

By means of this secret, you seem to be able to reveal the telephone number of a person you have never met before.

Method: Hold the deck so you can see the faces of the cards. Beginning at the top of the deck, spread the cards to the left and note the tenth card from the top. Write it on a piece of paper. Continue spreading cards. Note the twentieth, thirtieth and fortieth cards from the top. Write each on the piece of paper. As you go through this procedure, explain to the spectator that you are going to try to guess his telephone number.

Square the deck and hold it face-down in the left hand and say, "We're going to concentrate on the four digits in your telephone number, not the exchange. Beginning with the first digit, is it a nine?" As you ask this question, deal the top card of the deck to the table. If the spectator says yes, deal nine cards onto the tabled card.

If the spectator says no, deal the top card of the deck onto the tabled card and say, "Is it an eight?" If he says yes, deal eight cards onto the tabled card. If the spectator says no to "eight," deal the next card onto the tabled heap and the next, and so on until you get a "yes" answer. Whatever number he says "yes" on, deal that many cards off the top of the deck onto the tabled heap.

Proceed in the same way with the second digit of his telephone number, forming a second heap in the process. Deal a third heap for the third digit, and a fourth heap for the fourth digit, always following the format described above. Turn up the top card of each packet. Then have someone read off the names of the four cards you wrote on the paper. It is a perfect match.

If you are able to set the card ahead of time, arrange to have the four aces at positions ten, twenty, thirty and forty. In this case, nothing is written down. Follow the above procedure to form four packets. Then turn up the top card of each to reveal that the spectator's telephone number found the four aces.

46. The Name's the Same

Say, "I met a psychic who said her name brings good fortune. To a magician, good fortune is when a card trick works successfully." The magician has a borrowed deck of cards shuffled and then cut into two heaps. Picking two cards from one heap, he writes the name of a card on one, the psychic's name on the other.

The psychic's name is Eve. Spelling E-v-e and dealing a card for each letter from the other packet (the one never touched up to this point), the spectator turns up the card on the last letter. This card might be the ♣4. It is seen to have matched the magician's prediction.

Method: Have the deck shuffled and then cut into two heaps. The spectator hands you either heap. Place it behind your back or below the edge of the table. Say, "I'm going to pick two cards at random." When the cards are out of sight, silently push over the top three cards of the packet. Turn them over and replace them on top of the packet. Let's say the top face-up card is the ♦2. This card will become the card you predict. Of course, you don't know the identity of this card yet. Say, "On second thought, why don't you pick two cards for me."

Bring the packet into view so that the top card, the ♦2 in our example, is concealed from the audience's view. The packet is held as shown in Figure 44. Remove cards from the face of the packet with the right hand as shown in Figure 44. Each card is dealt to the table. Continue doing this until the spectator calls "stop."

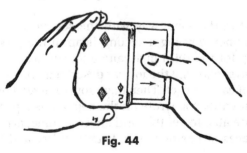

Fig. 44

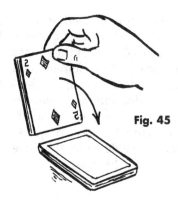

Fig. 45

When "stop" is called, deal the next two cards to one side, saying that you will write your predictions on these cards. Grasp the packet with the right hand. Lower it onto the other packet as shown in Figure 45. The ♦2 and the two cards directly above it will now be face-down. The rest of the cards above these cards will be face-up.

On one of the prediction cards write, "Two of diamonds." You can abbreviate it to "2D" if you like. On the other card write "Eve." Say, "Of course, I wouldn't predict any of these face-up cards because I handled them. It gives me too much opportunity to cheat." As you speak, pick up the deck and push over all of the face-up cards into the right hand. When you get to the first face-down card, stop. Place the face-up cards in the right hand to one side. Place the face-down packet in front of the spectator.

Turn up the "Eve" prediction and say, "This is the psychic's name. Please deal one card for each letter in her name." The spectator deals three cards into a heap on the table.

"And this is the card Eve told me was her favorite card." Turn up the other prediction. It says "Two of diamonds." Have the spectator turn over the top card of the three-card heap. It will be the prediction card, the ♦2.

47. Tomorrow's Cards

The magician writes a prediction and places it in full view. A packet of cards is handed to a spectator. He turns some face-up and some face-down. This is a random process and is not in the magician's control.

When the prediction is opened, it is seen to have correctly predicted how many cards would be reversed, and then goes on to reveal the identity of each of these cards. This baffling mystery is based on ideas of Bob Hummer and Charles Hudson.

Method: Hold the deck face-up in the left hand. Push over eight cards. As you do, note and remember the card that lies second from the face of the packet, and the card that lies sixth from the face. In Figure 46, they are the ♦3 and ♣2. Square the packet and place it face-down on the table. The deck is put off to one side as it will not be used.

Fig. 46

Pick up a piece of paper, and write, "There will be two reversed cards . . ." Fold the paper and place it on the table. Say, "That was a general description of a future event. This second prediction will be more specific." On a separate piece of paper write, ". . . and they will be the three of diamonds and the two of clubs." The cards you write down are the two cards you remembered being at positions two and six from the face of the packet.

Pick up the packet. The cards have to be mixed in a particular fashion to set up the desired outcome. The following procedure was devised by the author. Hold the packet face-down in the left hand. Use the left thumb to push five cards to the right. Without disturbing the order of the cards, grasp them with the right hand, turn them over and replace them on the balance of the packet.

Push off four cards. Take them with the right hand, turn them over and replace them on the balance of the packet. Finally, push over three cards. Take them with the right hand, turn them over and replace them on top of the packet. As you perform these maneuvers, remark that you want to reverse some cards in a random way. Spread the cards to show some face-up and some face-down, as in Figure 47.

Fig. 47

Hand the packet to the spectator. Invite him to cut the cards and complete the cut. Then he pushes over two cards, grasps them with the right hand, Figure 48, turns them over, Figure 49, and replaces them on the balance of the packet.

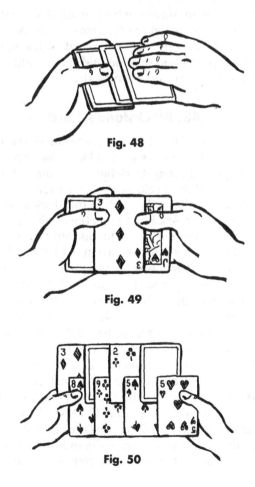

Fig. 48

Fig. 49

Fig. 50

Again he gives the packet a straight cut, pushes over two cards, turns them over and places them on top of the packet. He does this maneuver as often as he likes. When he is satisfied that the cards are well mixed, take the packet from him. Remark that you will try to find your predicted cards sight unseen. Place the packet behind your back. When the cards are out of sight, upjog every other card as indicated in Figure 50. Strip out the upjogged cards, turn them over and place them on top of the other cards.

Bring the packet out into view and spread the cards on the table. One of two situations will present itself. Either you will have six cards face-down and two face-up, or two cards face down and six face-up. Have the first prediction opened. It says there will be two reversed cards. Point to the two cards that face opposite the others. Slide them out of the spread. Then have the other prediction opened and read aloud. It correctly predicts the identity of these two cards.

48. Blackstone's Card

The magician says, "The famous magician Harry Blackstone invented a card trick that, as far as I know, has never been performed. Tonight it makes its debut." As you speak, deal ten cards off the top of the deck. Do not call attention to the number of cards dealt. Place the rest of the deck aside. Give the packet to a spectator. Ask him to mix the cards and give them a cut. Then he is asked to look at the bottom card of the packet. He then holds the packet face-down in his left hand.

Say, "Since this is Harry Blackstone's trick, I would like you to spell the word H-a-r-r-y and deal one card for each letter from the top to the bottom of the packet." After the spectator has done this, say, "Now spell B-l-a-c-k-s-t-o-n-e and deal one card from top to bottom for each letter." After the spectator has done this, take back the packet. "We're going to eliminate all but one card by means of a random process." Transfer the top card to the bottom of the packet. Deal the next card to the table. Transfer the next card from the top to the bottom of the packet. Deal the next card to the table. Continue this process until you have one card left. It will be the chosen card.

The trick can be personalized in the following way. Introduce the trick by saying that Harry Blackstone invented a card trick.

You know that one of the spectators has a five-letter name like Kathy or Diane or Peter. Invite that person to participate. Say, "We will use your first name and Blackstone's last name." Hand the packet to the spectator. Invite him to spell P-e-t-e-r, dealing a card for each letter from the top to the bottom of the packet. Then have him spell B-l-a-c-k-s-t-o-n-e, dealing a card from top to bottom for each letter. When he has done this, take back the packet.

Perform the elimination deal described above by dealing the top card to the bottom of the packet, the next to the table, the next card to the bottom of the packet, the next to the table, and so on until you have one card left. It will be the chosen card.

49. Impulse

"Impulse" is based on a trick invented by Herb Runge.

Method: Hold the deck face-up so you can see the faces. Spread the cards from left to right and note the top and bottom card. Say these are the ♠3 and ♥6. Find the cards that are the same color and value. In this example you would find the ♣3 and ♦6. Toss these two cards out face-up onto the table. Put the deck face-down between these two cards as shown in Figure 51.

Fig. 51

Remark that you're going to test the spectator's ability to act on impulse. Ask him to place the deck on either of the face-up cards. He shouldn't think about his decision. Rather, he should do it on impulse. Let's say he puts the deck on top of the ♦6. Ask him to pick up the deck (with the ♦6 now face-up on the bottom) and place it in his left hand. Invite him to deal cards onto the other face-up card. In this case he will deal onto the ♣3. Figure 52. He is to continue to deal until some impulse tells him to stop.

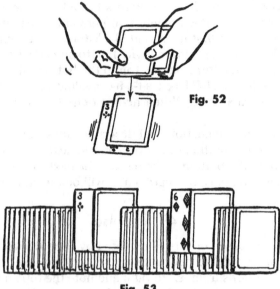

Fig. 52

Fig. 53

When he has stopped dealing, tell him that he has one more decision to make. He is to place the deck on the table. Ask him to place either the deck onto the dealt packet or the dealt packet onto the deck. Let's say he places the dealt packet (including the ♣3) on top of the deck. Cut the deck at the mid-point and complete the cut. Spread the deck face-down from left to right on the table. Slide the ♦6 and the card directly above it halfway out of the spread. Slide the ♣3 and the card above it out of the spread. The situation is shown in Figure 53.

Remove the four outjogged cards, and say, "Let's see how good you are on making impulsive decisions. The face-up cards are a red six and a black three." Turn over the other two cards. "Congratulations! You picked the other red six and the other black three!"

50. Ultra Match-Up

Tricks in which the spectator ends up with four cards of the same value are usually such that the magician must start with the four-of-a-kind at the top or bottom of the deck. John Murray worked out a version which uses any shuffled deck.

Method: Hold the deck so you alone can see the faces. Remark that you are looking for a special card. Beginning with the top card of the deck, spread the cards slightly so that the index corner of the top card is visible. Suppose this card is a jack. Beginning with the top card of the deck, silently spell j-a-c-k as you transfer cards from right to left, pushing over one card for each letter. In the case of the top card being a jack, you will have spread four cards to the left. Take this four-card packet with the left hand and place it face-down on the table. Say, "It's not among these."

Continue spreading cards from right to left, always beginning with the rearmost card of the deck, until you get to the next jack. Break the deck at this point so that the jack is the face card of the left-hand packet, Figure 54. Place this packet on top of the tabled packet as you say, "Not here, either." If you were to check the cards on the table at this point, there will be one jack fourth from the bottom and another jack fifth from the bottom.

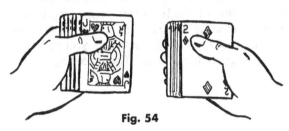

Fig. 54

Keep spreading the cards until you get to the third jack. Place all the cards to the left of it onto the tabled cards, and say, "Still looking." Continue spreading the cards in hand until you get to the last jack. Upjog this jack, and say, "Success at last." Place this jack face-down on the table to one side. Then put the cards in hand on top of the tabled heap. If you were to check the deck, there is a jack on top, a jack that is fourth from the bottom, and a jack that is fifth from the bottom.

Pick up the deck and turn it face-up. Deal cards off the face into a face-up heap on the table. When you have dealt past the first two jacks, say, "Call stop at any time." When the spectator calls stop, turn the dealt packet face-down on the table. Then turn the packet in hand face-down and put it on the table alongside the dealt packet.

"I'd like you to make one more decision. Point to either

packet." The spectator has a free choice of either packet, but you will interpret his decision in such a way that the outcome is always the one you want. If the spectator points to the packet with the jack on top, turn up the top card to show the jack. If he points to the dealt packet, slide it in front of him and say, "Keep an eye on those cards for the moment." Then turn face-up the top card of the other packet. It will be a jack.

Point to the face-up jack. "Since this is a jack, we'll spell it out." Pick up the other packet. Spell j-a-c-k, dealing a card for each letter into a heap on the table. Place the balance of the heap on the table alongside the dealt heap. There are now three heaps on the table, one with a face-up jack on top. Point to that card and say, "Here's one jack." Turn up the top card of each of the other heaps as you say, "And another jack, and *another* jack."

Tap the face-down card you placed aside earlier. "And here's the card I picked." Turn it face-up to reveal the fourth jack.

At the beginning of the trick, when you first spread the cards and spot the value of the top card, make sure there is not another card of the same value among the cards you spell. Should this happen, give the deck a shuffle as you say, "I want to be sure the cards are really mixed." Then start again.

MINDS IN DUPLICATE

Some card tricks are developed around the fact that playing cards are manufactured with different color backs. Red-backed and blue-backed decks are the most popular and can be obtained in any store that sells playing cards. The tricks in this chapter use red-backed and blue-backed cards to produce interesting and novel card effects.

51. A Friendly Ghost

"Ghosts live in shadow. There is one lurking just in back of this fellow here. Under the right circumstances ghosts influence our actions. We shall see if this particular ghost is so inclined." Picking up a blue-backed deck of cards, the performer has the gentleman choose a card in a manner that is fair and honest.

"Now the ghost has moved over to the vicinity of the lady here. We're going to see if our friendly ghost can influence the lady's choice." The lady picks a card from a red-backed deck. This too appears to be a fair and free choice.

When the two cards are turned face-up, they prove to be the same card.

"Further," the magician says, "I receive an odd delivery in the mail. Here it is, a sealed envelope bearing no address." The envelope is displayed. It is sealed and has a stamp and postal markings, but the envelope is otherwise blank. "I take it the envelope was delivered from the land of shadows to our friendly ghost." The envelope is opened and a piece of paper removed. When it is read aloud, it correctly predicts the card that both spectators would choose.

Method: On a piece of paper write in a shaky handwriting style, "They will each choose the ace of hearts." Fold the paper and seal it in an envelope. Write your name and address on an address label, and affix the label to the front of the envelope. Put a stamp on the envelope and mail it to yourself. When you

75

get it in the mail, carefully peel off the label. The envelope is now blank. Bring this envelope with you to the performance.

The other preparation concerns the two decks of cards. Stack the decks so that the top four cards of each are a 2, 3, ace, and 4 of mixed suits. Stack the bottom four cards of each deck with a 5, 2, 4, and 3 of mixed suits. The stack for each deck is shown in Figure 55. In each deck place the ♥A fourteenth from the top. This completes the preparation.

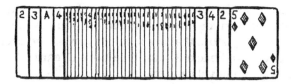

Fig. 55

At the time of performance place the envelope on the table. Ask the gentleman to indicate either deck. Let's say he decides to use the red-backed deck. Ask him to pick either the top card or the bottom card. Whichever he chooses, deal that card to the table. In other words, if he wants the top card, deal the top card of the deck to the table in front of him. If he wants the bottom card, take the bottom card off the deck and place it in front of him.

Again, ask him to choose either top or bottom. Put his choice on the table. Do this twice more. There will be a total of four cards on the table in front of the gentleman. Turn the cards face-up. Add their values. You might get a total of thirteen. Deal thirteen cards off the top of the deck into a heap on the table. Place the thirteenth card aside face-down.

Using the other deck, repeat the same procedure for the lady. On each round she can pick either the top or bottom card of the blue-backed deck. She does not have to pick the same four cards as the gentleman. The total of her four cards might be eleven. Deal eleven cards off the top of the blue-backed deck. Place the eleventh card aside.

Turn up the two chosen cards to reveal that each person was influenced by the ghost to pick the ♥A. Call attention to the envelope. Open the envelope, remove the prediction and have it read aloud, thus concluding the trick with the revelation that the friendly ghost knew all along what cards would be chosen.

52. Tea-Time Mystery

For this offbeat mystery you will need two decks of cards, and a cup of tea or similar beverage. The spectator shuffles each deck. He picks a card from one deck. The magician picks a card sight unseen from the other deck. Though the spectator's choice is unrestricted, the magician divines the name of his card. Then, without looking, he reveals the name of the card from the other deck.

The trick is not over just yet. Each card is returned to its own deck. With a snap of the fingers, the magician causes the backs of the two cards to change places.

Method: The trick should be done after a meal, when tea or coffee has been served. Your cup of beverage is part of the secret, so you want it to be at hand without raising suspicion. Secure two decks of contrasting back color. Secretly place a pencil dot or other mark on the back of one card, say the ♣3, in each deck. The marks should be at opposite ends of the card as shown in Figure 56.

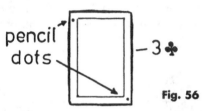

Fig. 56

Ask the spectator to shuffle each deck. When he has done this, have him pick one deck, say the red-backed deck. Ask him to spread his deck face-down on the table. While you say this, spread the blue-backed deck face-down on the table in front of you.

Spot the pencil-dotted card in your deck and slide it out toward you. Ask the spectator to slide a card out of his deck without looking at it. By means of a secret used by psychics to gain information, you are going to find out the name of his card without looking directly at the face of the card. Take his card with your right hand and transfer it to your left hand. In the process, bring the card over your cup, Figure 57. Glance down into the cup. The surface of the liquid acts as a reflecting mirror, allowing you to see the face of his card. Do not stop or

Fig. 57

hesitate as the card moves over the cup. To the audience, it should appear that you have simply transferred the card from hand to hand. Assume the spectator's card is the ♥A.

The left hand now holds the card. Keep it face-down and parallel to the floor. Glance off into space, pretend to concentrate, and then say, "I get the impression that you picked a low value card, a club. Yes, I can see it clearly now, the three of clubs." The card you name is the *other* card, the one you had previously pencil-dotted. Now pick up the blue-backed card with the right hand and transfer it to the left hand, but make sure it goes under the other card, Figure 58. Say, "And my card was the—hmm, let's see, yes, it looks like the ace of hearts." Here you name the card seen reflected in the cup of tea.

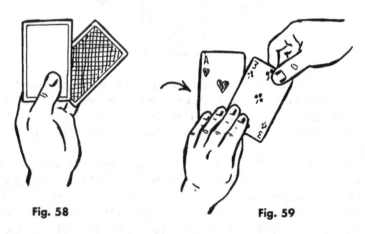

Fig. 58   **Fig. 59**

Turn the left hand palm-down, but in the process use the left thumb to slide the ♥A to the right. At the same time, use the left fingers to slide the other card to the left. When the left hand has turned palm-down, take the ♣3 with the right hand, Figure 59,

and say, "Let's put your card back into the red deck." Place the
♥A face-up on the table. Turn the red-backed deck face-up. Drop
the ♣3 onto the face of the red-backed deck. Cut the deck and
complete the cut.

Turn the blue-backed deck face-up. Drop the ♥A onto the face
of that deck and say, "We'll return my card to my deck." Cut the
blue-backed deck and complete the cut, then remark, "The curious thing about this trick is that if we switch decks, we switch
backs." Put the blue-backed deck in front of the spectator. Take
the red-backed deck and place it in front of you. Spread the red-
backed deck face-down on the table. There is now a blue-
backed card in the middle of his deck. Say, "This is something
of a curiosity. This card has my back." Turn the card over. "But
your face." The ♣3 appears to have changed into a blue-backed
card.

"And over here it's just the opposite." Spread the blue-backed
deck face-down on the table. There is a red-backed card in the
middle. "This card has your back." Turn the card over. "But my
face." It looks as if the ♥A has changed into a red-backed card.

53. Dupe-licates

J. K. Hartman devised a version of the two-deck card trick
which is impromptu and makes use of two decks that may be
borrowed.

Method: Ask the spectator to shuffle each deck and hand one
to you. As you take the deck and square it up, secretly glimpse
the bottom card. Let's say this card is the ♦A. The ♦A will serve
as a key card you will put to use later in the trick.

State that you and the spectator will deal cards from the tops
of your respective decks. You will deal your cards at the same
pace as the spectator, matching him card for card, until he says
stop. When he has called stop, there will be a pile of cards in
front of each party.

Reach over and look at the top card of his pile. He then looks
at the top card of your dealt pile. He drops his undealt cards on
top of his tabled pile, and follows up by giving his deck a complete cut. Drop your undealt cards on top of your tabled pile.
Invite the spectator to give your deck a complete cut.

Say, "Each of us has chosen a card. Please look through your
deck and remove your card. I will do the same with my deck."

Turn your deck face-up and spread the cards from left to right between your hands. Look through your deck for your original key card (the ♦A in our example). Remove the card just to the right of it and place that card on the table. The spectator does likewise with the card he chose, removing that card from his own deck and placing it face-down on the table. Say, "If we each do the same thing, we should arrive at the same card." Turn over both cards to show a perfect match.

54. Trapped in Time

Magic tricks usually have surprise endings. This trick is different. The magician reveals the ending before the trick begins.

Removing a wallet from his pocket, the magician shows that it contains a red-backed card, the ♠2, and that the card is signed on its face. The card is returned to the wallet. "I've had that card for weeks," the magician says. "It's a souvenir of how the trick ended the last time." A card is chosen from a blue-backed deck, signed by the spectator and cut back into the deck. Let's say this card is the ♥4. Its exact location in the deck is unknown to all present. The red-backed card is removed from the wallet and cut into the deck. When the cards are examined, it is seen that the red-backed card has located the spectator's ♥4.

The red-backed card is returned to the wallet. The deck is put in the pocket. The magician says, "The next time I perform this trick, that card in the wallet will remind me of the occasion when I did this trick for you. It has an odd way of doing so." He withdraws the red-backed card from the wallet and turns it face-up. Just a moment ago it was the signed ♠2, but it has changed into the ♥4, complete with the spectator's own signature.

Method: Write someone's initials in the center of a red-backed ♠2. Place this card in the wallet, Figure 60. Place the

Fig. 60

blue-backed ♥4 on top of the blue-backed deck. Position the red-backed ♥4 eleventh from the bottom of the blue-backed deck. This completes the preparation.

To present the trick, remove the wallet and show the red-backed card front and back. Comment that the card is a souvenir from the time you did this trick for Norman Jones (or whoever is represented by the initials). Put the card back in the wallet and leave the wallet on the table.

Place the blue-backed deck face-up on the table, and say "Please take a few cards off the face of the deck, any number less than ten." After the spectator has removed a few cards, count ten cards off the face of the deck into a face-up heap on the table. Ask how many cards he took. Say the number is five.

Deal five cards off the face of the packet. The fifth card will be the ♥4. Ask the spectator to sign his initials in the center of the ♥4. While he does this, gather all of the counted cards, including those taken by the spectator, and replace them on the face of the deck. Then put the signed ♥4 on the face of the deck. With the deck still face-up, lift off about three-quarters of the deck and place it on the table. Put the balance of the deck on top. Turn the deck face-down, and say, "Here's the magic card. It will seek out your card." Slide the red-backed card out of the wallet. Put it face-down on top of the deck. Cut the deck as close to the center as you can and complete the cut.

Pick up the deck and hold it in the left hand. Spread cards from left to right until you get to the first red-backed card. Take care not to spread past this point because you don't want to expose the other red-backed card. The cards above the first red-backed card are transferred to the bottom of the deck.

Fig. 61

Put the red-backed card back in the wallet without showing the face of this card. Push the top card of the deck forward about one inch, Figure 61, and say, "This should be your card."

Lift the deck so the audience can see the face of this card. "Is this the four of hearts?" you ask. When the audience says yes, square up the deck and put it in your pocket.

"Next week I plan to do this trick at a party. I'll have no trouble remembering that I did the trick for you because that card I carry around will remind me of this occasion." Remove the red-backed card from the wallet. The audience thinks it is the ♠2. They will be surprised when you turn it over to reveal that it has changed to the ♥4 and now bears the spectator's signature.

55. Cue Cards

This is a minimalist version of the two-deck card trick, each "deck" consisting of just five cards. It is a good trick to perform on those occasions when two decks are not readily available. It was devised by the author.

Method: Remove any ace through ten in mixed suits from the deck. Ask the spectator to shuffle the packet and remove five cards. Invite him to think of one card and remember its position from the top of the packet. He may think of the ♥A, and remember that it is second from the top of the packet. He does not disclose this information to anyone.

State that you too will think of a card. Take the packet from him. Fan the cards so you can see the faces. Memorize the order of the five cards from top to bottom. You do not need to remember suit; memorize value only. It helps to think of the five cards as a telephone number. If, for example, the cards were in the order 5-8-7-9-4, you would remember 58-794.

Close up the packet and drop it on top of the other five-card group. Pick up the ten cards and hand them to the spectator. Turn your head to one side, and say, "Whatever position your card occupies in the hand, transfer that many cards, one at a time from the bottom to the top of the packet. In other words, if your card is fourth from the top, you would transfer four cards from bottom to top."

After the spectator has done this, take back the packet. "Let's mix the cards a bit." Upjog or outjog every other card beginning with the second. The process is similar to that depicted in Figure 50 (see p. 69), except that in this case all cards are face-down.

Strip out the upjogged cards as a group, taking care not to

disturb the order of the cards. Put the remaining cards face-down on the table, and say, "Let's see if my card is here." Fan the five cards with the faces toward you. The memorized order of the cards in this example is 58-794. You will use this information to determine the identity of the card thought of by the spectator. If the first card in the packet is a five, that is the chosen card. If the second card in the packet is an eight, that is the chosen card. If the third card is a seven, that is the chosen card, and so on. In other words, there will be one card (and only one) that is in the same position that it occupied originally. Remove this card from the packet and place it face-down on the table. Place the remaining four cards on the table.

Pick up the five-card packet, and say, "I guess your card must be in here." Fan the five cards so the spectator can see the faces. "Is your card here?" He will say no. Pick up the four-card group and fan it. "Then it has to be here." The spectator says his card isn't there either. "What card did you think of?" When the spectator names his card, say, "Gosh, so did I!" Turn up the single card on the table to reveal that you both thought of the same card.

56. Synchronism

The effect was invented by Martin Gardner. This subtle version is by Tony Bartolotta. Two decks are used. We will assume that one deck is blue-backed and the other red-backed. Secretly pencil-dot or otherwise mark the back of the ♥2 in each deck. Either deck may be used for other tricks.

Method: To perform, invite a spectator to shuffle each deck and choose one for himself. Take the other deck, and say, "Both decks have been shuffled. Let's each give our cards a cut." We will assume that you have been given the red-backed deck. Spread the cards between the hands. Spot the pencil-dotted card. Cut the deck and complete the cut so that this card is on top of your deck. The spectator has, in the meantime, given the blue-backed deck a straight cut.

Remark, "Scientists speculate that people can sometimes act on the same wavelength. The process is called synchronism. It means that if two people do the same thing at the same time, they will obtain the same result."

Exchange decks with the spectator. "Spread your cards

face-down. Remove any card, look at it and place it on top of your deck. Then give your deck a cut." After the spectator has done this, you pretend to do the same thing, but the handling of your deck is slightly different. Spread the blue deck between your hands until you spot the pencil-dotted ♥2. Break the deck three cards above the ♥2, Figure 62. Place the right-hand

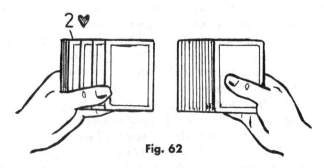

2 ♥

Fig. 62

packet on the table. Pretend to look at the top card of the left-hand packet. Place this card on top of the tabled cards. Then place the remainder of the left-hand packet on top of all. The result is that the ♥2 is third from the top of the blue-backed deck.

"To maintain the synchronized bond, we exchange decks again." Give the spectator the blue-backed deck. Take the red-backed deck in exchange. Invite the spectator to look through the blue-backed deck, and remove his card without disturbing the order of the rest of the deck. Then have him place the blue-backed deck face-down on the table. Direct him to place his card on top of the blue-backed deck.

Spread the red-backed deck from left to right between your hands with the faces of the cards toward you. When you find the ♥2, note the card to the left of it. Say this card is the ♦5. This is the card chosen by the spectator. Beginning with the card to the left of the chosen card, count a number of cards equal to the value of the chosen card. In this example, you would count five cards. Cut the deck at this point and complete the cut. Place the deck face-down on the table. Unknown to the audience, there are five random cards on top of your deck, then the spectator's ♦5, then your card.

Say, "Here's how synchronism works." Turn up the top card of the spectator's deck, and place it face-up on the table to the left of his deck. "Your card is a five, so we count five cards." Deal five cards off the top of your deck into a heap on the table near the spectator's deck, Figure 63. Put the balance of your deck on top of your dealt packet. Turn up the top card of your deck, revealing the matching ♦5. Place this card on the table to the left of the red-backed deck.

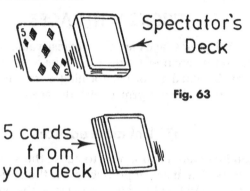

Spectator's Deck

Fig. 63

5 cards from your deck

Say, "My card is the two of hearts," and wave your hand over the red-backed deck. Turn up the top card, revealing the ♥2. "My card is a two, so we count two cards." Pick up the blue-backed deck, count two cards off the top onto the table. Put the deck on top of the dealt cards. Turn up the top card to reveal the matching ♥2.

TRICKS WITH ACES

In many card games, aces are the highest value cards. Each of the tricks in this chapter makes use of the aces. The first three tricks may be used in order, forming a routine of different effects which can be performed with the aces.

57. Unbalanced Aces

Bill Simon invented a subtle way to cause the spectator to find the four aces. The magical production of the aces is always an exciting trick, and this handling of a classic theme is one of the best.

Method: Prior to the performance, place the four aces on the top of the deck. Then place any other card on top of the aces. When ready to perform the trick, place the deck on the table in front of a spectator. Invite him to cut the deck into thirds. Keep track of where the top third goes. Ask him to point to one heap. If he points to the top third of the deck, remark that you will use that heap and one other. Invite him to indicate another heap. The heap not chosen is placed aside.

If, when you first ask him to point to a heap, he points to any heap but the top one, pick up the chosen heap and place it aside, saying that this is the one you won't use. In either case, no matter what choice the spectator makes, you will be left with the top heap plus one other heap.

Say, "In order for this to work, the cards can't be in balance. Frankly, they look a little too balanced right now, so let's take care of that." You should do a little acting here. Crouch down so you are looking at the cards from a distance a few inches above the table. Pretend to study each heap. Pick up the top card of the top heap (the one that contains the aces) and transfer it to the top of the other heap.

Study both heaps again. Shake your head, and say, "They're still not right." Transfer another card from the top heap to the top of the other heap. Look at the cards. Act as if you're still not satisfied. Transfer one more card from the top heap to the top of the other heap and say, "That should do it." Hand a heap to each of two spectators. Ask each to deal his cards into two heaps, alternating a card to each as he deals. When they are finished, there will be four heaps on the table. Say, "It's time to see if the numbers worked out right." Turn each heap face-up to reveal the four aces.

58. Attraction Aces

Remark, "It's well known that there's a magnetic attraction between people. The saying is that opposites attract. With playing cards the opposite is true." Ask the spectator to remove three aces from the deck. They are placed on the magician's palm, Figure 64. The magician turns his hand palm-down. The aces mysteriously cling to his hand as if attracted by a magnet, Figure 65-B. Giving his hand a shake, the magician causes two of the aces to fall to the table. The ace that remains is the odd-color ace of the three.

Method: Ask the spectator to remove three aces from the deck. Point out that two are of one color and one the opposite color. We will assume that the three aces are the ♠A, ♣A, and ♦A. The two cards of the same color are the black aces. Rub the left palm on the right sleeve, as if to create static electricity. Place the black aces on the left palm, then place the ♦A on top of them at right angles. Hold the three aces in place with the left

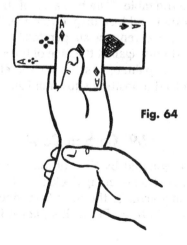

Fig. 64

thumb as shown in Figure 64. Make sure that the ♦A is closer to the wrist than the other two aces.

Grasp the wrist with the right hand, Figure 64. Turn the left hand palm-down. Keep the right hand stationary. As the left hand rotates to the palm-down position, secretly allow the right first finger to slide over so it contacts the ♦A, Figure 65-A.

Remove the left thumb from the ♦A. Spread the left thumb and fingers wide apart as shown in Figure 65-B. It appears as if

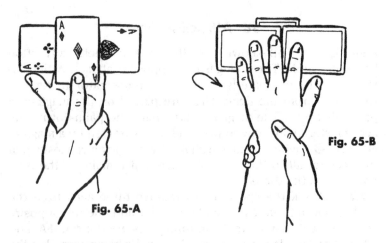

Fig. 65-B

Fig. 65-A

the aces are suspended under the hand. Gently shake the left hand back and forth. Do not release the right first finger's grip on the ♦A, but ease pressure, allowing the black aces to slide away and fall to the table. "The two aces of the same color cancel out one another and lose magnetic force. The opposite ace is always the one that remains suspended."

Place the left thumb against the face of the ♦A. Pivot or rotate the left hand so it is palm-up. As you do, secretly bring the right forefinger back to the position shown in Figure 64. Toss the ♦A to the table.

59. Carbon Copy

For this trick, originated by the author, you will use the four aces from each of two matching decks.

Method: Openly arrange the aces from one deck in ♣-♥-♣-♦ order from top to bottom. Place this packet face-down on the table. Arrange the other four aces in the same order. Drop this packet face-down on the table next to the first packet. As you do this, say, "Cards can be programmed to produce copies of themselves. I'll show you how it works. Please choose one of these groups of cards."

It makes no difference which group the spectator picks. Grasp it from above with the right hand, and say, "We'll mix these cards up." Deal the top card of the packet to the table. Place the next card under the packet. Deal the next card onto the tabled card. Deal the next card under the packet. Deal the next card onto the tabled cards. Then deal the last card onto the tabled cards. This method of mixing a group of cards is called a down/under shuffle.

Drop the other packet on top of the mixed packet. Point out that only one group of cards has been mixed, and say, "Now we're going to program the cards to act like a copying machine." Grasp the combined packet from above with the right hand. Draw off the top and bottom card with the left hand as shown in Figure 42 (see p. 63). Place this pair of cards on the table. Draw off the next pair in like manner and place it onto the tabled pair. Do the same with each of the remaining pairs.

Pick up the eight-card heap and perform a down/under shuffle just as you did before, the top card going to the table, the next card under the packet, the next card onto the tabled card, and so on until all cards have been dealt. Remark, "That should do it." Deal the top four cards into a face-down row. Deal the remaining cards into a face-down row below them. Turn up the cards in each row, calling them out as you do so. The cards in the bottom row will exactly match the cards in the upper row, Figure 66.

Fig. 66

If eight aces are not available and you wish to perform a similar trick with cards from a borrowed deck, use the ♥A through ♥4 as one group, and the ♠A through ♠4 as the other. The handling is otherwise the same.

60. One Chance in Four

British card expert Jack Avis developed an offbeat prediction that is the basis for this trick.

Method: Eight aces are used. Four of them are red-backed and four blue-backed. Deal the red-backed aces to the table. Arrange them in ♥-♣-♠-♦ order. Turn them face-down. Using a marking pen, write the number 5 on the back of the ♥A, the number 10 on the back of the ♣A, the number 15 on the back of the ♠A, and the number 20 on the back of the ♦A. The preparation of the red-backed aces is shown in Figure 67. The prepared aces may be kept in the wallet.

The blue-backed aces are stacked in the blue-backed deck such that the ♥A is fifth from the top, the ♣A sixth, the ♦A thirty-seventh, and the ♠A thirty-eighth. The deck is kept in the card case until the time of performance.

To perform the trick, remove the red-backed cards from the wallet. Deal them face-down to the table. As shown in Figure 67, the cards are dealt such that the numbers on the backs are in the order 5-10-15-20. Remark that the cards are marked in an obvious way so the audience can clearly follow the trick, and that, "There's one card in this deck—I emphasize one and *only* one—which matches one of these aces. Pick one of the aces."

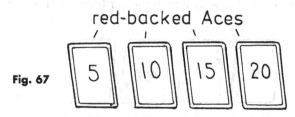

red-backed Aces

Fig. 67

If the spectator picks the card with the 5 or the card with the 10 on the back, remove the deck from the card case and hold it face-down in the left hand. Deal the top five cards in front of the card with the 5 on the back. Deal the next five cards in front of the card with the 10 on the back. Deal the next five cards in front of the card with the 15 on the back. Deal the next five cards in front of the card with the 20 on the back.

If the spectator chose the card with the 5 on the back, turn up the top card of each heap. Then turn over each of the red-backed cards. The only two cards that match (i.e., occupy the same positions in their respective rows) will be the card chosen by the spectator, and the matching ♥A from the blue-backed deck.

If the spectator chose the card with the 10 on the back, turn each packet face-up. Then turn up each of the red-backed cards. The only two cards that match will be the card chosen by the spectator and the matching ♣A from the blue-backed deck.

The other possibility is that the spectator will have chosen the card with the 15 on the back, or the card with the 20 on the back. In this case, remove the deck from the card case so that it is face-up. Deal twenty cards off the face of the deck into a heap on the table. Put the rest of the deck aside.

Turn the twenty-card heap face-down. Then deal five cards in front of each red-backed card as described above. If the spectator chose the card with the 15 on the back, turn up the top card of each packet, then turn up each of the red-backed cards. The only matching cards will be the card chosen by the spectator and the ♠A from the blue-backed deck.

If the spectator chose the card with the 20 on the back, turn each packet face-up. Then turn each of the red-backed cards face-up. The only two cards that match will be the spectator's chosen card and the matching ♦A from the blue-backed deck.

61. Cut and Match

The spectator and the magician each take half the deck. The cards are placed out of sight under the table to guarantee that the choices made will be random. Each person cuts off a group of cards, turns them face-up and places them under the remainder. The two packets are brought into view and spread on the table. It is seen that each person has cut to a red ace. The trick appears to be over, but then the black aces are produced in a surprising fashion.

Method: Place a red ace on the top and bottom of the deck. Position the black aces so they are 26th and 27th from the top of the deck. When ready to present this trick, count twenty-six cards off the top of the deck into a heap on the table. The spectator is seated across the table from you. Ask him to take either half of the deck. Each person puts his cards under the table.

Instruct him to lift off some of his cards, turn this group of cards face-up and place it under the remaining cards. State that you will do the same thing with your cards, but really proceed as follows. Take the top card of your packet (an ace), turn it face-up and place it on the bottom of your packet. Then take the top half of your packet, turn it face-up and place it on the bottom of your packet. Tell him you will exchange your packet with his so that he has control of your cards. Before handing your cards over to him, you perform a secret action suggested by Oscar Weigle for a similar trick. Secretly turn your packet over, then hand it to him. Take his packet in exchange, but as soon as you get it, turn it over.

Both parties bring their packets into view. Say, "Let's see how many cards we cut off." You are holding a packet of cards which consists of a face-down group on top of a face-up group. Deal the face-down cards in your packet to the table, counting aloud as you deal. When you get to the end of the face-down group, you may have counted twelve cards. Say, "Twelve cards. Perfect." The first face-up card is a red ace. Deal the ace to the table. Place the counted cards on top of your packet.

Instruct the spectator to spread the cards he holds until he gets to the first face-up card. It will be a matching red ace. Have him deal this red ace to the table. He then squares up his cards. His packet will consist of a face-down group of cards on top of a face-up group, just like yours. Say, "Here's what would have happened if we had done it the other way around." Turn both halves of the deck over. Spread each half. There will be a run of face-down cards, then a run of face-up cards in each packet. But this time, the first face-up card in each half will be a black ace!

62. Knockout Poker

This is a simplified handling of a baffling trick invented by mentalist Larry Becker. The spectator picks five cards for himself and five for the magician. The spectator's cards are drawn from a face-up packet and there is no force. He can pick any cards he likes. The magician's cards are taken from a face-down packet at the spectator's discretion. It looks like the zenith of fairness,

but when the magician's cards are turned over, it is revealed
that he has the four aces.

Method: Beforehand, place the four aces on top of the deck.
Remark, "Mind readers have an unfair advantage in gambling
casinos. Rather than use sleight of hand, they influence the outcome in mysterious ways." As you speak, place the deck face-up
on the table. Cut off about three-quarters of the deck and place
it nearer the spectator, Figure 68. Lift off the face card of the
larger packet and place it on the smaller packet. Continue doing
this until the spectator calls stop. When he does, take the
stopped-at card off the larger packet, turn it face-down and
place it on top of the smaller packet, Figure 69.

Cut the smaller packet in half, and complete the cut, Figure
70. The spectator's face-down card is now in the center of the
smaller packet. Say, "Wherever your card ends up, that will
mark the place where my card will come from." Turn the small
packet over and spread the cards from left to right until you get
to the face-up card. Put the cards above the face-up card under
the packet. Deal the face-up card in front of the spectator. Deal
the top card of the packet in hand nearer to you. Do not turn
this card over. Place this packet face-up on the table in front of
you.

You are back to the starting point. Deal more cards from the
larger to the smaller packet until the spectator calls stop. Turn
that card face-down and place it on top of the smaller packet.
Cut the packet, complete the cut, and go on as described above
to deal the reversed card to the spectator and the next card to
yourself. Repeat the same plan until each person has five cards.
Remark that the spectator has given himself a promising poker

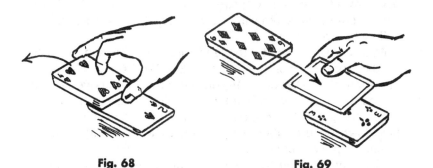

Fig. 68   **Fig. 69**

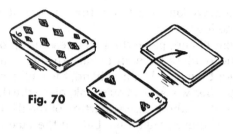

Fig. 70

hand. Then say, "And here's the hand you gave me." Turn your cards over to reveal the four aces.

At the beginning of the trick when the spectator is asked to call stop as you deal, caution him to do so fairly promptly because he is going to say stop five times and you don't want to run out of cards.

"Knockout Poker" can be routined together with the previous trick, "Cut and Match." After the four aces have been produced in "Cut and Match," say that you'd like to try a little guessing game. The object of the game is for you to guess when the spectator is going to say stop. Place the deck under the table. Pick up one of the aces and pretend to place it at a precise location in the deck. Really, the ace goes on top. Repeat with each of the other aces. The result is that the spectator thinks the aces are randomly distributed, but you know they are on top of the deck. Proceed from here with "Knockout Poker." At the conclusion, it appears as if you really were able to guess when the spectator would call stop.

63. Four-Card Monte

Say, "You've heard of three-card monte. A new version has just been invented called four-card monte. The slogan is, 'More cards, more chances to win.' I'm not sure if that's true, but I'm willing to give it a try."

Method: Unknown to the audience, you have previously stacked three aces on top of the deck in ♥-♠-♦ order. The ♣A is anywhere else in the deck. As you speak the lines above, spread the cards from hand to hand so you alone can see the faces. When you get to the ♣A, remove it from the deck and place it face-down on the table. Say, "The card we're going to move around is the ace of spades."

Place the deck on the table in front of the spectator. Invite

him to cut it in half, then to cut each half in half, forming four
packets. Make sure the portion with the stacked aces on top is
the leftmost packet. We are going to refer to the packets as
A-B-C-D. Packet A is on your left and has the aces on top.

Drop the supposed ♠A (really the ♣A) face-down on top of
packet A and say, "I'm going to mix the cards around. See if you
can keep track of the ace of spades." Place the left hand on top
of packet A, the right hand on top of packet B as shown in
Figure 71.

Lift up at least four cards with the left hand and a few cards
with the right hand. Cross the hands, Figure 72. Deposit the left-
hand cards on top of B, the right-hand cards on top of A.

Don't lift the hands away from the table. Grasp the top card
of A with the right hand, the top card of B with the left hand.
Uncross the hands. Place the card from the left hand on top of
A, the card from the right hand on top of C. Grasp the top card
of B with the left hand, the top card from D with the right hand.
Cross the hands and deposit the card from the left hand onto D
and the card in the right hand onto C.

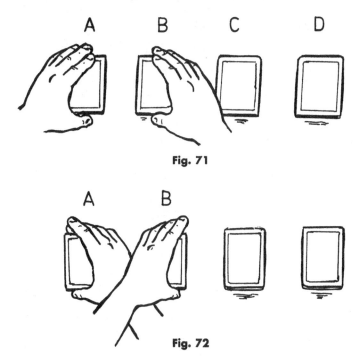

A   B   C   D

Fig. 71

A   B

Fig. 72

Don't uncross the hands just yet. Grasp the top card of D with the left hand, the top card of B with the right hand. Uncross the hands. Deposit the card from the left hand onto C, the card from the right hand onto D, and say, "Okay, I'll bet you a million dol— uh, better make that a million good wishes, that you can't tell me where the ace is."

The spectator never saw the ♠A to begin with, so he is skeptical that he can find it at all. Usually he will point to the card on top of packet A. Say, "That's a good guess, but the ace of spades is really over here." Turn up the top card of packet D, and remark, "But the catchword is, the more cards you have, the more chances to win. When it comes to picking an ace, it sounds to me as if you can't lose." Turn up the top card of each of the other packets to reveal that each is an ace.

There are only four moves, but the moves should be practiced so they can be done quickly and without thinking. The appearance of all four aces at the finish will come as a real surprise to the audience.

ROUGE ET NOIR

The faces of playing cards come in two colors, red and black. Many tricks have been devised in which the magician appears to exert control over the distribution of colors. Each of the tricks in this chapter evolved from classic principles in color control.

64. Your Card Is Red

This trick may be done at any time with any complete deck.

Method: Remove all twenty-six red cards from the deck. Hand them to the spectator with the request that he give them a good shuffle. Turn your back. Ask him to think of a number from one to ten. When he has a number in mind, he silently deals two heaps of cards, each containing the thought-of number. If, let's say, he thought of five, he would deal two heaps of five cards each. He does not tell you how many cards he dealt.

At this point, there are two heaps on the table and a packet of undealt cards in his hand. Ask him to pick either heap, look at the bottom card, and drop this heap on top of the red cards he holds in his hand. Then, turn and face him. There is a small packet of red cards on the table and a large packet of red cards in the spectator's hand. Take the packet he holds, and say, "There are two statements I can make about your card." Deal thirteen cards off the top of the packet into a heap on the table. Do not call attention to the number of cards you dealt. "Your card is positively one of these." As you speak, tap the packet just dealt to the table.

Pick up the dealt packet of thirteen cards. Place it on top of the cards you still hold in your hand. Then pick up the remaining small packet from the table. This is the second packet the spectator dealt. In our example it would contain five cards. Put it on top of the cards in your hand. You now hold a packet of twenty-six cards. Say, "The second thing I know is positively true is that your card is red." This is not a shocking statement; *all* the cards used in this trick are red.

Spell Y-O-U-R, dealing a card for each letter from the top of the red heap. Then spell C-A-R-D, dealing a card for each letter. Spell I-S, dealing a card for each letter. Finally, spell R-E-D, dealing a card for each letter. Ask the spectator for the name of his card. Turn up the top card of the packet still in your hand and it will be the chosen card.

65. Transposed Thoughts

This trick was devised by the author. A spectator is given a packet of cards from any shuffled deck. While the magician turns his head to one side so he can't see what is being done, the spectator sorts reds from blacks, giving one packet to another spectator. We will call the spectators Albert and Beatrice. Assume that Albert has the black cards and Beatrice the reds. Each person counts their cards and remembers the number. Then each person initials the face card of their respective packets.

Albert returns his packet to the top of the deck. Beatrice places her packet on top of all. The deck is given to the magician behind his back. The magician says, "I'll try to find your signed cards and change their positions so that each occupies the position of the other person's card." The deck is brought into view. Albert is asked for his number. Suppose he says five. The magician counts five cards in front of him. Then Beatrice is asked for her number. She says ten. The magician counts ten cards in front of her.

The magician calls attention to Albert's packet. He removes the top card and turns the other cards in the packet over. All cards are black. The magician says, "Albert, here are your black cards . . ." Then he turns over the top card. ". . . and *Beatrice's* red card." The card is indeed the red card that Beatrice initialed.

He removes the top card of Beatrice's packet. The other cards are turned over. "Here are your red cards . . ." He turns over the top card. ". . . and *Albert's* black card." The top card is turned over to reveal that it is Albert's signed card.

The deck may be borrowed and shuffled by the spectators. The magician does not know which spectator has which color cards, nor does he know how many cards of each color are in play. He does not know the signed cards, nor does he have to know their positions. The signed cards are the only cards that change places. All other cards go back to the original spectator, and in their original order. There is no prior preparation, and the deck need not even be complete for the trick to work.

Method: When the shuffled deck is handed to you, deal off fifteen cards, counting silently as you deal. To make it seem as if you are using a random number of cards, push two cards off the deck with the left thumb, then three, then two, then three, then two, then three. Hand the packet to Albert and have him give it a shuffle.

Turn your back. Ask Albert to sort reds from blacks. He takes either color and hands the cards of the other color to Beatrice. Each person counts their cards and remembers the number. Each then shuffles the cards they hold. Direct them to sign their initials to the face (or bottom) card of their packets.

Albert replaces his packet face-down on top of the deck. Beatrice places her packet face-down on top of all. The deck is given to you behind your back. Turn and face the audience. Remark that you will try by means of color-sensitive fingertips to gauge who took which card, and further that you will exchange these two cards and no others.

It seems a difficult task, but the procedure is easy. Silently count fourteen cards from hand to hand, dealing one on top of the other so their order is reversed. The number you deal is always one less than the number of cards handed to the spectator originally. Replace the dealt packet on top of the deck.

Bring the deck into view. Ask Albert how many cards he had originally. Deal that many cards in a heap in front of him. Ask Beatrice how many cards she had. Deal that many cards in a heap in front of her. Turn attention to the packet in front of Albert. Lift off the top card with the right hand, but don't turn it over just yet. With the left hand, turn all of the other cards in this heap face-up. Spread them to show all cards of one color. If Albert had the black cards to start with, he has them back. Then turn over the card in hand to reveal Beatrice's signed red card.

Lift up the top card of the packet in front of Beatrice. With the other hand, turn over all the other cards. Beatrice has her red cards back. Turn over the card in hand to reveal Albert's signed black card.

66. Color by Touch

This is a double mystery in which the magician correctly guesses the colors of cards that have been shuffled by the spectator.

Method: Arrange twenty cards so that the colors alternate red-black-red-black from top to bottom. If you do this trick with a borrowed deck, one way to achieve the necessary set-up is to spread the cards between the hands so you alone can see the faces. Spot a red card that has a black card just to the right of it. Remove this pair of cards and place it on the table. The top card of the pair is red and the bottom card black. Find another red card that has a black card just to the right of it. Remove this pair and place it on top of the tabled pair. Continue adding pairs to the tabled packet until there are ten pairs.

Ask the spectator to give the packet a straight cut and then another. After he has done this, take back the packet. Push over the top ten cards without reversing their order. Place this packet on the table. Turn the other packet face-up and put it alongside the first packet. Invite the spectator to riffle shuffle the two packets together, Figure 73.

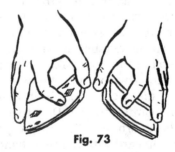

Fig. 73

After the shuffle, take back the packet. Deal the top ten cards into a heap on the table. Spread them enough to reveal the mixture of face-up and face-down cards. Push the face-up cards out of the spread, but don't disturb the order of the face-down cards. Square up the face-down cards and put this packet to one side for the moment. Count the number of face-up reds and the number of face-up blacks. Let's say there are two reds and three blacks.

You still hold a packet of ten cards in the left hand. Remark that Russian scientists have tested subjects who claim to be able to detect color by sense of touch alone. In an attempt to duplicate this experiment, you will turn some cards face-up and some face-down so that they match the cards on the table.

Place the ten-card packet under the table. When it is concealed from audience view, secretly turn it over. That is all you need do. Bring it into view again. Spread the cards from hand to hand. Toss the face-up cards to the table as you come to them. Don't disturb the order of the face-down cards.

When all of the face-up cards have been dealt to the table, you will have some face-down cards in the left hand. Hold onto these for the moment. Call attention to the number of reds and blacks you have just dealt. The number of reds will equal the number of face-up reds in the first packet. The number of blacks will equal the number of face-up blacks in the other packet.

The trick appears to be over, but there is one more trick to come. Call attention to the group of face-down cards in your hand. Say, "I'm going to try it with these cards." Place this group of cards below the edge of the table. When the cards are out of sight, upjog every other card. Strip the outjogged cards from the packet, bring the cards into view, and spread them face-up on the table to reveal that you have the reds in one hand, the blacks in the other.

There is another packet of face-down cards on the table. Place these below the tabletop. Upjog every other card and strip out this packet. Bring the cards into view, one face-down group in each hand. Spread them face-up to show all red cards in one hand, all black cards in the other. You have separated the colors in an impressive manner.

67. Guess Again

This trick was worked out by the author. Say, "Some people have a strong sense of intuition that guides them to make the right decision." The spectator is given a packet of eight cards, with the rest of the deck spread on the table. To test his intuitive powers, he is asked to push the eight cards one at a time into the deck as shown in Figure 74. Each card is left outjogged for about half its length.

After he has done this, the deck is squared side for side,

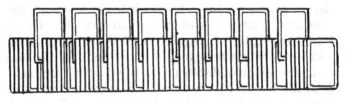

Fig. 74

leaving the eight cards still outjogged, Figure 75. Pairs of cards are dealt off the top of the deck. When the performer gets to a pair of cards containing one of the jogged cards, that pair is placed to one side. He continues dealing pairs of cards off the top of the deck. When he gets to another pair containing a jogged card, he puts it aside. At the completion of this process, there will be eight pairs of cards placed to one side.

Fig. 75

The performer turns over the jogged card in one of the eight pairs. Say, "This card is black. You could have paired it with a red card, but some intuitive sense told you to find a card of the same color." The card paired with the black card is turned over. It too is black. The procedure continues with each of the remaining pairs. In each case, the spectator succeeds in placing a card next to a card of the same color.

Method: Secretly stack the deck so the colors alternate. That is the only preparation. When ready to perform this trick, place the deck in front of the spectator. Invite him to cut the deck and complete the cut. He may give the deck any number of straight cuts, but three is about right.

Place the deck in your left hand. Push over the top eight cards without reversing their order. Place the eight-card packet on the table. Spread the balance of the deck face-down on the table. Invite the spectator to take the top card of the eight-card packet and insert it into the spread. Explain that he is going to do this eight times, so he should start near the top of the deck.

After he has done this, he takes the new top card of the packet and inserts it into the deck a few cards below the first card. He continues this process with each of the remaining cards. In all cases, the cards the spectator inserts into the deck remain outjogged so they can be identified later on. Also, the cards must be inserted into the deck in order, each card going under the cards that are already outjogged. When all eight cards have been placed into the deck, the situation will look like Figure 74.

Square the deck side for side, Figure 75. Do not square the outjogged cards into the deck. Deal the top two cards off the deck. Place them on the table. Continue dealing pairs until you get to a pair of cards containing the first outjogged card. Place this pair on the table to one side.

Continue dealing pairs of cards off the top. Whenever you get to a pair containing an outjogged card, put it to one side. When you have gone through the deck, you will have eight pairs of cards on the table. Pick one of these pairs at random. Turn up one card in the pair, then the other to reveal a color match. Pick another pair at random and repeat the process. Do not pick pairs in order because that will reveal the secret. When you have finished, congratulate the spectator on having excellent powers of intuition.

68. She Read Your Mind

A spectator cuts the deck into three heaps, picks one heap and places a chosen card into the heap. He is the only person who knows the identity of the chosen card. He shuffles the heap and hands it to a lady. She picks one card from the heap and places it face-down on the magician's palm. The magician divines the name of the card without looking at it. The card may be the ♣A. He then turns to the gentleman and says, "Which card did you pick?" The card he picked was indeed the ♣A. This trick was worked out by Tony Bartolotta and the author. Although a double mystery is performed, the trick is obtained by a simple means.

Method: Beforehand, sort the deck so the twenty-six red cards are on top of the deck and twenty-six black cards are on the bottom. Remember the top card of the black group (that is, the card that is now twenty-seventh from the top of the deck). Let us say this card is the ♣A.

When ready to perform, place the deck on the table. Invite Neal and Nancy to participate. Ask Neal to cut the deck into three heaps. Point to the top heap and ask Neal to shuffle it. While he does this, place the middle heap on top of the bottom heap, and say, "I want to make sure we have enough cards, so I'll count a bunch of them to the table." Count twenty-six cards off the combined heap into a packet on the table. The rest of the packet will not be used. Drop it in your pocket.

Ask Neal to deal his cards one at a time onto the table. You do likewise with the twenty-six-card heap, matching him card for card as you form a separate heap. When Neal has dealt his last card, point to the last card you dealt. Ask him to look at it and place it anywhere in his packet. Unknown to the audience, the card he looks at will be the ♣A.

Neal shuffles his packet and hands it to Nancy. Instruct her not to say anything that might give a clue as to what is going on in her mind. Say to Neal, "I get the impression that your card is a black card. Is that true?" Neal says yes. Turn to Nancy. "Please look through those cards and pick out a black card. Don't show your choice to anyone." When Nancy fans her cards, she will see a group of cards that is all red except for one black card. That black card is Neal's selection, the ♣A.

Hold out your hand palm-up. Instruct Nancy to place the black card on your palm. When she has done that, take the rest of Nancy's packet with your other hand and place the cards in your pocket. Pretend to concentrate your mental energies on the card that rests on your palm. Say, "When I do this trick, I usually get blurred images, but right now the image is as clear as it's ever been. I see an image of a club, in fact the ace of clubs. Neal, what card did you pick?" Neal admits he chose the ♣A. All that remains is to turn over the card to show that it is indeed the ♣A.

69. Psychic Map

Fifteen cards are dealt out into an array like the one shown in Figure 76. A spectator mixes the cards and turns some face-up. The apparatus is covered with a newspaper. The magician reaches under the newspaper and makes some adjustments. When the newspaper is removed, it is seen that all of the face-up cards are black. The face-down cards are then shown to be all red. Thus, without looking at the cards, the magician has succeeded in sorting red from black. This trick is the author's handling of a brilliant invention of Bob Hummer's.

Method: Fan the deck so you can see the faces. Remove eight red cards and place them in a face-down heap on the table. Remove eight black and place them on top of the reds. Do not show the faces of the cards. Simply state that for this experiment you will use some reds and some blacks.

Place the rest of the deck aside. Grasp the packet of sixteen cards from above with the right hand. Draw off the top and bottom card as shown in Figure 42 (see p. 63). Place this pair on the table. It will consist of one red and one black card. Draw off seven more pairs in a similar way onto the tabled cards.

Pick up the packet. Turn it face-up and spread the cards in bunches from hand to hand to show a mixture of reds and blacks. Turn the packet face-down and hand it to the spectator. Ask him to give the packet two or three straight cuts. He then deals out three rows of five cards each, dealing from left to right, a card at a time. This accounts for fifteen cards. The last card is returned to the top of the deck.

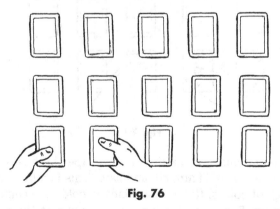

Fig. 76

Demonstrate what you want the spectator to do by grasping the two cards at the lower left, Figure 76, exchanging them, Figure 77, and then turning them over, Figure 78. As you do this, explain to the spectator that he is to pick two cards that are

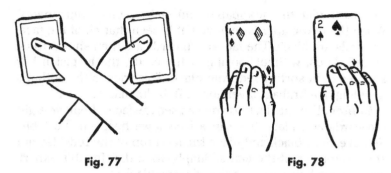

Fig. 77   **Fig. 78**

next to one another, exchange them, and then turn them over in place.

"The cards can be face-up or face-down, one can be face-up and one face-down, it doesn't matter." As you say this, grasp the second and third cards in the bottom row, Figure 79, exchange them and turn them over. Turn your head to one side. The spectator goes through the exchange-and-turn procedure four or five times.

Fig. 79

When he is finished, ask that a newspaper be held over the cards to hide them, Figure 80, and say, "This layout of cards is like a map of colors. Red is hot, black is cold. By scanning the map with my fingertips, I will read the colors in the map you have drawn and turn certain cards over. If I follow the contours of this map correctly, the face-up cards will all be of the same color."

Fig. 80

The system is to turn over the second and fourth cards in the upper row, the first, third and fifth cards in the middle row, and the second and fourth cards in the lower row. Make it look complicated and demanding as if you have to struggle to receive psychic thought patterns from the cards. When you are finished turning over cards, ask that the newspaper be removed. The audience will see a number of face-up cards and they will all be of the same color. The face-down cards are then gathered and turned over to reveal they are all of the opposite color.

GAMES OF CHANCE

New gambling casinos have been established in many states. The success of these enterprises is an indication that games of chance are more popular than ever. The subtleties of tactics and strategy at the gaming table are of interest only to expert players. In order to entertain the audience, the magician should strive to present gambling tricks that show in a clear, uncluttered way what it looks like when the game is under the control of an expert. It is the dream of many to win the lottery, to hit the jackpot, to be dealt the winning hand. The tricks in this chapter give the audience a glimpse into the world of the winning player.

70. Thought-Card Poker

Three poker hands are dealt out. The spectator merely thinks of a card in any hand. The magician infallibly finds the chosen card. This handling of an Eddie Joseph trick was developed by Frank Garcia.

Method: Deal out three poker hands of five cards each. While you turn your head to one side, the spectator chooses any hand, spreads the card so he can see the faces, and thinks of one of the cards in the hand. He drops this hand onto one of the others. Then he puts the remaining hand on top of all. Finally, he places the packet on top of the deck.

Pick up the deck and deal five poker hands, dealing a card at a time from left to right until each hand has five cards. As you deal the cards, remark that expert poker players are trained to keep track of the cards even when those cards are only thought of by other players. Pick up the hands one at a time. Fan them so the spectator can see the faces of the cards. Ask the spectator if he sees his card in that hand. If he doesn't, pick up another hand and show those cards to the spectator.

When he says he sees his card in a particular hand, hold the

poker hand face-down. Deal the top card to the table. Place the
next card on the bottom of the hand. Deal the next card to the
table. Place the next card under the hand. Deal the next card to
the table. Place the next card under the hand.

You are holding two cards at this point. Take the top card in
the right hand. Ask the spectator to name the card he merely
thought of. Pretend you have to decide which of the two cards
is the thought-of card. Then turn over the card in the right
hand. It will be the chosen card.

71. Beginner's Luck

Gamblers debate whether beginner's luck can beat skill at the
card table. The magician offers to test someone's luck, with surprising results.

Method: A simple set-up makes this a mysterious trick. Put
the four kings on top of the deck. Then remove the four aces
and place them on top of all. Do not show the audience what
you are doing. Merely state that you are going to use cards that
have a way of testing whether or not a person is really lucky.

Deal eight cards in a circle as shown in Figure 81. The numbers under the cards indicate the order in which they are to be
dealt, i.e., the first card is dealt to the no. 1 position, the next to
the no. 2 position, and so on clockwise around the circle.

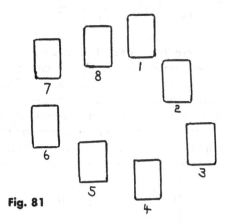

Fig. 81

Say, "There were eight players in the game. Pick a card to
indicate which place you took at the card table." It makes no

difference which card the spectator takes. Slide the chosen card to the middle of the circle. Gather the remaining cards, beginning with the card at the no. 1 position. Put it on top of the card at the no. 2 position, these on top of the card at the no. 3 position, and so on clockwise around the circle so that the aces are back on top. If the spectator chose the card at the no. 1 position, then begin gathering cards with the card at the no. 2 position going onto the card at the no. 3 position, and so on. Place these cards on top of the deck.

Say, "You picked a card at random. We're going to introduce another random element to really test your luck." As you speak, deal cards off the top of the deck into a heap on the table. Deal at least seven cards before you say, "I'd like you to stop me at any time." When the spectator calls stop, put the rest of the deck aside. Pick up the dealt heap. "Now we're going to spell the name of the card you chose a moment ago in our imaginary card game." The card the spectator chose can only be an ace or a king. If it is a king, spell k-i-n-g, dealing a card at a time to form a row of four cards, Figure 82. Then deal the remaining cards in

Fig. 82

K   I   N   G

the packet onto these four cards, dealing a card at a time from left to right until you have dealt out all the cards.

Say, "The king was the first card dealt to you. This is the test of beginner's luck. Here are the other four cards in your hand." Turn up the top card of each packet to reveal the four aces. If the spectator's card is an ace, spell a-c-e, dealing the top three cards to the table in a row, Figure 83. Then deal the remaining cards onto these three cards, dealing a card at a time from left

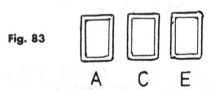

Fig. 83

A   C   E

to right to form three heaps. Continue the deal until the cards have been exhausted.

Point to the card the spectator chose. "That is the first card in your hand, an ace. Here are three more." Turn up the top card of each heap to show the other three aces. In either case, congratulate the spectator on having exceptional beginner's luck.

72. A Perfect Strike

Mel Bennett invented a test that measures how well someone can expect to do at the bowling alley.

Method: The ace through ten are dealt out face-up as in Figure 84. This is the way the ten pins are positioned at the start of the game. The magician says, "In bowling, you get a particular score depending on how many pins you knock down in any one frame. I'll write the score I think you're going to achieve on this piece of paper." On a piece of paper write the number 30. Fold the paper and place it on the table.

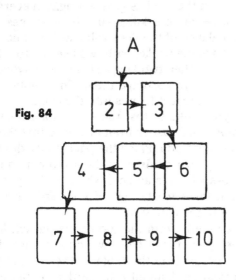

Fig. 84

Invite the spectator to turn over any card in the layout. Remember whether the card is an even-valued or an odd-valued card. Gather the cards by turning the ace over onto the two, then these onto the three, then these onto the six, these onto the five, and so on, following the arrows in Figure 84. Remark that turning over cards like this is symbolic of the way bowling pins are knocked down.

If the card that the spectator turned face-down was even-valued, state that you will add the value of his card to the total of the face-up cards in the packet. Otherwise, say nothing. Spread the packet on the table. Add together the values of the face-up cards. Then add the value of the card chosen by the spectator at the beginning of the trick if the card had an even value. You will always arrive at a total of 30.

Say, "In bowling, a perfect strike is awarded a score of thirty. You achieved a perfect strike. I had a hunch you would." Open the paper to show the number 30.

73. Poker by Perception

The magician holds a packet of four kings and four aces in his hand, but does not tell the spectator the order of the cards. The spectator tries to guess which cards are aces. When the cards are shown, it is seen that he has guessed right in every case.

Method: Remove the four kings and the four aces from the deck. Place the balance of the deck aside as it will not be used in this trick. Arrange the packet with two aces on top, then two kings, then two aces, then two kings. Do not let anyone see the faces of the cards as you arrange them. The empty card case should be handy because it figures into the trick.

Explain that you'd like to test the spectator's poker sense. Position the empty card case in front of you so that the open or flap end points toward you. Place the packet face-down on the table. Take the top two cards, mix them around and ask the spectator to guess which is an ace. Whatever his guess, place that card on the table to the left of the card case. Put the remaining card into the card case.

Take two more cards from the top of the packet. Mix them around. Ask the spectator to guess which is a king. Whatever his guess, put that card on the table to the right of the card case. Put the discarded king into the card case, but *under* the card that is already there. Because the open end of the case is away from the audience, no one can see exactly where the card goes when it is placed inside the card case.

Take the next two cards, mix them around and ask the spectator to guess which is an ace. Put that card on top of the card that is to the left of the card case. Put the discarded ace into the card case, but on *top* of the cards already there. The spectator guesses which of the next two cards is a king. His guess goes on top of the card to the right of the card case. Put the discarded king into the card case, but under the cards already there.

Remove the four cards from the card case. Take the top two and ask the spectator to guess which is an ace. Put his guess on top of the ace heap. Put the discard into the card case. Ask him to guess which of the remaining two cards is a king. Put his guess on top of the king heap. The discard goes into the card case, but under the card already there.

Finally, remove the two cards from the card case. Ask the spectator to point to one of them. You know the top card is an ace. If he points to that card, put it on top of the ace heap and the other card on top of the king heap. If he points to the king, put that card on top of the king heap and the other card on top of the ace heap.

For the finish, turn over the four cards in the left heap to show all aces. Turn over the cards in the right heap to show all kings.

74. Underground Poker

The magician places a joker into a poker hand at a location unknown to the spectator. The spectator removes one card from the hand. It is found that he successfully located the joker.

Method: The trick is best done when seated at a table. Secretly place a jack of any suit in the lap. That is the only preparation. To perform the trick, remove three aces and two jacks from the deck. Don't show the faces of these cards. Merely remark that this is a full house, aces and jacks.

Remove a joker from the deck. Say that you will place the joker into the poker hand at a location that is unknown to the spectator. Hold the full house in one hand, the joker in the other. Lower the hands behind the near edge of the table so the cards are out of sight. Place the joker in the lap. The jack that was placed in the lap earlier is now picked up and inserted anywhere in the poker hand.

Mix up the cards a bit. Hand the six-card poker hand to the spectator under the table. "One card doesn't belong. I'd like you to remove one card from the hand and give it to me, but keep the cards under the table so you have no clue as to the where-abouts of the unwanted card."

Whatever card the spectator gives you, leave it in your lap and take the joker. Bring the joker into view, but keep it face-down. Say, "If you got rid of the correct card, you should be back to the full house, aces and jacks." The spectator brings the poker hand into view and spreads the cards face-up on the table. He will have a full house. It may be three aces and two jacks, or two aces and three jacks, but either way it matches your words.

The card in hand is then turned face-up to show the joker.

75. The Blackjack Player

Remark, "Gamblers are superstitious and bet hunches. Blackjack players especially believe that some dates bring good luck. Write down any four years in your life that you consider lucky. It may be the year you graduated school, the year you got married, the year your child was born."

When the spectator has done this, he totals the four dates. He might choose $1958 + 1976 + 1984 + 1999 = 7917$. The total is used to deal four piles of cards. The first heap will contain seven cards in our example, the next heap nine cards, the next heap one card, and the last heap seven cards.

When the four heaps are turned over, they form two perfect blackjack hands, i.e., an ace and a ten-count card. The outcome is always the same. When the perfect blackjack hands appear, they seem to have dropped in from nowhere. This ingenious trick was originated by Mel Bennett, based on an idea of Stewart James.

Method: From the top of the face-down deck, the stack is ace-any six-spot cards-ace-ace-ten-all twelve picture cards-ten-ten-ten-rest of deck. Follow the above procedure to arrive at four dates. It appears as if the spectator can arrive at thousands of different totals, but whatever the total, the first digit must be a 7 or an 8. The other digits will vary, but there is no danger of running out of stack. The four heaps A-B-C-D are dealt into a square as shown in Figure 85.

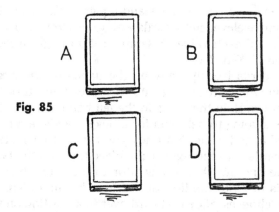

Fig. 85

After the four heaps have been dealt out, invite the spectator to remove the bottom card of heaps A and C, and place this pair aside face-down. Then have him remove the bottom card of heaps B and D. He then turns over each pair of cards to discover that he has given himself a blackjack in each case.

Before starting the trick, explain that if a "0" shows up in the total, you will substitute the number one. The trick works even for dates after the year 2000. For example, assume the trick is done in the middle of the 21st century. The spectator writes these dates:

> 2002
> 2008
> 2011
> <u>2025</u>
> 8046

Try it for these and other dates to satisfy yourself that the stack will work.

76. Pick 'Em Poker

When doing a poker demonstration, it is not always necessary to deal yourself a royal flush or the four aces. Gamblers will settle for any hand that is a winner. This trick is a good example. The audience decides who gets which cards in a three-handed game. The dealer finds he has been dealt a pair of kings and a pair of tens—not much of a hand, but good enough to beat the other players.

Method: Remove a pair of kings and a pair of tens from the deck. Also remove eleven more cards with values from 2 to 9, no more than two of each value. A sample set-up is given here: 4-5-9-4-K-10-2-6-8-7-K-10-2-3-5.

Spread the cards face-up between the hands to show that there is no apparent order. Close up the spread and turn the packet face-down. Hold the cards in the left hand. Explain that the audience is going to help you form poker hands in a high-stakes, three-handed game. Naturally you expect to win. Take the top two cards with the right hand. Place them on the table alongside one another. Ask a spectator to indicate which of these cards is to go to the first player. It makes no difference which one he chooses. Slide that card over to a position on the left. Put the other card of the pair on the bottom of the packet.

Push off two more cards. A spectator decides which of these two cards goes to a second spectator. Slide his choice over to a position on the right. Place the card not chosen on the bottom of the packet. Push off two more cards. Ask a spectator to decide which of these is to go to the dealer. Slide his choice to a position in front of you. Place the other card on the bottom of the packet. Each player now has one card.

Repeat the same process with one more round of cards. At the conclusion, each player will have two cards. Then, to save time, deal the remaining cards out as you would deal a game of poker: beginning with the player on the left, deal clockwise a card at a time until each person has five cards.

Turn up the hands dealt to the first two players to show average hands. Finish by saying, "And you gave the dealer all he needs to win." Turn up the dealer's hand to show two pair, kings and tens, not spectacular, but enough to win the hand.

77. Poker Logic

The trick is a matching effect where the magician correctly predicts the way the spectator will arrange five cards. This is a self-working version of a classic effect perfected by Hen Fetch.

Method: Before the trick begins, place any spot card in a back trouser pocket. That is the quick and simple preparation that sets up an impressive feat. When ready to perform, remark that poker experts have to think a step ahead of the competition. Ask the spectator to call out any royal flush. Say he chooses the royal flush in spades. Remove the ♠A-♠K-♠Q-♠J-♠10, and lay them out in that order in a face-up row on the table.

Remove the other royal flush of the same color, in this case clubs. Arrange the cards in the same order. Put the deck on the table between you and the spectator. Hold the club flush behind your back. Secretly remove the extra card from your trouser pocket and put it on top of the club packet.

Say, "We're each going to pick cards. I'll try to guess which card you plan to choose, so I'll go first." Remove the top card of your packet and place it face-down on top of the deck. Invite the spectator to pick one of the face-up cards in front of him and place it face-down on top of the deck. Let's say he picks the ♠K. Your cards are in order so you know where the matching card lies. Reach behind your back and take the matching card—in this case the ♣K. Place it face-down on top of the deck. Invite the spectator to pick a card from his royal flush and place it face-down on top of the deck. Let's say this card is the ♠10. Reach behind your back and remove the matching card, the ♣10. Place it on top of the deck.

Proceed in the same way twice more. There will be one card in front of the spectator and two behind your back. Let us say that the card in front of the spectator is the ♠J. Behind your back place the matching card, the ♣J, on top of the other card. Carefully square the two cards so they appear as one. Bring the double card out from behind your back and drop it on top of the deck. Invite the spectator to place his card on top of all.

Say, "I think I guessed correctly on most of the cards, but I'm not sure about the last one." Deal off the top two cards. Put them on the table to one side, and say, "We'll get back to those cards in a minute."

Remove the top two cards of the deck. Mix them around. Turn them face-up to show, for example, matching aces. Place this pair face-up on the table. Follow exactly the same process with the next three pairs, in each case revealing a perfect match. Finally, turn attention to the pair of cards placed aside. Turn them over to show a final matching pair for a perfect score.

THOUGHT CONTROL

Magic tricks which seem to demonstrate the reality of psychic forces have built-in audience appeal. Although magicians who perform mental magic customarily issue disclaimers to the effect that what is being demonstrated is not of supernatural origin, many in the audience will think otherwise. There is no better example than that of Harry Houdini. A tireless debunker of fraudulent spirit mediums, Houdini was nevertheless credited with using supernatural powers to escape from chains and handcuffs. The tricks in this chapter were chosen because they create the impression that occult forces are at work.

78. Secret Spell

This is Sam Schwartz's revelation of a thought card using any borrowed, shuffled deck. No questions are asked, there are no key cards, and the working is so well concealed that the trick may be repeated.

Method: Ask the spectator to think of a short name, say the name of a family member or friend. It will work with Bartholomew or Wilhelmina, but the trick moves along a little faster if a short name is thought of. Turn your head to one side. The spectator thinks of the name of a loved one and deals cards off the top of the deck to the table, one card for each letter in the name. If the name is S-U-S-A-N, he would deal a heap of five cards. He looks at the face or bottom card of the heap and drops the heap on top of the deck.

Turn and face the spectator, and say, "I want you to deal cards one at a time from top to bottom, a card for each letter in the name you thought of. For example, if you thought of Sam, you would put one card on the bottom for 'S,' another for 'A,' and another for 'M.'" As you speak, transfer three cards from the top to the bottom of the deck.

Hand the deck back to the spectator and turn your head to

one side again. He transfers the appropriate number of cards from the top to the bottom of the deck. Unknown to the spectator, if the above procedure has been followed exactly as described, his chosen card will be fourth from the bottom of the deck.

Take the deck from him. Deal a card off the top to the table, then a card off the bottom, then another off the top, another off the bottom, and so on. Don't turn any card face-up. Instead, rub the face of each card with the fingertips as if searching for psychic vibrations. When you hold the card that was fourth from the bottom, start to place it on the table, change your mind, rub the face of the card with the fingertips, and say, "What card did you think of?" The spectator might name the ♠6. Turn over the card in hand to show it is the ♠6.

79. Topper

Walter Gibson developed a trick which is a perfect complement to "Secret Spell." It is only necessary to secretly determine the identity of the top card of the deck. This can be done at the conclusion of a previous trick, or by the expedient of spotting the top card as you look through the deck to remove any jokers.

Place the deck on the table. Turn your head aside. Ask the spectator to think of the name of someone close to him. He is then to spell out that person's name, silently dealing a card at a time into a tabled heap for each letter in the name. After he has done this, ask him to shuffle the balance of the deck and cut it into two heaps. Direct him to pick up the dealt packet (the one he used to spell the name), look at the bottom card, place it on one heap and put the other heap on top of all. This last action is shown in Figure 86.

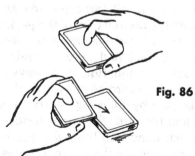

Fig. 86

Turn and face the spectator. Pick up the deck and spread it face-up on the table. Slide your fingertips along the cards as if to pick up vibrations of a psychic nature. After a while, shake your head, and say, "I'm not getting a clear enough impression. What name did you spell?" The spectator might say Kathy. Nod and say, "Ah, Kathy. It's clear now." Study the cards again and push out one card. It is the chosen card.

The chosen card will be the card that was originally the top card of the deck. This is the card you secretly glimpsed before the trick began. Normally it is difficult to force the top card, but the misdirection provided by having the deck shuffled and cut tends to disguise the real secret of the trick.

80. Without a Clue

Tony Bartolotta utilized a gimmicked card in subtle ways to produce baffling card mysteries. The gimmick is known as a thick card. To make it, glue two jokers together, taking care that the edges line up perfectly. Such a card looks like any other, but the double thickness means it can be detected by touch. Thus, unlike a traditional marked card, which must be detected by sight, the trick card can be detected by touch when the cards are out of sight. Two applications will be given in this chapter.

Method: The deck should contain fifty-two cards. Insert the thick card twenty-seventh from the top of the deck. To present the trick, place the deck face-down on the table. Invite the spectator to cut off the top third and place it in the card box. Point out that when this has been done, the deck will contain a random number of cards, making the trick that much harder to perform.

There is a packet of about thirty-five cards on the table. Ask the spectator to cut it in half. Direct him to take the bottom half, shuffle it and note the bottom card of the packet. He then drops this packet on top of the portion of the deck on the table. Finally, he gives the combined packet a straight cut.

Take the packet from him. Hold it face-down in the left hand. You have no idea which card he chose, nor do you know where it is in the packet, but by following a certain procedure, you are guaranteed to find his card. Turn your head to one side. Push cards from the left hand into the right. You can tell by touch when you have reached the thick card. Cut this card and all the cards to the right of it to the bottom of the packet. The thick card is now the bottom card of the packet.

More important, the spectator's card is now twenty-sixth from the top of the packet. Deal cards one at a time from the top of the packet to the table. Pretend to tune into mental wavelengths to find the card. Silently count the cards as you deal them to the table. When you get to the twenty-sixth card in your count, stop. Ask the spectator to name his card. When he does, turn over the card in hand to reveal the chosen card.

81. Number Affinity

This is Tony Bartolotta's handling of a classic trick in which a chosen card moves from one location to another in the deck. Each location is known to the audience but not to the magician. He does not know the chosen card, yet he is able to cause it to move to the correct position.

Method: The gimmick is the thick card described in the previous trick. It must be at the bottom of the deck when the trick begins. Turn your head to one side. Ask someone to lift off a group of cards from the top of the deck. The packet should contain about twenty-six cards, although the number is not important. We will assume the packet contains twenty cards. The magician does not know this number. The spectator gives some of the cards to a second spectator. Let us say the first spectator keeps eight cards and gives the other twelve to the second spectator.

The first spectator shuffles his cards, counts them and looks at the bottom card of the packet. He then drops this packet on top of the balance of the deck. The second spectator counts his cards and remembers the number. In our example, he would remember the number twelve. He places his packet on the table and drops the deck on top.

The deck is given to you behind your back. Remark that you will move the chosen card from the first spectator's number to the second spectator's number. All you need do is turn the deck face-up behind your back and deal cards off the face, one at a time, from the left hand to the right. When you get to the thick card, you will know it by touch. Leave the thick card on the face of the deck. Turn the deck face-down. The cards that were taken by the right hand are dropped onto the top of the deck.

Bring the deck into view. Point to the first spectator, and ask, "What was your number?" He says eight. Count eight cards off the top of the deck. Show him the eighth card. It is not his selection. Turn to the second spectator, and ask, "What was your number?" He says twelve. Count twelve cards off the top of the deck. The last card you deal will be the chosen card.

82. The Great Escape

Houdini was among the first to popularize a trick called the substitution trunk, a trick where an assistant locked in a wooden trunk changed places with Houdini. So persuasive was his presentation that spectators suspected that Houdini used teleportation to bring about the effect. The following is a miniature version with playing cards.

Method: Besides a deck of cards, you will need two hats or cardboard boxes to serve as containers for the cards. We will assume you use two hats. They are placed on the table, one to the right, the other to the left. On top of the deck are the ♥K and ♥Q, followed by five black spot cards.

The magician says, "In order to reenact this mystery, Houdini and his wife Bess will be represented by the king of hearts and the queen of hearts." Remove the top two cards. Show the faces, and say, "Houdini was locked in a box over on this side of the stage." Drop the ♥K into the hat on the right. "Bess was taken to the other side of the stage and locked into another wooden box." Drop the ♥Q into the hat on the left.

Continue, "Five members of the audience were asked to form a committee and inspect the boxes to make sure there was no trickery." Remove the five-spot cards from the top of the deck. Fan them with the faces toward the audience, then square the packet and hold it face-down in the left hand, and say, "They split up." Drop the first card into the hat on the left, the next card into the hat on the right, the next into the left hat, the next into the right hat, and the last into the left hat. It is important to alternate the cards left, right, left, right, left. At this point, there will be four cards in the hat on the left and three in the hat on the right.

Remark, "The committee was satisfied that all was on the up and up, so they withdrew to the center of the stage." Remove the ♥K from the hat on the right. Don't show the face. Simply reach into the hat with the right hand, remove the ♥K and place it in the left hand. Reach into the hat on the left, remove a spot card and place it *under* the ♥K. Take a spot card from the hat on the right and put it on top of the cards in the left hand.

Take the ♥Q from the hat on the left. Don't show the face. Put it on top of the cards in the left hand. Finally, remove a card from the hat on the right and put it on top of the cards in the left hand. Unknown to the audience, the ♥K and ♥Q are second and fourth from the top of the packet.

Say, "As soon as the committee had gathered in the center of the stage, a strange thing happened. Bess and Harry could be heard conversing over here." This is the first surprise. Reach into the hat on the left and remove two cards. This appears to be Houdini and his wife. Don't show the faces of these cards. Drop them back into the hat on the left, and say, "The committee knew something was wrong. They decided to inspect both trunks." Deal the packet in hand into the two hats, dealing left, right, left, right, left.

Continue, "That was when they realized that Houdini and his wife had teleported yet again." Pick up the hat on the left. Remove cards one at a time, showing the face of each card to the audience. There will be five-spot cards in the hat on the left. Then pick up the hat on the right. There will be just two cards in this hat. Remove them one at a time to show the ♥K and ♥Q. Bess and Harry Houdini had outsmarted the committee once again.

83. Cards Can Think

The tables are turned in this trick. It is a playing card that reads minds. The cards stay in the spectator's hands all the way through, yet there is a surprising outcome to the trick.

Method: Remark that playing cards can influence human behavior, and say, "I have a particular card in mind. It is a card that has power over the way we act." Ask the spectator to shuffle his own deck. Then have him take about five or six cards off the top of the deck. He fans them so you can see the faces, Figure 87. Pretend to look for the card you have in mind, but really remember the value of the face card and the suit of the next card. In Figure 87, the value you remember is five and the suit is spades. The card you are going to look for will be the combination that is produced, in this case the ♠5. If you don't see the ♠5 in this group of cards, say, "No, not there." The spectator places this group of cards face-down on the table.

Fig. 87

He fans another group of five or six cards. If the ♠5 is not there, direct him to place these cards on top of the first group. The process continues until your card shows up. Remove it and place it face-down on the table. Tap the back of this card and say, "This card has the power." Any remaining cards are placed face-down on top of the packet that is on the table. At this point, there is a face-down ♠5 on the table next to the deck. The bottom or face card of the deck is a five, and the card second from the bottom is a spade.

Ask the spectator to cut the deck into three heaps, Figure 88. Keep track of the heap that is the bottom third of the deck. Instruct the spectator to pick up this heap and deal the cards onto the other two heaps. He does this by alternating a card to each heap as he deals, and continues until all cards from the bottom heap have been dealt.

bottom   middle   top

Fig. 88

Call attention to the card that was placed aside, then turn it face-up and say, "The power card. Please drop it onto either heap." He puts it face-up onto one heap. Direct him to pick up the other heap and deal a few cards onto the face-up card. Then have him drop the rest of the heap on top of all. The deck has been reassembled. Say, "The five of spades influenced your actions, causing you to place it between a five and a spade." Invite the spectator to spread the deck face-down on the table. He removes the card on either side of the ♠5 and turns them over. One is a five and the other a spade.

84. Fate Deals the Cards

In this trick, you are going to perform a mental mystery invented by Warren Wiersbe.

Method: Say, "Some people say that luck plays the major role in our decisions. Others insist we are controlled by fate." As you speak, spread the cards face-up from hand to hand. Silently count to the twentieth card from the top of the deck. Let us say this card is the ♣A. The ♣A will serve as your key card later on. As you spread the cards, remark that you want to remove any jokers because they have a habit of interfering with the outcome.

Place the deck face-down on the table. Invite the spectator to cut off about three-quarters of the deck and place the cut-off portion to the right of the other portion. When he has done this, invite him to cut off about a quarter of the larger portion and place this packet to the right of the larger packet.

There are now three packets on the table. The center packet is the largest of the three. Ask the spectator to look at the top card of this packet, replace it on top of the packet and give the packet a straight cut. When he has done this, ask him to give it one more cut. Then pick up the larger packet. Remark that you will try to find his card. Spread the cards between the hands. Silently count from the top until you find your key card, the ♣A in this example.

You want to reposition the ♣A so it is twentieth from the top of the packet. If it is less than twenty from the top, transfer cards one at a time from bottom to top until it is in the correct position. If it is more than twenty from the top, transfer cards one at a time from top to bottom until it is twenty from the top. As you do this, say, "No, that's not it, nope, not this one either."

After the ♣A has been correctly positioned, say, "I can't get it by luck. Maybe I can find it by fate." Place the packet face-down on the table between the other two packets. Push the original top portion of the deck (the packet that is to the spectator's far right) in front of the spectator, and say, "You cut off a group of cards. It might be a random number of cards, but then again, it might have been directed by fate."

Invite him to deal cards one at a time off the top of this packet. Simultaneously, deal cards off the top of the larger packet. Match him card for card until he runs out of cards. Ask for the name of his card. Turn up the top card of your packet. It will be his chosen card.

85. Gambler vs. Psychic

Remark, "There is a debate as to whether the psychic can beat the gambler at the card table. Each side has advantages. For example, the psychic can read minds. He can even read cards by telepathy." The spectator shuffles the deck any way he likes. Then he cuts off about a quarter of the deck and looks through it to find and remove the highest value card in the packet. He keeps this card.

The magician drops the rest of the deck in his pocket, and says, "Here's how a psychic would focus on the card you have in mind." The magician reaches into his pocket, removes a card and glances at the face and asks, "Is your card black?" The spectator says yes. The magician removes another card from the shuffled deck, and continues, "A spade?" The spectator says yes. The magician removes one more card as he asks, "The ace of spades?" The spectator shows his card to the audience. It is the ♠A.

"That's the advantage to being able to read minds. The disadvantage is that it doesn't give you a winning hand. On the other hand, the gambler may not know what cards you have, but he knows what cards he wants." The magician snaps his fingers over the three cards he pulled out of the deck. When they are turned face-up, they have changed into the other three aces!

Method: The key to the success of this trick is a gimmick known as an edge-marked card. Prior to the performance, place the ♠A, ♥A and ♦A into your jacket pocket. Remove the ♠A from the deck. Rub the point of a pencil on one edge near the corner in order to darken the edge. Make the mark as small as possible, yet large enough to be seen by you, and mark only one corner of the ace. No matter where the ace is in the shuffled pack, its approximate location can be determined at a glance, as shown in Figure 89. This is the only preparation. It can be done any time you have a minute or two in which to prepare the card. The deck may be used for other tricks prior to the performance of this effect.

When ready to perform, place the deck on the table so you can spot the corner of the deck that contains the marked ace. Cut the deck a few cards above the ♠A, and complete the cut so that the ♠A is two or three cards from the top of the deck, Figure 89. Cut the deck in half, and invite the spectator to riffle shuffle the two halves together.

Fig. 89

marked Ace

After the shuffle, spot the position of the marked ace. If the shuffle was even, the ♠A should be ten or twelve cards from the top. In this case, direct the spectator to remove the top third of the deck. If the ♠A is lower down in the deck, have him cut off the top half. In any case, the portion he cuts off must contain the ♠A in order for the trick to work. Tell him to look through it and remove the highest value card in the packet. Just so there is no ambiguity, remark that deuces are low, aces high.

Pick up the remainder of the deck, and say, "If I look through this part of the pack, I could figure out your card. Psychics don't have to look at the faces of the cards. They can read cards by thought waves." Drop the deck into the pocket that contains the three aces. Pretend to struggle a bit getting a psychic impression, then remove one of the aces placed there earlier. Glance at the face of this card, and ask, "Is your card black?" The spectator must acknowledge this. Place this card on the table without showing its face. Fumble a bit in your pocket, withdraw another ace, glance at the face and ask, "A spade?" The spectator acknowledges that his card is a spade.

Finally withdraw the third ace. "An ace, the ace of spades?" You are correct. This seems to be the point to the trick, but there is an unexpected finish. The three cards pulled out of your pocket have not yet been shown to the audience. They assume these are three random cards. Remark that the gambler may not know another player's cards, but he makes sure he gets the cards he wants. Snap the fingers, then turn over the three cards one at a time to reveal the other three aces.

86. Mind Probe

If you could perform real mind reading, it might look something like this. Invite the spectator to shuffle the deck, cut off about a quarter of the deck, look over the faces of these cards and think of one card. He then removes the thought-of card and hides it in his pocket.

Assemble the deck and place it face-up on the table. Say, "I'd like you to think first of the value of your card. Deal cards off the face of the deck into a heap, like this, until you get to a card with the same value as the card you are thinking of. For example, we'll assume you were thinking of a five-spot."

As you speak, secretly memorize the face card of the deck. We will assume this card is the ♥A. To illustrate what you want done, deal cards off the face into a heap until you deal a five, Figure 90. "Let me know when you've done this." Place the undealt portion onto the dealt portion of the deck. Unknown to the audience, the card you memorized, the ♥A, is now the back card of the face-up deck.

Turn your head aside. Wait until the spectator tells you he has dealt a card of the same value as the card he has thought

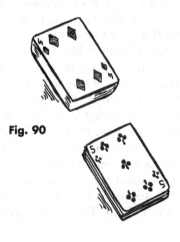

Fig. 90

of, and then say, "Good. Please concentrate on the card for a moment. Fine. Now place the rest of the deck on top of the packet you just dealt." After the spectator has done this, instruct him to deal cards off the face of the deck into a heap on the table until he has dealt a card of the same suit as the thought-of card. When he has done this, ask him to concentrate on the suit, then place the undealt portion on top of the dealt packet. Finally, ask him to give the deck a straight cut.

Turn and face the audience, and remark, "Thinking first of the value and then the suit is important because it clarifies the mental picture. I've got a card in mind. I'll show my card to the audience." Hold the deck so you can see the faces. Beginning at the top of the deck, spread the cards between the hands. When you get to the card you previously memorized, note the card just to the left of it. In Figure 91, the memorized card is the ♥A. The card just to the left of it is a nine-spot. This tells you that the spectator's thought card is a nine.

How do you establish the suit? You don't have another key card to refer to, but all is not lost. Continue spreading cards

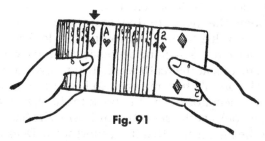

Fig. 91

from left to right. There will be three nines in the deck. The missing nine is the thought-of card. We will assume the missing nine is the ♠9. Frown and say, "I can't find my card. I'll write it down just so you know in advance." Write "nine of spades" on a piece of paper and toss it writing-side down to the table.

"For the first time, will you tell the audience the card you are thinking of?" The spectator names the ♠9. "Isn't that something. Here's the card I thought of." Turn over your piece of paper and show a perfect match.

87. Magic by the Book

This trick uses a deck of cards and the book you are now reading. Secretly place any seven-spot on top of the deck. Have *New Self-Working Card Tricks* handy and you are ready to begin.

Place the deck on the table. You are going to enact a force of the seven-spot by a means illustrated in Figures 33 and 34 (see p. 39). Ask the spectator to cut off about half the cards. In Figure 33, this would be packet A. Direct the spectator to place packet A on the table. He is then asked to place the remainder of the deck (packet B) on top of packet A, but at right angles, Figure 34.

Hold up the copy of *New Self-Working Card Tricks*. The reason you do this is to momentarily take attention away from the cards. "I've been studying this book lately. I think I've memorized most of the contents. Let's see if I can make use of my new-found knowledge." Hand the book to the spectator. Lift off the top packet (packet B in Figure 34). Ask the spectator to look at the top card of the remainder of the deck. The card he looks at is the top card of packet A. Since this was originally the top card of the deck, it is the seven-spot.

Say, "Open the book to the first page of any chapter. Whatever the value of the card you picked, look at the corresponding word in the opening sentence. In other words, if you picked a ten, look at the tenth word. If you picked a three, look at the third word. I'll turn my back so I can't see what you are doing." The spectator opens the book to the first page of any chapter and looks at the seventh word. When he has done this, say, "I get the impression that it's a short word. Does it contain the letter 'n'?" If the spectator says yes, the word is 'in.' Pretend to think a bit, then reveal the chosen word. If he says no, ask if the word contains the letter "s." If it does, the chosen word is "is." If he says no, then the chosen word must be "the."

88. Make the Cards Match

Howard Adams is the originator of this matching trick. The following version was suggested by Martin Gardner.

Method: Remove the ♥A through the ♥5 from the deck, arrange them in numerical order from top to bottom, and place the packet face-down on the table. Remove the ♦A through the ♦5, arrange them in numerical order and place the packet on top of the heart group. Do not show the faces of the cards to the audience. They see you arranging cards, but are unaware that the two groups of five cards are in the same order.

Ask a spectator to cut the packet and complete the cut two or three times. When he has done this, take back the packet and deal the top five cards into a heap on the table. Place the other group of five cards on the table without dealing them. The two packets are in reverse order with respect to one another.

Say, "This trick is called 'Make the Cards Match.' It gets its name from the fact that we are going to spell each word in the title. The first word is 'Make.' I'm going to spell m-a-k-e, and I will deal a card for each letter from top to bottom. But you choose which heap I deal from." Let's say the spectator picks the heap on the left. Spell m-a-k-e, dealing a card for each letter from top to bottom, a total of four cards.

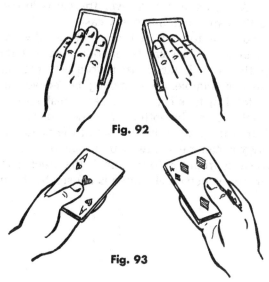

Fig. 92

Fig. 93

This next step is a touch that the author has added. After the spell, place the hands on top of the two packets, Figure 92. Then turn the packets face-up, Figure 93, and say, "No match yet." Turn the hands palm-down and replace the packets face-down on the table. Then take the top card of each packet and place this pair of cards to one side.

Say, "Now I'm going to spell 'the.' Which heap should I use?" The spectator might pick the same heap or the opposite heap. It does not matter. Pick up the chosen heap, spell t-h-e, dealing a card from top to bottom for each letter. At the conclusion of the deal/spell process, take the top card of each heap and place this pair of cards to one side.

Do exactly the same thing with the word "cards," and again with the word "match." Each time you finish the deal/spell, take the top card of each heap and place this pair of cards aside. After you have done this with each of the four words, you will have four pairs of cards placed aside, and one pair of cards remaining.

Point to the pair of cards remaining and say, "Wouldn't it be something if these two cards really did match?" Turn both cards face-up. They will be the same value. The trick appears to be over, but there is an even more unexpected result. Continue, "And wouldn't it be even more amazing if these matched, and these . . ." As you speak, turn over the cards in each pair to show that the cards match in every case.

You do not have to spell each complete word with one heap only. You can deal/spell some letters of a word with the cards in one heap, the other letters in that word with the cards in the other heap. For example, when spelling m-a-k-e, you are going to transfer a total of four cards. You can transfer the first three cards from the top to the bottom of the heap on the left, and the last card from the top to the bottom of the heap on the right. Alternately, you can transfer two cards from top to bottom of one heap, two cards from top to bottom of the other. The trick will work no matter which combination is chosen by the spectator.

MOVING MARKER

In a number of card tricks, the cards are dealt in a layout, and a coin or other marker moved randomly from card to card by the spectator, with a surprising outcome. Some of the best such tricks are described in this chapter.

89. Mental Case

This is an impromptu trick that packs a double wallop. Like a number of tricks in this chapter, it is based on a parity principle invented by Bob Hummer.

Method: When you first remove the deck from its case, leave one card behind. It can be any card, but we will assume it is the ♦A. Close the flap of the card case and put it aside. Perform two or three card tricks with the rest of the deck. When ready to perform "Mental Case," say, "You've been a good audience. I'd like to try one more trick, something a little different."

As you speak, hold the deck so you alone can see the faces of the cards. Run through the cards and remove four picture cards of the same value, plus the card that matches the card hidden in the card case. In our example the card hidden in the card case is a red ace, so you would remove the ♥A and, let's say, four kings. Do not show the faces of the cards to the audience. Place all five cards face-down in a heap on the table. The remainder of the deck is put aside.

Deal the five cards in a face-down row on the table such that the ace is the middle card in the row. In Figure 94, it would occupy position number three. Drop the card case on the card at position number two in the row, Figure 94, and say, "I'm going to turn my head aside and ask you to move the card case back and forth a certain number of moves. Let's say I call out the number three. Move the case three times, each time moving it to the card next to it, either right or left. Here, I'll show you."

133

Fig. 94

Move the card case to position three, then four, then five. "Or you can move it like this." Move it to position four, then position five, then back to position four. "Or like this." Move it to position three, then position two, then back to position three. The card case must always end at position three (i.e., the middle position in the row).

Turn your head to one side and say, "All right, move the card case three times." Wait for the spectator to do this. "I'm going to guess that the card case is not on the card that is at the far right end of the row. Take the card that is at the far right end and slide it away from the row. There will be four cards left." When the spectator has done this, say, "Now I'd like you to move the card case four times." The spectator moves the card case from card to card a total of four times. "Good. I'm going to say that the card case does not rest on the card that is at the far left end of the row. Slide that card out of the way."

When the spectator has done this say, "There are three cards left. Move the card case a total of five times." When this has been done, pause as if thinking things over. "Hmm, I'm going to say that the card case is not on the card that is at the far left end of the row. Remove that card." Wait for the spectator to do this and then say, "There are two cards remaining. Move the card case six times." After this has been done say, "It's a fifty-fifty chance where the card case is now, but I'm going to guess that it is not at the right end of the row. Remove the card that is on the right."

When this has been done, say, "There is one card left under the card case. Is that correct?" The spectator says yes. Say, "Lift the card case and look at this card. I believe it is an ace." Turn and face the spectator. He acknowledges that the card is an ace. Remark, "Some people say the trick is easy because all the cards are the same." Tap the four cards that were placed aside.

"As a matter of fact, they *are* all the same." Turn them over. "They're all kings." This is the first surprise.

Continue, "The card you ended up on is a red ace. It's a funny thing, but when you pick a red ace, another red ace materializes, right here inside the card case." The spectator opens the card case, removes the card and discovers that it is indeed the matching red ace.

90. Stover's Game

This clever trick was invented by Mel Stover. Eight face-up cards are placed in a circular layout. A spectator moves a glass or cup around the layout in a random way. The magician gives instructions for turning certain cards face-down. If the glass rests on a card he names, or if a card he names is already face-down, he loses and must pay up. Although the magician never knows the position of the glass, he never loses. When just one face-up card remains, the spectator is directed to a folded piece of paper in the glass. When unfolded, it correctly predicts the identity of this card.

Method: Remove the ♦A through the ♦8 from the deck. Arrange them in numerical order with the ace at the top. Hand the packet to a spectator. Invite him to give the packet several straight cuts. Take back the packet and deal the cards into a circle, dealing clockwise, all cards face-up. The layout will look like Figure 95.

Fig. 95

Say to the spectator, "I'm going to turn my back. I'd like you to place the glass on any card, like this." Put the glass on the ♦3. "For example, if you picked the three, you would move the glass three cards in either direction. You could move it like this." Move the glass three cards clockwise to the ♦6. Then put the glass back on the ♦3 and say, "Or three cards like this." Move it three cards counter-clockwise to the ♦8. "Or any combination." Put the glass back on the ♦3. Move it one card counter-clockwise, then two cards clockwise.

Write "two of diamonds" on a piece of paper, fold it and place it inside the glass. Hand the glass to the spectator and say, "The choice is yours. Just make sure you move the glass from card to card, and don't skip any card." Then turn your back. The spectator might choose to put the glass on the ♦6. Since this card is a six, he then moves the glass six cards to a new card.

Say, "Here's the bet. After each move, I'm going to ask you to turn a card face-down. If the glass is on the card I name, or if that card is already face-down, I lose a buck. Otherwise, we keep going." You don't know where the glass is. Nevertheless, the sequence of instructions you give the spectator is always the same. They can be written on a piece of paper for easy reference. The instructions are as follows:

1. "To start things off, I don't think the glass is resting on the ace. Place turn the ace face-down." The spectator does so.

2. Ask the spectator to move the glass 3 cards. Then have him turn the eight face-down.

3. He moves the glass 3 cards and turns the seven face-down.

4. He moves the glass 5 cards and turns the four face-down.

5. He moves the glass 1 card and turns the three face-down.

6. He moves the glass 3 cards and turns the six face-down.

7. He moves the glass 1 card and turns the five face-down.

There will be one face-up card, the ♦2. Turn and face the audience, and say, "I put a piece of paper in the glass earlier. I don't want to touch it. Please open the paper and show the audience what I wrote." The spectator opens the paper, which correctly predicts that the ♦2 would be the only face-up card in the layout.

91. Strange Voyage

The magician offers to reveal the technique psychics use to find hidden articles. While he turns his back, a spectator deals a row of seven cards. One of the cards is an ace. The other six cards can have any value. While the magician turns his head to one side, the spectator exchanges the ace with the card on either side of it. He makes several exchanges. The magician tells him to eliminate certain cards. The process of elimination continues until there is just one card left. It will be the ace. This trick was concocted by Stewart James.

Method: Ask the spectator to remove an ace and six other cards from the deck and deal them in a face-up row on the table. Say, "When I turn my back I'd like you to note the position of the ace from the left end of the row." In Figure 96, it is second from the spectator's left. "Since the ace is in the number two position, I'd like you to make two exchanges. An exchange consists of exchanging the ace with the card on either side of it. If the ace was third from the left, you would make three exchanges. We know where the ace is now, so why don't you shuffle the cards and deal them out while I turn my back."

Fig. 96

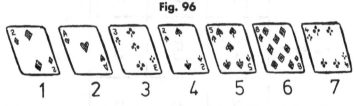

The spectator mixes the cards and deals them into a face-up row. He notes the new position of the ace. Say it is fifth from his left. Without telling you its position, he makes five exchanges. Each exchange is with the card on either side of it. If the ace is at one end of the row, it can only be exchanged with one other card, but otherwise the spectator can make the exchange with the card to the left or to the right of it.

When he has finished doing this, say, "The ace will represent an object hidden from the psychic. He wants to get extraneous cards out of the way, but he has to be careful to keep the ace in play. Let's see, remove the card at the right end of the row and the card at the left end of the row."

When the spectator has done this, say, "Now I'd like you to

exchange the ace with the card next to it. Good. Once again discard the end cards." After the spectator has done this, say, "Exchange the ace with the card next to it. Good. Once more exchange it with the card next to it. Excellent. One more time, I'd like you to exchange the ace with the card next to it. Terrific. We're down to three cards, so I have to be careful to keep the ace in play. Please discard the end cards. You should be left with the ace." The ace is the only card remaining in the row.

92. Mind Matrix

Martin Gardner conceived of the idea of arranging cards in a square layout to exploit the basic premise. His approach has been popular with magicians. This version incorporates a clever idea of Bob Brethen's.

A	2	3
4	5	6
7	8	9

Fig. 97

Method: Besides a deck of cards, you will also use a glass. Arrange the ace through nine in the layout shown in Figure 97. On a piece of paper write, "The glass will end up on the five." Fold the paper and put it inside the card box.

"There's a new game called portable roulette. Instead of a roulette table we will use a layout of nine cards. In place of a bouncing ball we use a glass. I'm going to ask you to move the glass from one card to an adjacent card. You can move it horizontally or vertically, up or down, but not diagonally."

Place the glass on the ace. Turn your back. "To start, think of

a number from one to five. Move the glass that many cards."
When the spectator has done this, say, "Good. Please move it
the same number of cards again."

When this has been done, say, "Here's where the element of
chance comes into play. I'm going to call out the name of a card
that I'd like you to remove from the layout. If the glass is on the
card I name, I lose. We keep playing as long as my luck holds
out. The odds are too heavily in my favor if I name just one card,
so I'll take a chance and name two. Please remove either the
two or the six, your choice. Don't tell me which one."

After the spectator has done this, you will give him a set of
instructions that never varies, no matter which card the glass
rests on in the layout. The instructions are:

1. When the spectator has removed a card as instructed
above, have him move the glass 7 times. The blank space
doesn't count. He must move from card to card. When he has
done this, say, "Now remove either the ace or the nine."

2. He moves the glass 4 times and removes either the three or
the seven.

3. He moves the glass 6 times and removes either the ace or
the nine, whichever card was not removed earlier.

4. He moves the glass 4 times and removes either the three or
the seven, whichever card was not removed earlier.

5. He moves the glass 3 times and removes either the four or
the eight.

6. He moves the glass twice and removes the four or the eight,
whichever card was not removed in the previous step.

7. There are two cards left. Ask him to move the glass 4 times.
Pause and say, "That doesn't seem quite right. Move it once
more." Again hesitate, as if thinking things over. "It still doesn't
feel right. Move the glass one more time." When he has done
this, say, "I have a hunch the bouncing ball ended up on the five.
Please remove the other card."

Turn and face him. The glass rests on the five, and it is the only
card remaining in the layout. Have the card case opened, the prediction removed and read aloud to verify that it is correct.

93. Four-Card Magic

A clever trick by card expert Jack Avis is the basis for this version.

Method: Remove an ace, two, five and jack in mixed suits from the deck. Without showing the faces of these cards, arrange them in A-5-J-2 order from top to bottom, and place them off to one side of the table. Remove another set of cards with the same values, also in mixed suits. Arrange them in 2-A-5-J order, and deal them in a face-down row on the table such that the two is the left-most card in the row, the Jack the right-most card.

Remark that this is a different version of three-card monte called, for some reason, four-card monte. As you speak, pick up the top card of the heap placed aside. This card is an ace. Turn it face-up. Drop it onto one of the cards in the row. It does not matter which one. Tell the spectator that you will ask him to move the ace from card to card. He can move it to the left or to the right. If the card is at the end of the row, it can move in only one direction, but otherwise it can move in either direction. Demonstrate with the ace, but arrange it so the ace ends up on the second card from the left, Figure 98.

Fig. 98

Turn your head to one side, and say to the spectator, "I'd like you to move the ace one card to the right or left. Don't tell me which direction you choose." When he has done this, ask him to move it three more times. Then say, "I will now ask you to remove a card from the row and place it on top of the card case. If the card I name is covered by the ace, I lose. Otherwise, we will keep playing as long as my luck holds. Let's see, I'm going to take a chance and ask you to pick up the card at the far left end of the row and place it on top of the card case."

That card will not be covered by the ace, so you are successful so far. With your back still turned, direct him to move the ace three times. "We have only three cards now, so the odds are not as good. I don't think the card at the far right end of the row is covered by the ace. Please remove that card and place it on top of the card case." After this has been done, ask him to move the ace one card. "Now it's fifty-fifty. I'm going to say that the card at the right end is not covered by the ace. Please place that card on top of the card case."

When he has done this, turn and face him. "I had no way of knowing how you would move the ace or where it would end up, but I made a little prediction." Turn up the top card of the heap you placed aside. It will be a five. Turn up the top card of the group on top of the card case. It too will be a five. Turn up the next card from each group to reveal matching jacks, and the next card to reveal matching deuces. Continue, "That leaves one more." Tap the face-down card under the ace. Turn it over to reveal a matching ace.

94. Magic Maze

On one of his televised magic specials, David Copperfield performed an intriguing effect for the television audience. An adaptation of that trick is described here.

Method: Remove any nine cards from the deck. Spread them face-down between the hands. Ask the spectator to pick four. He fans them so he can see the faces and thinks of one card. We will assume his thought-of card is the ♥4, although the identity of this card is never revealed to the magician.

After the spectator has one card firmly in mind, ask him to shuffle the four cards again. Take them back. Fan them with one hand. Fan the other five cards with the opposite hand. Interweave the nine cards as shown in Figure 99. The process must look exactly as shown in the diagram. From the audience's point of view, you are merely mixing two random groups of cards together.

Fig. 99

Square up the packet and deal the cards into three rows. Deal
the first card at position 1, the next at position 2, and so on,
Figure 100. Unknown to the audience (and the key to the success of the trick), the spectator's thought-of card must lie at one
of the even positions.

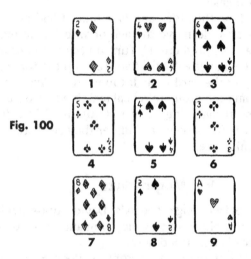

Fig. 100

As you deal the cards, remark that the layout represents a
maze. Explain that when you turn your back, the spectator is to
start on his thought-of card. You will not look at the cards, but
you will attempt to guide him through the maze to a card you
will predict. Note the card that lies at position 4. In the example
of Figure 100, the card at position 4 is the ♣5. Write the name of
this card on a piece of paper, fold the paper and give it to someone to hold for the moment.

Turn your back, and say, "Your card represents a random
starting point. Place a coin on your thought-of card." The path
through the maze to the desired card is arrived at through the
following instructions to the spectator:

1. Make 4 moves. A move consists of transferring the coin
from card to card, left or right, up or down, but not diagonally.
After he has made 4 moves, state, "I get the feeling the coin is
not on the card at position 9. Please remove that card."

2. Make 5 moves. Remove the card at position 6 from the
maze.

3. Make 2 moves. Remove the card at position 8.

4. Make 3 moves. Remove the card at position 3 and the card at position 7.

5. Make 3 moves. Remove the card at position 2.

6. Make 1 move.

When the spectator has done this, turn and face the audience and say, "I didn't know where you started, but let's see if I was able to guide you correctly through the maze." If the spectator followed your instructions properly, the coin should now rest on the ♣5. The spectator who holds the piece of paper now reads what you wrote, verifying that you did in fact predict where the coin would end up.

95. Revelation by Design

In this trick devised by the author, the spectator places a marker on a card in the layout. He then slides the marker up or down, left, right, or diagonally to the nearest card of a particular color. There is no counting. After several moves, the marker would appear to be on a random card, but it is a card that was correctly predicted by the performer.

Method: The layout of sixteen cards is shown in Figure 101. "B" means any black card, "R" any red. The only card whose identity is specified is the first card in the second row. It can be

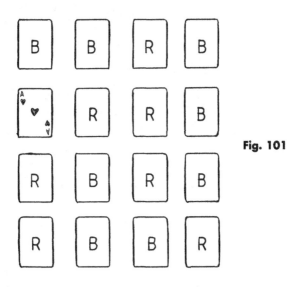

Fig. 101

any red card, but we will assume it is the ♥A. This is the card you write as your prediction. The marker can be an odd coin or a ring or a clear glass. If a glass is used, the prediction can be written on a piece of paper, the paper folded and dropped into the glass. The prediction is thus in full view at all times.

The instructions are always the same, and may be printed or typed on a card and carried in the pocket until the time of performance. The instructions are as follows:

1. Place the marker on any red card.
2. Slide the marker left or right to the nearest black card.
3. Slide the marker up or down to the nearest red card.
4. Slide the marker diagonally to the nearest black card.
5. Slide the marker up or down to the nearest red card.

No matter what choices the spectator makes, he will end up on the ♥A. Have the prediction read aloud to verify that you are correct.

More
Self-Working
Card Tricks

CONTENTS

INTRODUCTION

Card magic is the most popular area of legerdemain, accounting for at least half of the tricks published and performed by magicians. Part of the fascination card tricks hold for magicians is the fact that there are a seemingly endless number of possibilities in the ways that playing cards can be manipulated and controlled.

Card tricks are popular with laymen because laymen equate card routines with sleight-of-hand ability and gambling expertise. The tricks in this book give the impression of expert manipulation but they are self-working and can be performed by almost anyone, even the beginner.

Although this book is a sequel to *Self-Working Card Tricks* (Dover 23334-0), it is not necessary to know the material in that book to follow the routines described here. All of the tricks in the present volume are completely detailed.

The intent here is the same as in the earlier book, to present some of the best contemporary thinking on self-working card tricks while avoiding all sleights, even rudimentary moves like the Hindu Shuffle. Tricks involving complex setups or special apparatus have been avoided. The tricks here are easily learned yet they are strong enough to fool magicians as well as laymen.

The text includes chapters on some of the newest areas of card magic, Riffle-Shuffle Setups and Topological Card Tricks, as well as modern thinking on important fundamental techniques like Card Forces. The chapter on gambling contains the latest information on the Omega Bet and Face-Up Poker, two contemporary betting games.

The real enjoyment in magic comes from baffling friends with tricks. The card routines in this book were collected with this thought in mind: to provide the reader with entertaining card tricks that are easy to learn and easy to do, yet mystifying to the audience.

IMPROMPTU CARD TRICKS

The strongest magic is that which just seems to happen. If you are able to borrow a deck of cards and immediately perform strong card magic, the audience cannot but be impressed. The tricks in this chapter were chosen for two reasons. The first is that they require no preparation and can be performed impromptu under almost any circumstances. The second reason they were chosen is for novelty of effect. If the plot is novel and easy to follow, the audience will be that much more receptive.

Although the tricks are self-working, you should practice them until the working is smooth. When you feel confident that you know all the details and don't have to stop and think what comes next, you can proceed to baffle your audience.

1   GEMINI TWINS

This remarkable trick takes place with the deck in the spectator's hands from start to finish. The magician claims that he can cause the spectator to stop dealing when he hears a *mental* command.

The magician removes two cards from the deck and places them aside face up. We'll assume they are a red five and a black eight. The deck is then given to the spectator. He deals cards off the top one at a time, stops whenever he wants to, and places the red five at that point. The balance of the deck is then dropped on top of the cards on the table.

The spectator then deals cards off the top, stops when he likes, and drops the black eight at that point. He then places the balance of the deck on top of the cards on the table.

Now the spectator himself spreads the deck on the table and finds that he placed the red five directly adjacent to the other red five in the deck, and further, to prove it was no accident, that he placed the black eight directly adjacent to the other black eight in the deck. Note that the trick uses a borrowed, shuffled deck and that the spectator can stop anywhere. Note too that the magician never touches the deck.

METHOD: When the borrowed deck is handed to you, turn it face up so you alone can see the faces. Then run through the cards, saying you are going to look for two prediction cards. In fact you secretly take note of the top and bottom cards of the deck and find their mates. If, say, the top card is a red five, find the other red five and toss it out face up on the table. If the bottom card is a black eight, find the mate of this card (the other black eight) and toss it out onto the table.

Square the deck and hand it to the spectator. From this point on you never touch the deck again. Have the spectator hold the deck face down in his left hand. He is to deal cards off the top one at a time into a face-down heap. He can stop anytime he chooses, but you caution him that you will try by telepathic waves to cause him to stop at a particular card.

He deals and stops when he likes. It makes no difference how long he deals but to keep the handling simple he should stop before he has dealt no more than 17 or 18 cards. When he does stop, direct him to drop the black eight face up onto the dealt packet on the table. Then he drops the balance of the deck on top of all and squares the deck.

He picks up the deck and once again deals off the top into a face-down heap. He can stop anywhere before he comes to the face-up black eight in the deck. When he stops, have him drop the red five face up onto the top of the dealt packet on the table. Then he drops the balance of the deck on top of all.

Have him spread the deck face down from left to right. There are two face-up cards in the pack. Have him remove the face-up red five and the face-down card directly to the right of it. These two cards are placed to the left. Then he removes the face-up black eight and the card directly to the right of it. This pair is placed to the right on the table. The rest of the deck is gathered and placed aside.

The success of the trick depends on this next point. The audience does not know what to expect, so you have to prepare the way. Point to the face-up red five and say, "I chose a red five. Wouldn't it be amazing if you happened to stop at the other red five?" Now have the spectator turn over the face-down card paired with the red five. He finds that it too is a red five.

Then say, "That could have been luck. It's not likely, but it might have been luck. If it really was telepathy that caused you to stop at the red five, then it should also work for the second card you stopped at." Point to the face-up black eight and say, "Wouldn't it be truly incredible if you happened to stop at the other black eight?" The spectator turns over the face-down card paired with the black eight and finds that it is indeed the other black eight.

2   COMPUTER DATING

Computers are much in the news these days. This trick and the closing trick in this chapter use the theme of programming the cards to act like a computer. "Computer Dating" is a new effect that has not previously been published.

From a packet of two kings and two queens the spectator chooses any card and reverses it in the packet. Explaining that the cards came from a computer dating service and are programmed to produce the mate of any card, the magician drops the packet into a card case, gives the packet a shake and removes it. There is still one reversed card in the packet but it is the correct mate of the card chosen by the spectator!

METHOD: Remove the ♣K, ♣Q, ♥K and ♥Q and place them in a packet on the table. The rest of the deck is not used, so it may be placed aside. With the four cards face up explain to the spectator that the mate of the ♣K is the ♣Q and that the mate of the ♥Q is the ♥K.

Tell him to place the cards behind his back and mix them. As if to illustrate, you place the four cards behind your back. When the cards are out of sight, turn the ♥K and ♥Q face down so they are face-to-face with the ♣K and ♣Q. The setup at this point is shown in Figure 1.

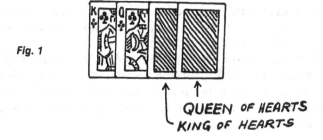

Fig. 1

QUEEN OF HEARTS
KING OF HEARTS

Square up the packet and hand it to the spectator. Tell him to place it behind his back and mix the cards thoroughly. While he mixes the cards, explain that computer dating has made it possible for people to meet compatible companions through electronics. When the spectator is satisfied that the cards are well mixed, tell him to turn over the entire packet three times.

Now ask him to bring one card forward. The card may be face up or face down. If it is face up, have him note the card and turn it face down. If the card is face down, have him turn it face up and note it. After the card has been turned over, he is to replace it in the packet in the reversed condition. This is to say that once he turns the card over, he does not turn it back; it goes into the packet in a reversed condition.

With the cards still behind his back, he is to further mix them. Then hand him the card case behind his back and tell him to put the packet into the card case and close the flap.

Take the card case from him. Give it a shake as you remark that this enables the computer program to sort through the cards. Ask him to name his card. Say he names the ♣K. Remind him that the packet contains only one correct mate to his card. In this case the correct mate is the ♣Q. He now removes the packet from the card case. There is still a reversed card in the packet but now it is the mate to his chosen card.

This trick is a good example of a principle known as a self-adjusting setup. Regardless of how the spectator mixes the cards, and regardless of which card he chooses, the packet will always produce the correct mate to his chosen card.

3   THE DATING GAME

If asked to repeat "Computer Dating," you may want to switch to this effect. It is similar in terms of what the audience sees, but different in method. In this effect the spectator mixes cards face up and face down, yet at the finish only a matching king and queen are face up. All other cards are face down.

METHOD: Remove the ♣K, ♣Q, ♥K, ♥Q, ♠K, ♠Q, ♦K and ♦Q from the deck. Have the spectator shuffle these eight cards. Take back the packet. Fan it so the spectator can see the faces, and have him remove a matching king and queen. Say he chooses the ♦K and ♦Q.

Lower the fanned packet so it is face down. Insert the ♦K so it is fifth from the top of the packet. Then insert the ♦Q so it is seventh from the top of the packet. Square up the packet. All eight cards are face down at this point.

Explain that the spectator is to mix the cards by the following process. Openly take the top two cards and turn them over onto the packet as a unit so they are face up. (So that you do not reverse their order, take care to push them over to the right with the left thumb, take the two cards together with the right hand and turn them over onto the packet.) Then tell him to cut the packet anywhere and complete the cut. As you say this, as though demonstrating, cut the top two cards to the bottom.

Push over the next two cards with the left thumb. Take them as a unit and flip them face up onto the top of the packet. Remark that the spectator can flip the same two cards over and over. As you say this, flip the same two cards face down on top of the packet. Then add, "Of course you are to do this with the cards behind your back." As you say this, place the packet behind the back. Take the top face-down card and insert it face down between the two face-up cards on the bottom of the packet. The situation now is that the top five cards are face down, the next card is face up, the next face down, and the bottom card is face up.

The spectator takes the packet behind his back. He turns over the top two cards on top of the packet, then gives the packet a cut. He continues this process as long as he likes. When he is satisfied that the packet is well mixed, he turns it over a few more times for good measure.

Take the packet and place it behind your back. When the cards are concealed from the audience's view, quickly and silently upjog every other card. Strip out the upjogged packet, turn it over and place it on top of the remaining cards. Then bring the packet into view.

Have the spectator call out the two cards he chose. In our example he will name the ♦K and ♦Q. Spread the packet on the table. Two cards will face one way and six will face the other way. If the two cards are face down, flip over the packet and respread it. The spectator sees that in spite of the random mixing, only two cards are face up and they are the very cards he chose.

The basis for this trick is the Hummer-Page "Odd Color Out" described later in this book. To see why the trick works, deal a row of eight cards face down on the table. Every other card is then turned face up. Pick up two adjacent cards, one in each hand, turn them over, cross the hands and replace the two cards in the vacant spaces in the row. By crossing the hands you are exchanging the two cards.

Pick up two more adjacent cards, one in each hand, turn them over, cross the hands and replace them in the vacant spaces in the row. Repeat as often as you like. You will find that face-up and face-down cards still alternate perfectly.

If every other card were now turned over, all eight cards would face the same way. That is, all eight cards would either be face up or face down.

To see how the result of "The Dating Game" is brought about, deal out eight face-down cards. Turn up every other card. Now pick up the last two cards in the row and exchange them *without* turning them over. Say these cards are the red kings.

Now pick up two adjacent cards, turn them over, cross the hands and replace the two cards in the vacant spaces in the row. Repeat several times. Then turn over every other card. The result will be that six cards face one way and two the other. Further, the two cards will be the red kings.

4 PENNY PLAIN

This is a card revelation done under seemingly impossible conditions. It is the author's handling of a principle first published by Alex Elmsley.

Have a spectator take his own deck and deal two heaps containing the same number of cards. He shuffles one heap, notes the top card and places the heap on the table. Then he shuffles the other heap and places that on top of the first heap, thus burying the chosen card somewhere in the packet.

Another spectator is asked to guess where he thinks the chosen card will end up. If he thinks the card will end up twelfth from the top, he deals 12 cards off the deck onto the tabled packet. He does this while you turn your back. You have no idea of how many cards he dealt.

Now you take the packet, grasping it from above in the right hand. The left thumb draws the top card off while the fingers of the left hand simultaneously draw the bottom card off as shown in Figure 2. This pair of cards is placed on the table.

Fig. 2

Draw off another pair of cards in the same way and place them onto the tabled cards. Continue drawing off pairs of cards until all of the cards have been drawn off and placed onto the tabled cards. Then place the top card at the bottom of the packet. This transfer of a card from top to bottom is done openly.

Ask the spectator for his number. In our example he would say 12. Deal 12 cards off the top of the packet. Turn over the next card and it will be the chosen card.

5 MIRASKIL

The invention of Stewart James, Miraskil is a classic of modern card magic. The following version was devised by Joseph K. Schmidt and the author. The only requirements are a deck of 52 cards and a slip of paper.

On the paper write, "You will end up with four more face-down cards than face-up cards." Fold the paper and drop it into a drinking glass so it is in plain view.

Remove the deck from its case and silently deal 28 cards off the top. Turn the balance of the deck face up and shuffle face-up cards into face-down cards. Square up the deck and place it before a spectator.

Invite him to shuffle the deck until he is satisfied it is completely mixed. When he has done this, pretend to study the deck. Then pretend to make a mental calculation. Nod as if satisfied, then say, "Give the deck one more shuffle and it should work."

He is now to deal the cards two at a time off the top. If the dealt pair contains two face-down cards, he places them in a heap to the left. If both cards are face up he deals them into a separate heap to the right. If he deals a pair which contain one face-up card and one face-down card, he deals them into a pile in the center.

The spectator deals pairs of cards until he has gone through the entire deck. He will have three heaps of cards on the table: one consisting of face-down cards, one of face-up cards, and one a mixture of face-up and face-down cards. Have him count aloud the number of cards in the face-down heap. Then have him count aloud the number of cards in the face-up heap. When he reads the prediction he will find that it is correct. There are four more face-down cards than face-up.

There is a simple way to repeat the trick so that the outcome is different. When the spectator counts the cards in the face-up heap and the face-down heap, pick up the heap containing the mixture of face-up and face-down cards. Cut it and complete the cut so there is a face-up card on top of this heap. The right hand takes this card, places it under the heap, and uses it to scoop up the heap and flip it over into the waiting left hand, as in Figure 3.

Fig. 3

Then place the face-up card on top of the heap and immediately give this heap a riffle shuffle. The handling allowed you to turn over the heap but not the card used as a scoop.

To repeat the trick, shuffle the face-down heap into this heap, then shuffle the face-up heap into this heap. Hand the deck to the spectator for further shuffling. On a separate slip of paper write, "You will end up with two more face-down cards than face-up cards."

Have the spectator shuffle the deck and deal the cards into three heaps as described above. Then have him open the prediction slip. Once again the prediction is correct.

6   THE SEVEN-UP MYSTERY

Impromptu mental effects are invaluable on those occasions when you are handed a deck of cards and want to impress people with your mind-reading abilities. This routine smacks of mentalism but in fact it's based on a simple premise.

The trick is introduced as the Seven-Up Trick. Before anything else is done you explain that the trick gets its name from the fact that you will later spell "Seven Up" to arrive at the chosen card.

Note that at the very beginning of the routine you've told the audience what you intend to do. This would seem to eliminate the possibility of cheating later on but there are ways and ways of spelling "Seven Up."

The spectator is given a packet of 13 cards. While you turn your back the spectator shuffles the packet and notes the face (or bottom) card. Whatever that card is, he mentally spells the suit, transferring a card for each letter from top to bottom. If for example the card was the ♣7, he would spell C-L-U-B-S, and silently transfer a card for each letter from top to bottom.

Take the packet and state that you will try to find his card. Place the packet below the level of the tabletop or behind your back. With the cards out of sight, count down to the fifth card, turn it face up and exchange it for the bottom card of the packet. Bring the packet into view. Ask for the name of the chosen card. Depending on the suit, proceed as follows:

If the spectator's card was a club, spell "Seven Up," dealing a card for each letter from top to bottom. When you've completed the deal, turn over the next card and it will be the selected card.

If the spectator names hearts or spades, spell "Seven Up," dealing a card for each letter from top to bottom. Turn up the last card dealt and show it to be the chosen card.

If the spectator names diamonds, spell "Seven," transferring a card for each letter. Then pause and say, "We spell *seven* and your card turns *up*." Spread the cards to show the chosen card face up in the center of the spread.

It is true that there will be a face-up card in the packet if the spectator's card is anything other than a diamond, but this should give you no trouble. At the conclusion of the trick simply place the packet on top of the deck, cut the deck and complete the cut. If a face-up card is later spotted in the deck it will never be connected with the Seven-Up Trick.

7 THE OPEN PREDICTION

A card problem suggested by Paul Curry has become a classic in contemporary card magic. The effect appears to be impossible. As seen by the audience, the magician writes a prediction on a slip of paper and places the paper in full view. The prediction, which can be seen by all present, reads: "You will choose the ace of spades," for example. Note that the prediction is known at the start, making it impossible for the magician to change his mind or switch predictions.

The spectator is given a deck of cards. He deals cards off the top one at a time into a face-up heap on the table. At some point he deals one card face down. Then he deals the rest of the deck face up. As he deals he is asked to look for the ♠A among the face-up cards. The ♠A never shows up.

There is one face-down card on the table. It is the only card the spectator did not turn face up. When the spectator turns this card over, he sees that it is the ♠A, the very card predicted by the magician.

Many solutions to this card problem have been proposed. The following, based on ideas of Lin Searles and Ed Balducci, is one of the simplest. The magician never touches the deck once the prediction is written.

METHOD: Take any well-shuffled deck and look through it as if to study the cards. Say you are going to try to guess where the spectator is going to stop. All you really do is note the top card of the deck. We will assume it is the ♠A. Square up the deck, place it face down on the table and write the prediction mentioned above. Make sure the spectators see exactly what you write.

Hand the deck to the spectator. Tell him to cut off about a third of the deck, turn it face up and place it on top of the rest of the pack. When he has done this, instruct him to cut off about two-thirds of the deck, turn this portion over and place it on top of the balance of the deck. If correctly done, there will now be a face-up portion on top followed by a face-down portion.

Tell the spectator to deal the face-up cards off the deck into a face-up heap, dealing one card at a time. Instruct him to deal the first face-down card off the deck so it is kept face down and no one sees its face. Then have him turn over each of the other face-down cards in the deck. At the finish there will be one face-down card. The rest of the deck is face-up.

It appears as if the face-down card was selected by a completely random process, but it will be the ♠A. Have the spectator turn this card over to show it matches your prediction.

8   FLIP TOP

In this classic effect the deck is tossed face down onto the table, whereupon an ace turns face up on top of the deck. Although the effect is well known among magicians, the correct technique is not.

We will cover the technique first and then extend the principle to a number of previously unpublished applications.

Begin with any ace on top of the deck. The card can be any card but aces are more dramatic. Hold the deck face down in the left-hand dealing position. As the right hand picks up the deck from above, the left thumb pushes the top card to the right about an inch as shown in Figure 4. This is done as the hands are raised above eye level. The action is covered by the right hand, which is above the deck at this point as shown in Figure 5. The right hand then holds the deck about 18 inches above the tabletop. The deck is parallel to the table. It is best when learning the technique to have a tablecloth covering the table because the soft surface will absorb the impact and the cards won't scatter.

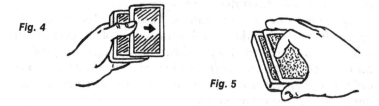

Fig. 4

Fig. 5

If you drop the deck, the ace will turn over because it is offset over the side of the deck and air pressure will cause it to flip face up. But if you just drop the deck, the ace will turn over at the last instant, making it obvious to the audience what happened. Instead of dropping the deck, toss it gently. The ace will flip over faster and the effect will appear magical.

After you try the effect a few times, you may want to consider a variation. The left thumb does not push the top card over to the right as in Figure 4. Instead, the fingers of the left hand slide under the deck and push the bottom card to the right, as in Figure 6. As before, the right hand is above the deck and covers the action.

Fig. 6

You will have to push the bottom card over about 1½ inches. Otherwise the technique is the same. Work on a soft surface (either a tablecloth or a rug) until you get the knack.

A simple application is to have an ace on top and bottom of the deck. Perform the first technique to cause the topmost ace to turn face up as you toss the deck onto the table. Leave that ace squared and still face up on top of the deck as you pick up the deck and replace it in the left hand. Then use the second technique to cause the bottom card of the deck to turn face up. This will puzzle those who know or suspect the first method.

A subtle application is the following. Secretly reverse the bottom card of the deck. Have the spectator choose a card. Then tell him to place it on top of the pack. Use the technique of Figure 6 to get the deck ready to flip over the bottom card. Toss the deck onto the table. A card will fly off the deck face down.

Say, "Your card was supposed to turn over. Let me try that again." Place the face-down card in the center of the deck, acting as if *this* card is his card. Then perform the technique of Figure 4 to get the deck ready to flip over the top card. Toss the deck onto the table. It will appear as if his card slid out of the center of the deck, turned face up and landed on top.

9 TELEVISION DICE

It is well known that the picture you see on a television screen is really a series of images. If the set is turned off, an image will remain on the screen for a fraction of a second and then dissolve. Images can be captured in a variety of ways, some of them most mysterious.

The magician drops two dice onto the table. While he turns his back he asks the spectator to roll the dice several times to verify they are not loaded. Then the spectator rolls the dice one final time.

He notes the topmost number on one die. Say it is four. He picks up any shuffled deck of cards and notes the card fourth from the top. The deck is given to the magician behind his back. The chosen die is hidden under a cup.

The magician turns around and faces the spectator. "There is one die on the table," he says. "Obviously it can't give me any information because you chose a card by means of the die hidden under the cup. Still, the die on the table contains a mental image of what number showed on the other die. Sometimes one can pick up impressions."

With the deck behind his back the magician studies the visible die, then makes an adjustment to the cards. Then he places the deck on the table. "Without looking at the deck I was able to find your card and place it in a new location," he says. "For the first time, uncover the die you used."

The cup is lifted. The number on top of the die is four. "You threw a four on this die and a six on this die," the magician says. "The total is ten, right?"

The spectator agrees. "Count down to the tenth card," the magician says. The spectator counts ten cards, turns up the next card and discovers that it is his previously chosen card.

METHOD: The trick is a swindle. The visible die on the table does indeed tell the magician all he needs to know, but in an offbeat way. When the magician gets the deck behind his back he turns and faces the spectator. Whatever number shows on the visible die, he transfers that many cards from the bottom to the top of the deck. Then he transfers one more card. In our example a six would show on the visible die. The magician transfers six cards from bottom to top, then one more card. The deck is then handed to the spectator.

He uncovers the chosen die. The uppermost numbers on the two dice are added together. The spectator counts down that many cards, turns up the next card and discovers it is his chosen card.

10　DECKSPERT

If asked to repeat the above trick on another occasion, and four dice are available, you can perform an even stronger version of "Television Dice." The presentation angle was taken from a routine of Stewart James.

If possible use dice of two different colors, say two red and two green. This is not strictly necessary to the working but it adds to the mystery. While your back is turned a spectator rolls all four dice. He chooses one color. We'll assume he picks red. Mentally he adds together the top numbers on the two red dice. Then he notes a card at the corresponding position from the top of his deck of cards. If he rolled three on one die and six on the other, he would add these numbers together, getting nine, and note the card that is ninth from the top of the deck. Once he has done this he covers the two red dice.

The deck is handed to you behind your back. Turn and face the spectator. Glance at the white dice and note the topmost numbers. Say these numbers are a three and a two. Mentally add them together, getting five. Subtract five from 28 (the sum is always subtracted from 28). Whatever number you get, deal that many cards off the top of the deck. Deal one card at a time and deal each card onto the last, thus reversing the order. The cards are dealt from the left hand into the right hand. When you finish the deal, place the dealt cards back onto the top of the deck.

The intriguing part of the routine comes in at this point. Place the deck on the table in full view. Then have the spectator uncover the two red dice. Tell him to turn all four dice over to bring new numbers uppermost. Then have him point to one of the dice. Say he points to a die with the number four uppermost. Deal four cards off the top into a heap on the table. Then the spectator points to another die. Say it shows a one uppermost. Deal one card onto the tabled heap. Continue in this way with the other two dice. The spectator can point to the dice in any order. When you have dealt cards corresponding to the top number on each of the four dice, turn over the top card and it will be the chosen card.

If dice are not available there is an impromptu substitute. Using a paper clip, attach a three back-to-back with a four. Then attach a one (ace) back-to-back with a six. Then attach a two back-to-back with a five. Repeat this same procedure with the remaining aces through sixes. The result will be that you have 12 pairs of cards. The spectator may mix the pairs and choose any four pairs. Proceed from here with the trick exactly as written.

11 CRAZY CLOCKS

Novel effects are always remembered by the audience. Fred Taylor here describes an offbeat trick that originally appeared in a European magazine. The magician writes a prediction, folds it and places it under the spectator's watchband for safekeeping. The spectator is asked to think of any full hour from one to 12. When he has an hour in mind, 12 cards are dealt off the pack face up and arranged in the form of a clock dial as shown in Figure 7.

The spectator is asked to remember the card that appears at the position of his thought-of hour. The performer correctly reveals the hour. Then the prediction is removed from under the spectator's

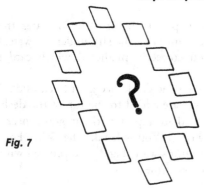

Fig. 7

watchband, opened and read aloud. The performer has correctly predicted the card chosen by the spectator.

The trick may be immediately repeated without the performer going near the deck.

METHOD: Go through the deck and remark that you want to discard any jokers that might be in the pack. As you look through the cards note and remember the thirteenth and twenty-fifth cards from the top of the pack. Say the thirteenth card is the ♣4 and the twenty-fifth card the ♦8. The ♣4 will be the first card you predict.

Place the deck face down on the table. On a slip of paper write, "You will choose the ♣4." Fold the slip and have the spectator place it under his watchband for the time being. Now have the spectator mentally decide on any hour between one and 12. Have him look at his watch when he does this, and say that the slip of paper might influence his choice by telepathic suggestion.

Turn your back. The spectator is to deal off the top of the deck a number of cards corresponding to his thought-of number. If, say, he thought of five o'clock, he would deal five cards off the top of the deck. He places these five cards in his pocket so the magician has no clue as to the number dealt.

The magician then takes the deck and deals 12 cards to represent a clock face. The cards are first dealt singly into a heap on the table. Then they are placed around an imaginary clock face, beginning at the one o'clock position, the cards being arranged face up. Mentally note the position of the previously noted thirteenth card, the ♣4 in our example, and you know the selected hour. Jot this on a second slip of paper.

Have the spectator announce the chosen hour. He then notes the card at that hour on the clock face. In our example he would note the card at the five o'clock position. This card will be the ♣4. Have him open the second slip, which correctly indicates the hour he thought of. Then have him open the slip under his watchband. He will discover that you correctly predicted which card he would choose.

The cards representing the clock face are placed aside. The cards in the spectator's pocket are added to the top of the deck. You are now ready for an immediate repeat without going near the deck. On a sheet of paper write, "You will take the ♦ 8." Fold the slip, place it under the spectator's watchband, and proceed with the trick exactly as you did the first time.

12   TO LIE OR TELL THE TRUTH

Jack Avis devised an excellent trick which will quickly establish your reputation as a card expert. The plot, originally suggested by Martin Gardner, is one where the spectator is asked a series of questions about a chosen card and is encouraged to lie or tell the truth in answer to the questions. The deck has been programmed like a lie detector. It provides the correct answers to his questions, and then it goes on to produce the chosen card!

It is only necessary that you secretly note the bottom card of the deck before the trick begins. This can be done under cover of the excuse that you want to check that the deck contains 52 cards. Simply glimpse the bottom card while you count the cards. The glimpsed card becomes your key card.

Spread the deck face down and have the spectator remove any card. He notes the card, puts the card on top of the deck, then cuts the deck and completes the cut. Take back the deck. Turn it face up, spread it from left to right, find your key card, and note the card just to the right of it. This will be the spectator's chosen card. Cut the deck between the key card and the chosen card. Complete the cut. His card will now be on top.

You're now going to make a series of setting-up moves. While doing this, tell the spectator you are programming the deck to act like a lie detector, and that once programmed it is infallible and will produce the right answer no matter how he tries to trick it with false answers. Once the deck has been programmed you will invite the spectator to assist, and he is to try to beat the lie detector by giving it incorrect information. In other words, he may lie or tell the truth in answer to your questions.

The setting-up process is given here. It will take a bit of practice to get it to the point where it can be done smoothly and quickly. The deck is face up and you have cut the chosen card to the top of the deck. From the *face* of the deck and working to the *left,* upjog cards as follows:

> One card of the same *value* as the selected card.
> Three indifferent cards.
> Two cards of the same *suit* as the selected card.
> Three indifferent cards.
> One card of the same *color* as the selected card.
> One indifferent card.
> One card of the same *color* as the selected card.
> Two indifferent cards.

As an example, assume the spectator chose the ♣K. Beginning at the face of the deck and working to the left, upjog a king, then three indifferent cards, then two clubs, then three more indifferent cards, then a black card, then an indifferent card, then two black cards, and finally two indifferent cards.

Retain the deck in the right hand. With the left hand strip out the jogged cards as a unit, and allow them to drop into the left palm. Drop the deck on top of the cards in the left hand, square up the pack and turn it face down.

Ask the spectator if his card was red or black. Remind him that he can lie in answer to this and every other question. The idea is to trick the lie detector. Whatever his answer, spell it out a card at a time, forming a small packet. If for example he answers red, spell "R-E-D," dealing a card for each letter, forming a three-card packet.

The second question has to do with suit. If he said his card was red, now ask if it was hearts or a diamond. If in answer to the first question he said his card was black, now ask if it was clubs or a spade. Spell out his answer, forming a second packet to the right of the first packet.

The third and final question has to do with the value of the chosen card. Ask, "Was the card a court card or did it have spots?" As with each of the other two questions, the spectator may lie or tell the truth when answering. Spell C-O-U-R-T or S-P-O-T-S, which-ever he chooses, in answer to the third question, dealing these cards into a third packet to the right of the other two.

Now say, "You've done your best to fool the lie detector. Let's see what the real truth is." Working from left to right, turn up the top card of each packet. Your patter might run like this: "The computerized lie detector indicates that you chose a red card. It was a diamond. It was a court card. In fact this is your chosen card."

If the spectator chose hearts, the selected card will be on top of the deck at the finish. When you get to the line, "In fact this is your chosen card," turn up the top card of the pack. In all other cases the chosen card will be the top card of the third packet.

The spelling must be done exactly as described above. Master the details of this fine routine and you will have in your possession a truly baffling card trick.

RED-BLACK MYSTERIES

John N. Hilliard once observed, "The great majority of card tricks begin with a spectator choosing a card which he notes and then replaces in the deck. That card is then discovered and revealed by the magician in various ways."

It is wise to have on hand tricks which depend on a different plot idea. In this way the audience can be entertained with a wide variety of different card effects. Tricks involving reds and blacks are ideal because the effects are novel and quite different from card locations. This chapter describes some of the best contemporary mysteries with reds and blacks.

13   CHROMATIC CAPER

The only requirements for this unusual trick are a deck of cards and two slips of paper. Have the spectator shuffle the deck and deal it into two heaps of 26 cards each. Then tell him to turn either half of the deck face up and shuffle it into the face-down half of the pack. Let him give the deck two or three shuffles.

Ask him to name two of the suits. Point out that there are 12 answers he can give (clubs-hearts, spades-hearts, clubs-diamonds, etc.) and that you could have no way of guessing ahead of time which two suits he will choose. He might choose clubs and hearts. Jot these down on a slip of paper and place it before the spectator. Jot down the remaining two suits (spades and diamonds in our example) on the remaining slip and place this slip near you. The only reason for the slips is to remind the spectator of the two suits he freely chose for himself.

While you fill out the slips, have the spectator deal the deck into two heaps of 26 cards each. When he has done this, have him pick up one heap, go through it and remove the face-up cards of the suits he has chosen—clubs and hearts is our example. After these cards have been removed, take the remainder of the heap from him, turn it over and place it on the table.

Then have the spectator go through the other heap and similarly remove all the face-up clubs and hearts. He adds these to the clubs and hearts removed from the other half of the deck. When he has done this, take the remainder of the heap from him, turn it over and place it near the first heap. The situation is now as in Figure 8. There is a packet containing face-up clubs and hearts. Below it are two heaps containing a mixture of face-up and face-down cards.

Fig. 8

HEARTS
AND
CLUBS

Remind the spectator that he chose any two suits for himself and left the other two suits for you. Go through each of the heaps, remove all the face-up spades and diamonds, and place them in front of you. The situation now looks like Figure 9.

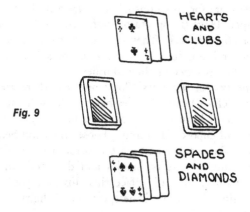

Fig. 9

HEARTS
AND
CLUBS

SPADES
AND
DIAMONDS

Have the spectator count the clubs and hearts in his packet. Then have him count the spades and diamonds in your packet. He will be surprised to discover that you have exactly as many cards in your packet as he has in his.

For the final surprise gather the balance of the two remaining heaps and spread them on the table to reveal that the *only* face-up cards in them are clubs and hearts, the two suits freely chosen by the spectator!

14 FLYING COLORS

The spectator gives an ordinary deck of cards a riffle shuffle. He then divides the deck into two heaps and gives the deck another shuffle. The magician removes a red card and a black card from the middle of the deck. Passing these cards over the deck, he causes all the reds to separate from all the blacks. The colors separate instantly, a startling trick in view of the fact that the deck was given repeated shuffles by the spectator.

METHOD: This routine is based on an idea of George Pierce and Charles Jordan. Beforehand place 13 red cards face down on the table. Place 13 blacks on top of that. Then place the joker on top of the blacks. Place the other 13 reds on top of that, and finally place the remaining 13 blacks on top of that.

When ready to perform the trick for the spectator, turn the deck face up and fan the cards so that only you can see the faces. Remove the joker at the center and discard it. Split the deck at that point so that one group of 13 reds and 13 blacks is in each half of the deck.

Place the packets face down on the table. Instruct the spectator to riffle shuffle them together (as shown in Figure 17) and square up the pack. The shuffle should be fairly even for best results, so choose a spectator who can give the deck an even riffle shuffle.

After he has shuffled the cards, have him deal them into two even heaps. He is to deal from left to right, dealing a card alternately into each heap, until he has dealt all 52 cards.

Once he has done this, tell him to riffle shuffle the two heaps together again. At the conclusion of the second shuffle, take the deck from him and spread it so that you alone can see the cards. Remark that you are looking for some important cards. As you spread the cards from left to right you will note a large number of black cards at the bottom of the deck and a large number of red cards at the top of the deck. Depending on how even the shuffle was, there will be a few reds and a few blacks intermixed in the center of the deck.

Remove these intermixed cards and place them on the table. Cut or split the deck at the division between the colors so that reds are in one half, blacks in the other. Place each half face down on the table.

Pick up the intermixed packet. Remove one red card and one black card. Remark that these cards have magical powers. Tap the red card against the top of the red packet. Pick up the red packet and spread it face up to show that all the cards are red. Pick up the black card, tap it against the black half, then spread that half to show that all the cards are black.

In many cases, if the shuffle is even, there will be no reds intermixed with blacks. In other words the colors will be perfectly separate at the conclusion of the second shuffle. In this case remove any red and any black. Cut the deck between the colors and proceed as described above.

To increase the chances for a perfect color separation, at the beginning stack the deck as follows from top down: 13 blacks, joker, 13 reds, 13 blacks, joker, 13 reds. Proceed with the trick as described above through the second riffle shuffle. When you then pick up the pack and look over the faces, you may find one or two cards intermixed at the center, but these are likely to be the jokers. Discard them from the deck. The colors should be perfectly separated at this point. If not, remove the few intermixed cards from the center and proceed as described above.

15 OIL AND WATER

The trick in which reds and blacks magically separate was noted as a card problem by the great nineteenth-century conjuror J. N. Hofzinser. A small-packet version was described by Walter Gibson in a magic magazine called *The Jinx*. Since its publication it has become a magic classic.

The effect is that four reds and four blacks are mixed together. Then they instantly separate. The simplest handling is described here.

Have four blacks in one pile and four reds in the other. Hold them as shown in Figure 10. Explain that there are numerous ways to mix reds and blacks, and that you will demonstrate one way.

The left thumb pushes over a red card so it drops face down onto the table. Then the right thumb pushes over a black card so it drops face down onto the table in a separate heap.

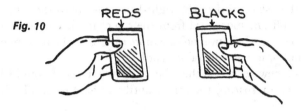

Fig. 10

REDS   BLACKS

The hands now cross, Figure 11. Thumb off a black card onto the tabled red card. At the same time the other hand thumbs off a red card onto the tabled black card.

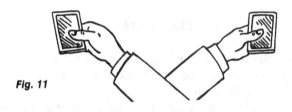

Fig. 11

Uncross the hands and thumb off another card from each packet onto the heaps that are on the table. Then cross the hands and thumb off the last card from each hand onto the tabled cards. You now have two packets on the table, each containing two reds and two blacks.

Pick up the left heap and place it on top of the right heap. Say, "That's how you mix the colors. It takes almost as long to unmix them." As you speak, deal the packet into two heaps, alternating a card to each, dealing from left to right. It appears as if you are separating the colors.

"Now I'll show you how magicians do it." Pick up the left heap and place it face down into the left hand. Pick up the other heap, turn it face up and place it into the right hand as in Figure 12. Turn the left hand palm down to show a black card at the bottom of the left hand heap. Turn the left hand palm up again, and turn the right hand palm down. Both packets are face down at this point.

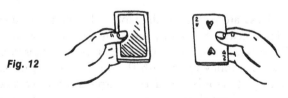

Fig. 12

Thumb off the top card of the left-hand heap onto the table. Thumb off the *bottom* card of the right-hand heap onto the tabled card. Thumb off one more card from the top of the left-hand heap onto the tabled cards. Thumb off one more card from the bottom of the right-hand heap onto the tabled cards.

Then start a new packet on the table. Thumb off a card from each heap as before, alternating the cards, until you have dealt all four cards.

Snap your fingers over the first heap. Turn it face up and show that all cards are of one color. Turn over the other heap and show four cards of the opposite color. The colors have instantly separated.

16   CHECKERS

This is an offbeat version of "Oil and Water" devised by the author. Alternate three reds and three blacks, then hold the six-card packet face down in the left hand.

Turn the top card face up on top of the packet. Then deal the top two cards into a heap on the table. Pick them up as a unit, turn them over and replace them on top of the packet.

Deal the top three cards onto the table. Pick up the dealt packet, turn it over and replace it on top of the packet.

Deal the top four cards into a heap on the table. Pick up the dealt packet, turn it over and replace it on top of the packet.

Finally, deal the top five cards into a heap. Pick up the dealt cards, turn them over and replace them on top of the card in the left hand.

You will find that the colors still alternate but now every other card is reversed. If you do the trick without turning over the packet at each step the colors will separate. Deal smoothly and quickly to give the illusion that the cards are being completely mixed.

17   INFLUENTIAL PAIRS

Two cased decks are placed on the table. The spectator chooses either deck. This deck is thoroughly mixed by the spectator and the magician. The spectator then sorts these cards face up according to color. The magician follows suit with the other deck and matches the actions of the spectator but he does it with his cards face down.

Although the magician's cards are randomly dealt, when they are turned over it is seen that the colors have separated; all blacks are in one packet and all reds in another.

METHOD: This routine is based on ideas of Roy Walton and the author. Required are two decks, one red-backed and the other blue-backed. Stack the red deck so there are 26 pairs of cards such that each pair contains two cards of the same color. The actual order of the pairs is unimportant, although there should be a fair mixture of reds and blacks. Thus the red-backed deck might be stacked BB-BB-RR-BB-RR-BB-BB-RR-BB, and so on, from top to bottom.

The blue-backed deck is then stacked in exactly the same order. Once this has been done, deal the blue-backed deck onto the table a card at a time, thus reversing the order of the cards in this pack. Place each deck in its own card case until the time of performance.

To present the routine, toss out both cased decks. Ask the spectator to choose one pack. It can be either pack, but we'll assume he chooses the red deck. Remove it from its case and hand it to the spectator. Ask him to deal it into two heaps. He deals cards from right to left, a card at a time, until there are 26 cards in each heap.

Ask him to take either heap. You take the other one. Each of you places your half of the deck behind your back and mixes the cards. Actually you do nothing. Just place the packet behind your back and pretend to mix the cards.

Now the two halves of the red-backed deck are placed on the table alongside one another. Both halves are face down. The spectator removes a card from the tops of both heaps simultaneously. He turns them face up. If both are red they go into one packet on the table. If both are black they go into a separate packet. If one card is red and one is black they go into a discard packet off to one side.

As the spectator does this, you remove the blue-backed deck from its case and hold it in the left hand. Deal the top two cards off and take them with the right hand. Don't look at the faces of these two cards. Just follow the actions performed by the spectator. If he places his two cards into a face-up red pile, you place your two cards near his in a separate pile. If he then turns up two cards, sees they are black and puts them into a separate black pile, you take your next two cards from the blue-backed deck and place them in a pile near his black pile. If the spectator turns up two, sees that the colors don't match and places them in a discard pile, you place your pair of cards in a discard pile near his.

The spectator's pairs of cards will or won't match. The outcome is random on each round. You merely follow what he does but without looking at your cards. Yet although he has sorted matching-color pairs visibly, your pairs of cards sort themselves invisibly. At the finish of the deal, when you turn over your packet near his all-black packet, it will be seen that all of your cards are the same color. Similarly, when you turn over your packet near his all-red packet, all of the cards in your packet are seen to be of one color.

If the spectator wishes to examine your discard heap (the one next to his red-black heap), pick up the heap and transfer the top card to the bottom. Now all of the pairs in this heap will be nonmatching pairs.

18 RED MAGIC

Using his own deck of cards, which the magician has never seen before, the spectator removes any number of red cards and places these in his left jacket pocket. He then deals the remainder of the pack into two heaps, chooses either of these, sorts out the red cards in the chosen heap, and then places these in his right jacket pocket.

All of these actions take place while the magician has his back turned. Yet the magician now picks up the remaining heap on the table, glances briefly through it and immediately tells the spectator how many cards he has in *each* jacket pocket.

METHOD: Begin as described above by having the spectator remove a number of red cards from the deck. Tell him to place them in his left jacket pocket. He must choose an even number for ease of working later on.

Now the spectator is directed to deal the remainder of the deck into two heaps, each heap containing the same number of cards. After the deal he can shuffle each heap.

He then chooses either heap, sorts out all the red cards and places them in his right jacket pocket. The magician picks up the remaining heap and mentally counts the number of reds and the number of blacks in it.

A quick mental calculation is performed as follows. To the number of red cards in this heap the magician adds *twice* the number of black cards and from the result subtracts 26. The number arrived at is the number of red cards in the spectator's right jacket pocket.

As an example, if the heap examined by the magician contains ten reds and 12 blacks, he would add 10 + 24, getting 34. From this he subtracts 26, getting 8. This tells him that the spectator has eight red cards in his right jacket pocket.

You have accounted for eight reds in the spectator's right pocket and ten reds in the packet you examined. Since the pack contains 26 red cards in all, the spectator must have eight reds in his left jacket pocket.

19 ODD COLOR OUT

A packet of cards is removed from the deck and handed to a spectator sitting across the table from you. He places the cards below the level of the tabletop, cuts them and completes the cut. Then he turns the top two cards face up, places them on top of the face-down packet and cuts the packet. He turns two more cards face up, places them on top of the packet and again cuts and completes the cut. The process continues as long as the spectator desires. Each time he turns over the top two cards, places them on top of the packet and cuts the packet. The result will be a random distribution of face-up and face-down cards in the packet.

When the spectator is satisfied that face-up and face-down cards are hopelessly mixed, tell him to glance at the top card of the packet and the bottom card. If these are of different colors, he remembers each card, turns each over, then returns each to its original position. Then he cuts the packet to lose these two cards. If the top and bottom cards are of the same color, he cuts the packet until he brings a card of each color to top and bottom of the packet.

With the two noted cards buried in the packet, the cards are handed to the magician under the table. He sorts through the cards briefly, then brings the packet into view and spreads it out on the table to reveal a surprising outcome. All of the face-up cards are red except for the previously noted *black* card. The packet is flipped over to reveal that all of the face-up cards now in view are black except for the previously noted *red* card!

METHOD: This excellent close-up mystery is based on ideas of Bob Hummer and Robert Page. You will need a stack of about 20 cards. The colors alternate red-black-red-black from top to bottom. This is the only preparation.

When ready to present the trick, hand this packet to the spectator. He places it below the level of the tabletop, cuts the packet and completes the cut. The trick then proceeds exactly as described above. When the spectator pushes over the top two cards and reverses them, he must reverse them as a unit. This is to say that the top two cards are pushed over, taken with the right hand, turned over and replaced on top of the packet.

After the spectator has noted the top and bottom card and reversed each in place, he cuts the packet and completes the cut. The position of the two chosen cards is not known to anyone, nor is the order of face-up and face-down cards in the packet.

The packet is handed to you under the table or behind your back. All you need do is reverse every other card. Then bring the packet into view and spread it on the table. All of the face-up cards will be red except for the previously noted black card. When the packet is flipped over, all of the face-up cards will be black except for the previously noted red card.

Performed seemingly on the spur of the moment with an unprepared deck of cards, this is an all but unfathomable mystery. There is another way to go directly into the trick using a shuffled deck of cards, but it is not impromptu. The idea is to have a packet of 20 cards on the lap already set up as described above. After doing a few card tricks with the deck on the table, cut off about 20 cards and have the spectator shuffle the packet. Take back the packet and give it another shuffle. Then hand it to the spectator under the table. Actually, when the packet goes under the table, switch it for the duplicate packet in the lap. Since this packet is stacked in the correct order with the colors alternating, the trick works exactly as described. You will have to put the cards away after the routine is done because the cards in this packet won't necessarily match the cards in the packet you cut off the deck, but you may find the effect worth the extra effort.

20   THE COLOR OF THOUGHT

In *Self-Working Card Tricks* a routine called "Opposites Attract" introduced a novel method of making kings and queens match. Here, in the closing routine of this chapter, Martin Gardner provides an ingenious application in which the spectator correctly guesses the color of every card in the pack!

Set up the deck so that all the reds are in the top half and all the blacks in the bottom half. Spread the deck face down on the table. Invite the spectator to push 26 cards out partially from the spread. Be sure to keep mental count of the number of cards he pushes out so you can stop him at 26. The situation might look like Figure 13 at this point.

Mention that, to make sure he has exactly 26 cards, you will count them. Take each card he pushed out, beginning at the top (or

Fig. 13

right-hand end) of the spread, and deal or place them into a pile, counting aloud as you take each card. This procedure secretly reverses the cards. Make sure the cards stay in order.

Square up the remainder of the spread. Pick up this packet. Tell the spectator you want to make a quick check of the count. Turn the packet so you alone can see the faces and fan them toward you. Pretend to make a quick count. Actually you spot the reds remaining in the top half and note the last card of this run. Say the last red card is the ♦ 7.

Place the two packets alongside each other. Say, "It seems you did rather well. Look." Deal cards simultaneously from the tops of both packets. In Figure 14 the packets are placed at *A* and *B*. You deal cards off the tops of the packets, turn them face up and place them in face-up packets *C* and *D* as shown in Figure 14. Continue dealing until your previously noted key card (the ♦ 7 in our example) turns up.

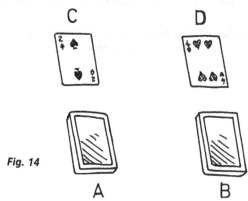

Fig. 14

By this time the audience assumes the entire deck has been correctly separated into reds and blacks by the spectator. As if in recognition of this, say, "Let's not waste time turning up single cards."

Pick up the packet at *D* and spread it at a spot above the layout.

Then spread *C* below it. The situation as it now looks is shown in Figure 15.

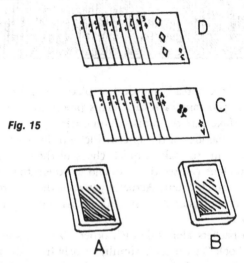

Fig. 15

A subtlety in the handling comes into play at this point. Pick up the packet at *A*, turn it face up and spread it as a continuation of the spread at *D*. The audience sees all cards of one color.

Finish by picking up the pile at *B*, turning it face up and spreading it as a continuation of the spread at *C*. All cards show the other color.

This is a simple, natural handling of an extremely strong card routine. In effect the spectator has correctly guessed the color of every card in the deck.

TELEPHONE TRICKS

In the early part of this century a new effect was introduced, based on the remarkable premise that it was possible to perform mind reading over the telephone. Since its inception, the telephone trick has inspired many variations and developments. Some of the best are described in this chapter.

21 TWENTIETH-CENTURY TELEPATHY

This is the original telephone trick, devised by John N. Hilliard and published in 1905. With attention to dramatic presentation, it is still one of the best demonstrations of telephone telepathy. The details of performance are important. Hilliard urged that the trick be done as an experiment in long-distance telepathy rather than as a card trick. The following description is taken from his original article.

Have someone go into the next room. Explain that this person will be a committee of one, delegated to call the medium at a later time. When he is out of the room, tell one of the spectators that you would like him to name a card. It can be any card in the deck but to make the demonstration meaningful the spectator should try not to name an obvious card.

We will assume the ♣K is named. The spectator in the next room is called back. He acknowledges that he is not a confederate and that he has no idea which card was chosen. He is given the name and telephone number of the medium. He dials the number and asks the medium to call out the name of the thought-of card. Immediately she names the exact card merely thought of by the spectator!

The magician never leaves the room and does not communicate

with the medium. The spectator may think of any card in the deck. There is no force and there is no confederacy involved. Properly performed it is an astounding trick.

METHOD: In a sense the method has been included in the above description of the effect but it seems such an incidental detail that the reader is likely to have overlooked it. The secret is that when you convey the medium's name to the spectator you have furnished a code which transmits the name of the chosen card to the medium. To say it another way, you choose one of 52 names for the medium and that name tells her the chosen card.

On a card write down the following information:

	Hearts	*Clubs*	*Diamonds*	*Spades*
Ace	Sidney	Dobson	Colt	Harris
Two	Smith	Darrow	Carver	Holmes
Three	Schmidt	Driscoll	Campbell	Hart
Four	Sanford	Dwight	Christopher	Hanford
Five	Scofield	Drew	Cartwright	Hamlin
Six	Stoddard	Draper	Caldwell	Haskins
Seven	Samson	Dayton	Cortland	Herne
Eight	Saddler	Dodge	Craig	Hicks
Nine	Seager	Davis	Cabot	Hoffman
Ten	Snyder	Drake	Case	Holt
Jack	Scranton	Dawson	Clark	Higgins
Queen	Sarles	Denton	Collins	Hodges
King	Spencer	Daley	Curtis	Hartz

On the back of this card write the medium's telephone number. The medium has a duplicate of this list of names which she keeps near the telephone.

Proceed as described above to have the volunteer spectator leave the room while you have a card named. As soon as the card is named, have the volunteer return to the room. Take the above card out of your pocket with the name side toward you. If the named card is the ♥A for example, have the spectator dial the number and ask for Mrs. Sidney. If the named card is the ♦6, have the volunteer ask for Mrs. Caldwell. In our example the named card is the ♣K. Here you would have the volunteer go to the phone, dial the number and ask for Mrs. Daley.

On her end of the phone the medium consults her list and sees that Mrs. Daley is the code for the ♣K. She then goes on with a dramatic revelation of this card.

In the original article Hilliard concluded with these wise words: "If worked in a dramatic manner, a single trial will convince the most skeptical that the experiment has a remarkable and totally inexplicable effect on an audience."

22 THE PERCIVAL CODE

In the original article Hilliard suggested an alternate code that is somewhat more brief. This code assigns letters of the alphabet to the values of the cards and letters to the suits. The letters A through M are assigned to the values ace through king, and the letters D, I, T, E to the suits clubs, hearts, spades and diamonds respectively.

Using this code, if the spectator chose the ♥A, the volunteer would be instructed to dial the phone and ask for Mrs. A. I. Smith. If the spectator chose the ♣6, the volunteer would ask for Mrs. F. D. Smith, and so on.

Another approach is this. Use Hilliard's Sidney through Spencer column to code values, and the following code for suits:

Alice	= clubs	Carol	= spades
Betty	= hearts	Ethel	= diamonds

If the spectator names the ♣A, the volunteer is to ask for Alice Sidney. If he named the ♦A, the volunteer would ask for Ethel Sidney. If the named card was the ♠J, the volunteer would ask for Carol Scranton, and so on. Thus the medium's first name codes the suit of the named card, while her last name codes the value. This cuts down on the size of the list and makes it easier to find the proper name. The method is related to one published by John Percival.

Still another method is to assign a different card to each week of the year. Since there are 52 weeks in the year and 52 cards in the deck, each card can be associated with a particular week. The medium keeps a calendar near the phone, looks up the card for the current week, and knows which card to name when asked. But note that although no code is used in this version, it is necessary to force the card for that particular week. The chapter on forces later in this book provides information on forcing any card you desire. In this version of the telephone trick the spectator cannot name any card in the deck, but the fact that no code is used might make this approach appealing to the reader.

23   CALLING MS. WIZARD

In this version of the telephone trick the medium's name and phone number are known from the start, yet she is able to name any thought-of card. The idea is this. Have someone name any card. You then go to the phone and dial the medium's number. When she picks up the phone she begins counting from one to 13. When she calls out the value of the named card, you say, "Hello?"

If for example she called out, "One, two, three, four——" and you said, "Hello?" she would know that the value of the thought-of card was four because you said "hello" immediately after the medium said "four."

As soon as she knows the value, the medium calls out the suits. When she calls out the suit of the thought-of card, you say, "Hello?" once again. For example, if she called out, "Clubs, spades——" and you said "Hello?" she would know that the suit is spades, because you said "hello" right after she called out spades.

Immediately hand the phone to the spectator. He asks the medium to name the chosen card. Since she now knows the suit and value, she can go on to reveal the card in dramatic fashion.

This trick once sold for a considerable sum. One of the simplest and best methods of transmitting any card in the deck to the medium without the use of a name code, it is credited to Bill McCaffrey.

24   THE GREAT PHONE MYSTERY

The spectator is given the deck behind his back. He removes the top card, turns it over and inserts it anywhere in the deck. Then he removes the bottom card, turns it over and inserts it anywhere in the pack.

Spreading the pack face down on the table, he finds the first reversed card and the card that is face to face with it. Then he finds the other reversed card and removes the card that is face to face with it.

There are now two random cards on the table. The spectator goes to the phone, dials the medium and calls out one of the two random cards. The medium immediately names the *other* random card!

There is no code. The spectator handles the cards from start to finish. He can know the medium's name and phone number ahead of time.

METHOD: This approach introduces the idea of a force. Beforehand you and the medium agree on a card that will be forced. Say it is the ♥9. Place the ♥9 near the bottom of the deck. Then place a card face up under it so the reversed card is face to face with the ♥9. Then reverse the bottom card. The prepared deck is shown in Figure 16. The ♦2 and ♣3 are face up in the drawing.

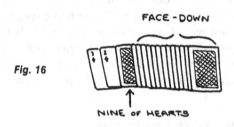

Fig. 16

FACE - DOWN

NINE OF HEARTS

To present the trick remove the deck from its case. Holding it face down, hand it to the spectator behind his back. Tell him to take the top card, turn it over and insert it anywhere in the pack. Then tell him to take the bottom card, turn it over and insert it somewhere else in the pack. Finally ask him to cut the deck and complete the cut.

He brings the deck into view and spreads it face down on the table. There will be two face-up cards in the pack. Have the spectator remove the card that is face to face with each of the reversed cards. Caution him not to turn either of these cards face up.

Since you knew at the start which card was facing the ♥9, you know which of the two cards on the table must be the ♥9. Have the spectator turn the other card face up. He dials the medium and names this card. She then reveals the identity of the other card, the ♥9.

25 A REMOTE MIRACLE

As this routine illustrates, the telephone trick has developed in an unexpected direction. In this version you do not call the medium. Instead you call a friend and perform the entire trick for him over the telephone, as follows:

Using his own shuffled deck, the spectator deals out two poker hands of five cards each. He chooses one hand, shuffles it and notes the top card. Then he takes a few cards from the top of the deck and places them on this hand to bury the chosen card. The deck is then dropped onto the hand containing the chosen card. Finally the deck is dropped onto the other poker hand.

The spectator calls off the cards in order from the top of the deck. When he has called off all the cards, the magician on the other end of the line immediately names the chosen card.

METHOD: All of the above is intended to make the trick appear more sophisticated than it really is. What the method comes down to is this: the chosen card will always be tenth up from the bottom of the deck, or forty-third down from the top. All you need to do is call a friend, have him follow the above instructions, then simply note the forty-third card he calls out. That will be the chosen card.

26 POKER BY PHONE

In this novel routine the magician remarks that he has a friend who can play Stud Poker by telephone. The spectator freely chooses a card. There is no force. The spectator signs his name on the card. Then he adds four more cards to it to make a Five-Card Stud Poker hand. He mixes the five cards and turns one of them face down for the hole card. Then he calls off the four face-up cards to the medium over the telephone.

Without asking a question she names the hole card, then she goes on to name the card signed by the spectator!

The spectator may call out the four face-up cards in any order. There is no code. The medium's name and phone number are known to the spectator ahead of time. The spectator has a free choice of cards, and the name of his card need not be known to the magician.

METHOD: The trick uses a force but the subtle angle is that the card chosen by the spectator is not the force card. In fact it is the only card that is not forced.

On top of the deck have four known cards. Say they are the ♣A, ♥4, ♠8 and ♦J. This is the only preparation. These four cards must be known to the medium ahead of time. She can jot them down on a slip of paper and have the paper near the phone in readiness for this trick.

When ready to present the routine, place the deck face down on the table. Ask the spectator to cut off about half and place it on the table. Then hand him the lower half, and ask him to shuffle it and place it on top of the tabled half, but at right angles. A view of the situation at this point is shown in Figure 46 on page 78.

Remove a slip of paper from the pocket. Written on it is the name and phone number of the medium. Place it in full view on the table. Then have the spectator take the top card of the top packet, look at it and sign his name across the face.

Lift off the upper packet and place it aside. Then deal the top four cards of the lower packet onto the table. These are the four cards you placed on top of the deck previously, but it looks as if they are four random cards from the middle of the pack.

Have the spectator add his signed card to the four dealt cards. Then tell him to mix them face up and turn one face down. If it is the signed card, have him turn three more cards face down so that only one card remains face up. Tell him this will be the hole card. The hole card must not be the signed card, but it can be any other card.

The situation now is that there are four face-up cards on the table and one face-down card. Remark that this represents a Stud Poker hand and that the medium has the ability to play Stud Poker by phone.

The spectator calls the medium and names the four face-up cards in any order. Knowing what the four force cards are, the medium notes which one was *not* called out. This is the hole card. If for example the spectator calls out ♣A, ♥4, ♠8 and ♣3, the medium notes that the ♦J was not called out so she knows this must be the hole card. Further, the spectator called out the ♣3, which is not one of the four cards on her list, so she knows this must be the signed card. She then goes on to reveal the identity of the hole card and the signed card.

In keeping with the poker theme, instead of having the spectator sign the face of his card, have him place an X on the back. Explain that this card represents a marked card since it is marked on the back. You further explain that you know someone who can play Stud Poker over the telephone and who has the remarkable ability of being able to detect marked cards via telephone. The medium is called, she names the hole card, then ponders a bit and goes on to identify the marked card.

27 SHYLOCK'S CARD

Whereas Sherlock Holmes always caught the guilty man by brilliant deduction, his infamous brother Shylock Holmes always sent the innocent man to the electric chair. The ♥J is used in this trick to represent Shylock, and the entire detective story is enacted over the phone.

1. Call a friend and have him bring a deck of cards to the phone. When he has done this, ask him to remove the ♥J and place it aside for the moment.

2. Tell him to remove three kings, say the ♥K, ♠K and ♦K, from the deck and arrange them in that order in a face-up row on the table.

3. The spectator mentally decides which king is to be the guilty party. He signifies this by placing the Shylock card (♥J) face up under the chosen king.

4. Then he turns the chosen king face down so that the king is face-to-face with Shylock. "Shylock gets an excellent look at the killer. In fact he can't get a better look. But you can bet he'll disgrace himself by picking the wrong man later on."

5. Ask the spectator to exchange the guilty party with one of the other kings. Then he exchanges the face-down king with the other face-up king.

6. This step is optional. Have him exchange the two face-up cards and call out their positions. Then have him exchange these two cards again. (The spectator, in calling out the positions of these two kings, need only say whether each is on the left, in the middle or on the right. Then have him exchange these two cards again.)

7. Have the spectator turn the two face-up kings face down. Say, "Shylock is face-to-face with one of the suspects. Since he's positive this fellow is the guilty man, we know he's wrong. Place this king back in the deck."

8. There are two kings left on the table. To name the guilty party you use the information of Step 6. If the spectator called out positions 1 and 2, you know the guilty party is not the king originally in position 3. That is, the guilty party is not the king in the position that was not called on. Since the kings were originally in heart-spade-diamond order in Step 2, you know the guilty party is not the ♦K. Have the spectator discard this king. The remaining king on the table is the guilty party.

If the spectator called out positions 1 and 3, the ♠K would not be guilty. If the spectator called out positions 2 and 3, the ♥K would not be the guilty party. Thus, whatever positions the spectator calls out in Step 6, you know who is not guilty.

As mentioned, Step 6 is optional. Instead of having the spectator exchange the two face-up cards and then exchange them again, you can have him simply call out the positions of the two face-up kings. The rest of the trick is as written.

This routine is the author's version of a principle suggested by Bob Hummer. A remarkable version of Hummer's idea is the routine that closes this chapter.

28 NO QUESTIONS ASKED

This clever version of the telephone trick was marketed by Richard Himber. Call a friend and tell him to take his own cards, shuffle them and deal out two heaps. He is to deal from left to right and he can stop whenever he likes, as long as there are the same number of cards in both heaps.

After he has done this, tell him to place the undealt portion of the deck in his pocket. Then tell him to lift up a portion of cards from the left-hand heap and note the bottom or face card of the cut portion. He then places this portion on the right-hand heap.

There will be some cards remaining in the left-hand heap. Have him call them off to you over the phone. When he's done this, say, "Your card is the —— Wait, I forgot, your card is in the *other* heap. All right, call out the cards in the right-hand heap."

He does this and you immediately name the chosen card.

The secret is this. When he calls out the cards in the small left-hand packet, list them on a piece of paper, one under the other. When he calls out the cards in the large right-hand heap, list them under the other cards you've written down.

You may have a total of 20 cards. Half of 20 is ten. The tenth card he called out is his chosen card. The chosen card is always at a position that is half the total number of cards. If, for example, he called out 24 cards, his card would be the twelfth card he called out.

As soon as you name the card, hang up. Chances are excellent the spectator will call you back and ask how you did it!

29 THE CONNECTION

Most of the tricks in this book require nothing in the way of special apparatus. This routine is an exception, although the apparatus is something you are likely to own. The gimmick makes possible miracle tricks like the following.

While at a friend's home ask him to remove a deck of cards from its case, spread the cards face up on the table and remove any card. He can change his mind as often as he likes until he finally decides on one card.

You then dial the medium's number but hand the phone directly to the spectator while the phone on the other end is still ringing. The medium picks up the phone and instantly announces the name of the chosen card!

There is no code and the effect may be repeated immediately. The medium can be in the next town or across the country. The spectator has an absolutely free choice of any card in the deck. He can even make up the name of a card, like the twenty of clubs, or he can think of some other object like a key or a picture or a coin. If he thinks of the title of a tune, the medium will pick up the phone on her end and immediately whistle the tune. Before proceeding you may wish to try to figure out a method that will answer the above conditions.

METHOD: The special apparatus mentioned above is a cassette tape recorder. All you do is have someone dial your phone, turn on the tape recorder and record the ringing phone. Then record the sound made when you pick up the phone. That completes the preparation. Rewind the tape, place it next to the phone, have your medium ready, and you can now perform a perplexing mystery.

When at the home of a friend, have him choose a card as outlined above. Make sure he has time to change his mind so that he won't think he merely picked an obvious card. When he has a card in mind, go to the phone and dial the medium.

As soon as the phone rings, she takes it off the hook and starts the tape recorder. Hand the phone to the spectator. He hears the sound of a ringing phone and thinks it is the medium's phone that's ringing. Actually it's only a *recording* of a ringing phone, but he doesn't know that.

Say to him, "Now remember to get a clear mental picture of the four of clubs" (or whatever card he chose). When you name the card to him, the medium on the other end of the line hears your remarks and thus knows the card.

The phone rings four or five more times. Then there is the recorded sound of the phone being picked up. The medium now comes on the line and merely names the card she just heard you mention. Properly built up, this is a trick of sensational impact.

30 LINEAR BLACKJACK

This is the game of blackjack played over the telephone. Though you never see the cards, never touch them and never ask a single question, you always win at this game.

Call a friend and have him bring a deck of cards to the phone. Tell him you and he are going to play a little game of blackjack. He is to deal a jack to himself and a jack to you. These represent the hole cards.

Then have him remove any ace, two and three from the deck. He is to place them in a row in any order. You do not know the order. Tell him to exchange the three with the card to the right of it. If there is no card to the right of the three, he does nothing.

Then have him exchange the ace with the card to the left of it. If there is no card to the left of the ace, he does nothing.

Finally have him exchange the two with the card to the right of it. If there is no card to the right of the two, he does nothing.

Remind the spectator that he dealt the three cards out in any order and that you had him mix them without your knowing which card was where. Now you will pick one of the three cards to go with your jack. Tell him you want the card on the far left. It will be the ace. If he takes either the two or the three, or even if he takes both the two and the three for himself, he cannot beat your score of 21.

METHOD: In the above trick, devised by the author, you need simply follow the instructions as given. The three cards can be in any order at the start. The spectator tells you nothing. Have him move the cards around as described, then tell him you want the card on the left. It will always be the ace.

31 THE ULTRA CODE

The spectator chooses any one of the four suits, then removes any five cards in that suit to form a poker hand. The magician gives him the name and phone number of the medium. He explains that he wants the spectator to choose one of the five cards and turn it face down. Then he is to read off the other four cards to the medium over the phone. He can read the cards in any order.

When he has done this the medium instantly names the value and suit of the face-down card.

This routine is somewhat similar to "Poker By Phone" (No. 26) but here there is no force. The spectator can choose any five cards. Since the method is completely different, it forms an ideal follow-up trick.

METHOD: This is the author's solution to a stud-poker problem proposed by Fitch Cheney. The curious feature of this approach is that although a code is used, the code is determined *before* the spectator chooses a card.

Have the spectator name one of the four suits. Then tell him to remove any five cards in that suit. Explain that you are going to try to transmit telepathic impressions of these cards and, to make it easier, the spectator should select spot cards rather than picture cards.

As he removes five cards from the face-up deck, mentally add together their values. If for example he removes the ♣5, ♣3, ♣7, ♣8 and ♣2, you would silently add together 5 + 3 + 7 + 8 + 2, arriving at a total of 25. You now remove a small book from your pocket, apparently to get the medium's telephone number. One page of the book contains the following information:

TOTAL	NAME	TOTAL	NAME	
15	Abbott	28	Hardin	
16	Thompson	29	Jaks	
17	Ashworth	30	Jordan	Clubs = Alice
18	Baker	31	Rodgers	
19	Buckley	32	Lyons	Hearts = Betty
20	Collins	33	Rawson	
21	Dalton	34	Stanyon	Spades = Carol
22	Davenport	35	Tarbell	
23	Downs	36	Walsh	Diamonds = Jean
24	Ducrot	37	Taylor	
25	Elliott	38	Nielsen	
26	Gardner	39	Simpson	
27	Horowitz	40	Palmer	

Since you know the total of the five cards, look up that figure and note the name opposite it. In our example the total is 25. The name opposite 25 is Elliott. This means that you will tell the spectator that the medium's last name is Elliott.

In our example the spectator selected clubs for the suit. Since the suit is clubs, you will tell the spectator that the medium's first name is Alice.

Jot down this information on a blank page of the book, write in the medium's phone number, tear out the page and hand it to the spectator. In our example he will be directed to phone the number you gave him and ask for Alice Elliott.

Close the book and put it away. There should be no suspicion attached to the book because the spectator has not yet chosen a card. Ask him to look over the five cards and choose one. He is to signal his choice by turning the chosen card face down. Have him go to the phone and dial the number you gave him.

When he asks for Alice Elliott, the medium knows that the suit is clubs (because Alice = clubs) and she knows that the total of all five cards is 25 (because Elliott = 25).

Now the spectator reads off the four remaining cards in any order. The medium jots down their values, totals the four numbers and subtracts this total from 25. Whatever the result, that is the value of the chosen card. If, say, the spectator called out 8, 2, 3, 5, the medium would note that the total is 18. Subtracting 18 from 25, she gets an answer of 7. Thus she knows that the chosen card is the ♣7.

To take another example, suppose the spectator dials the medium's number and asks for Jean Baker. The medium knows that the suit is diamonds (because Jean = diamonds) and that the total of all five cards is 18 (because Baker = 18). If the spectator then reads off four cards and they total 12, the medium would announce that the chosen card is the ♦ 6.

The trick can be done with any five random cards taken from the full deck of 52 cards. In this case suits would have to be given numerical values and summed the same way that values are handled. The details are left to the interested reader.

32 TIME SQUARED

We close this chapter with an outstanding telephone mystery. Calling the spectator on the phone, the mentalist asks him to note the time on his watch, and to remove three cards from the deck corresponding to that time. If, for example, the spectator's watch indicated it was 8:53, the spectator would remove an eight, a five and a three from the deck. He arranges them in a row on the table to indicate the correct time.

Remarking on the well-known phrase that time is money, the

magician tells the spectator to place a quarter on any card. He is then to exchange the other two cards. After the exchange there will be a new time indicated by the three cards. The spectator calls out this new time, whereupon the magician instantly reveals on which card the spectator placed the coin.

METHOD: This trick is the diabolical invention of Fr. Cyprian. Note that because the time on the spectator's watch is different from the time on your watch, you could not know which three cards he removed from the deck. Since you do not know the three cards, it is impossible to have enough information to conclude the trick without asking questions.

But in fact you do know something about the time on the spectator's watch. While it is true you do not know the exact setting, you know exactly where the hour hand points. Thus if your watch indicates 8:51, his watch might indicate 8:52 or 8:57 or 8:49. In each case the first digit is an 8, and it is on this subtle point that the ingenious method depends. When the spectator places three cards on the table to indicate the time on his watch, you know that the card on the left will be an 8.

The rest of the method derives from a Hummer principle. Have the spectator remove the three cards and place them in a row to indicate the time. Then tell him to place a coin on one card. When he has done this, have him exchange the other two cards. Then have him call out the new time to you.

In our example you call the spectator sometime between eight and nine o'clock so the first card on the left should be an eight. If it is an eight when he calls out the time, then the coin is on the eight. If the eight is in the middle, the coin rests on the rightmost card. If the eight is on the right end, the coin is on the middle card.

There is one final point. Do the trick between one o'clock and ten o'clock. This avoids the confusion of having to use picture cards to represent later hours.

RIFFLE-SHUFFLE SETUPS

Riffle-shuffle setups represent one of the newest areas to emerge in card magic. In tricks of this nature the spectator is allowed to shuffle the deck. Although it would seem that the deck is in random order after the shuffle, in fact the magician can control the distribution of cards in the entire deck. It is this surprising fact which leads to strong card tricks using shuffle setups.

Except where noted, the material in this chapter is from my own files. The chapter begins with simple ideas and then goes on to more sophisticated tricks using riffle-shuffle setups. Occasionally familiar plot ideas are employed but they emerge here in unexpected new ways.

Tricks using riffle-shuffle setups exploit a kind of thinking that is different from anything else in card magic. It is not unlikely to find that although you know how these tricks work, you are not sure why. This chapter represents a roundup of current thinking in a provocative area of card magic.

33 STACK A PACK

One of the basic principles of riffle-shuffle setups has to do with a method of controlling the distribution of colors. The idea is that the spectator shuffles the deck, but despite this, you know how the colors are distributed throughout. The following idea is too simple to fool anyone, but it will quickly and easily illustrate the basic method.

Two packets are used. One contains a red card on top followed by a black card. The other packet contains a black card on top followed by a red card. Place the two-card packets side by side. Riffle shuffle them together as shown in Figure 17, and square up the cards. Deal off the top two cards. You will find that one of these cards is black and the other is red. Look at the remaining two cards and you will see exactly the same situation; one of these cards is black and the other is red.

Fig. 17

This simple stunt represents a basic principle of riffle-shuffle setups, for it is true that no matter how unevenly the two packets are shuffled together you will *always* end up with a red and a black among the top two cards, and a red and black among the bottom two cards. No other result is possible. This idea is exploited in the following trick.

34 MAGNETIC COLORS

The spectator gives the deck a riffle shuffle. Although the shuffle appears to be completely random, the spectator finds on dealing off pairs of cards that *every* pair contains exactly one red and one black card!

METHOD: This routine was independently devised by Gene Finnell, Norman Gilbreath and others. Preparation consists of arranging the deck so that the colors alternate red-black-red-black from top to bottom.

Cut the deck at about the midpoint. The only stipulation is that there is a red card on the bottom of one half and a black card on the bottom of the other half. Place the two packets side by side. Tell the spectator you are going to control the way he shuffles the deck even though you will not touch the cards.

The spectator gives the deck one riffle shuffle. He then deals pairs of cards off the top and turns each pair face up. He should be surprised to discover that each pair contains one red card and one black card.

Laymen think that a riffle shuffle destroys any possible order of the cards. They are therefore baffled to discover that even though they shuffled the deck, the cards are still in order!

35 SELF-MATCHING COLORS

It is possible to alter the basic setup so that colors match up. You cannot say when a pair of the same color will show up but you can definitely say what the matching colors will be.

Arrange ten cards so the colors alternate red-black-red-black and so on. Then arrange another ten-card packet in identically the same order. Riffle shuffle the two packets together.

Deal a pair of cards off the top. It may contain two cards of the same color. If so, that color will be red. If the pair contains one red and one black, toss it aside. Deal off the next pair. If the first pair didn't match but the second did, then this pair will contain two reds. In other words, the first matching pair to turn up, even if it's the fifth pair you deal, will contain two red cards.

The next matching pair you turn up, whether it's the next pair or the last pair, will contain two black cards. You can't say when this new pair of matching colors will turn up, but you can say with certainty what colors it will contain.

Matching-color pairs will alternate throughout the shuffled packet. In other words, the first matching-color pair will contain two reds. The next matching-color pair will contain two blacks. The next matching-color pair (if there is one) must contain two reds. The next must contain two blacks, and so on. Of course there will be times when the packet will contain no matching-color pairs. But if there are pairs containing two cards of the same color, you can say positively what those colors will be.

36 A DEVILISH SECRET

Red and black cards seem to attract one another in strange ways. To illustrate, the magician has the spectator give the deck a riffle shuffle and begin turning pairs of cards face up, beginning at the top of the pack. When a pair of black cards is turned up, the magician states that the next pair of cards will be red. The spectator turns up the next pair and these cards are indeed red.

Continuing to deal pairs of cards, the spectator finds that every time he deals a matching pair of one color, the very next pair of cards will match and will be of the opposite color.

METHOD: The deck is stacked. The arrangement from the top down is red-black-black-red, red-black-black-red, and so on, this same sequence repeating through the pack.

To present the trick, cut the deck approximately at its midpoint, between two red cards. Place the two packets in front of the spectator. Invite him to riffle shuffle them together.

After the shuffle he deals pairs of cards off the top. Whenever a matching pair is dealt, the next matching pair will be of the opposite color.

37 ESP + MATH

The spectator shuffles two packets of cards together. Then he deals off the top three cards and hands them to the magician behind his back. If the packet contains at least two cards of the same suit, the magician reveals the matching suit. Then, with the packet still behind his back, he finds at least one of the matching-suit cards.

The process is repeated until there are no cards left. Each time the magician correctly reveals the matching suit and then goes on to find one card of that suit, always with the cards behind his back.

METHOD: This trick introduces a different idea in riffle-shuffle setups. Here you not only know *which* cards will match, you know *where* one of them will be, even though the cards have been shuffled by the spectator.

Stack one 12-card packet spades-diamonds-hearts, this same sequence repeated throughout the packet. Then stack another 12-card packet spades-hearts-diamonds, this same sequence repeated throughout the packet.

When ready to present the trick, hand the two packets to the spectator. Have him riffle shuffle them together. Turn your back. Tell him to deal the top three cards into a heap. Then have him pick up this three-card packet, turn it face up and note if it contains at least two cards of the same suit.

If it does, he hands you the packet behind your back. The first packet of matching-suit cards will contain two spades and, further, at least one spade will be at the bottom or face of the packet. When the packet is handed to you behind your back, pretend to concentrate, then reveal that the matching suits are spades. Pause, then say that you will try to find one of the matching spade cards by sense of touch.

Act as if great powers of concentration are required, but all you need do is remove the bottom card of the packet and bring it into view. Show that you were correct in finding one of the matching spades.

Bring the remainder of the packet out from behind your back. Toss the three cards face up onto the table. Simply note which suit is *not* represented among the three cards. This will be the matching suit in the next group of cards the spectator gives you. Assume the missing suit is diamonds.

The spectator deals off the next three cards into a face-down heap. While you turn your back, he notes if this packet contains at least two cards of the same suit. If it does, he hands it to you behind your back. If it doesn't, he discards it and deals three more cards. He continues to deal three-card packets until he finds one which contains at least two cards of the same suit. Then he hands you this packet behind your back.

In our example, when the spectator hands you the next matching pair packet behind your back, you reveal that the matching suit is diamonds. Then remove the bottom card and bring it into view to show that you have located one card of the matching suit. Continue in this way until all of the cards have been handed to you. With no change in handling you can have each three-card packet placed in an envelope and handed to you behind your back. You reveal the matching suit, then reach into the envelope and remove a card of the matching suit. The use of envelopes seems to isolate the cards, making the effect more difficult. Actually the envelopes do not affect the handling in any way.

38 COLOR PROPHECY

In this puzzling effect, devised by Gene Finnell, the spectator shuffles the pack and deals it into two heaps. He takes either heap and gives the other to the performer.

The performer runs through his cards and openly turns several of them face up. Then he places the heap on the table. The performer explains that he has made an odd sort of prediction with his cards. He and the spectator will deal cards simultaneously from the tops of the heaps. If the performer deals a face-down card, it will not match the color of the card dealt by the spectator. But when the performer deals a face-up card, it will match the color of the card dealt by the spectator.

The dealing commences and each time the performer deals a face-up card, it does in fact match the color of the spectator's card.

METHOD: Arrange the pack so that the colors alternate red-black-red-black throughout. Cut the deck so there is a red card at the face of one packet and a black card at the face of the other. Have the spectator riffle shuffle the two halves together and then deal the deck into two equal heaps, alternating a card into each heap as he deals.

Pick up either heap and run through it two cards at a time. Examine each pair. If the pair contains a red and black card, turn this pair over as a single card. Thus, if the rightmost card of the pair was red, then after the pair is turned over the red card will be on the left. It is important to turn over each pair separately, one pair at a time as you go through the packet.

At the completion of this process you'll have several face-up cards in the packet. Place the packet on the table. Then cards are dealt simultaneously off the top of both heaps. If the performer deals a face-down card, the pair will be a mismatch, that is, one red card and one black. But if the performer deals a face-up card, the spectator will deal a card of the same color.

The trick is automatic and never fails to impress the onlooker since he shuffled the cards at the very beginning of the trick.

39   BLIND CHOICE

This brilliant trick, invented by Roy Walton, is one in which both the spectator and the performer successfully guess the colors of the cards. The routine has not previously appeared in print.

Stack the deck so the colors alternate red-black-red-black from top to bottom. Hand the pack to a spectator and have him cut the deck and complete the cut a few times. He then cuts off about half the deck and riffle shuffles the two halves together. Spread the pack out face up to show how well mixed the cards are. As you do, find any two adjacent cards of the same color near the center of the deck. Cut the deck between these cards and complete the cut.

Square up the pack and turn it face down. Thumb off four cards and hand them to the first spectator. Thumb off four more and hand them to the second spectator. Continue to give four-card packets to each of the participating spectators. We will assume there are five spectators. For ease of explanation we'll refer to the spectators as A, B, C, D, E, from left to right.

Ask each spectator to mix his four cards and select any one from his face-down packet. He is to place it face down on the table. No one knows which card he chose.

When this has been done, tell the spectators to mix their cards. Then each looks at the faces of his three cards. Point out that the packets can consist of three cards of the same color or of two cards of one color and a card of opposite color. Say, "If they're all of the same color, select any one and place it face down on top of the one already on the table. But if you have one card of one color and two of the opposite color, remove the *one* card that does *not* match the color of the other two." The spectator does this, placing his card face down on the table on top of the card already there.

After they have all done this, take the remaining two cards from each of them, making sure you collect them in order so that E's pair is on the bottom, D's on top of it, C's on top of that, B's on top of that and A's on top of all.

Beginning with the top card, upjog every other card. Strip out the upjogged cards as a group without disturbing their order and place this group on the table. As you do this, remark that you want to mix the cards.

Point out the odds against the tabled pairs being of the same color. Then turn up each pair to show that the odds have somehow been beaten, because each pair contains two cards of the same color. This is the first effect. You are about to follow it with an even stronger finish.

At this point you have five face-down cards in your hand. Say you will try and sense the colors of these cards without looking at the faces. Slowly you deal them into two heaps on the table, sometimes pausing as if having trouble with a particular card. What you really do is look at the face-up color pairs in front of the spectators and deal according to those colors, reading from A to E. For example, if the color pairs in front of the spectators read red, red, red, black, black, you would deal the first card into a heap on the left, then the next card into the same heap (because the color of B's matching cards is the same as A's). You would deal the third card into the same heap (because C's matching colors are the same as A's). You would deal the next card into a separate heap (because D's matching colors are different from A's) and you would deal the fifth card into the separate heap (because E's matching colors are different from A's). Thus you would deal the first three cards into one heap and the last two into a separate heap.

Pick up the other five-card packet on the table and simply repeat the process, beginning by dealing the first card into the left-hand heap, the next two into this heap, then the final two into the other heap.

You have dealt your ten cards into two separate heaps. Build up the impossibility of what you are attempting, then turn up each heap to show all blacks in one and all reds in the other.

40   REPLICA POKER

Ten cards are placed in a face-up row on the table as shown in Figure 18. The spectator is invited to slide out of the row any ace, any two, any three, any four and any five. When he has done this the other five cards are gathered in order from left to right. The spectator's cards are also gathered in order and placed alongside the other packet.

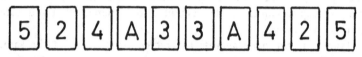

Fig. 18

Both poker hands contain identical cards, of course, but with a snap of the fingers the magician causes the cards in his hand to rearrange themselves in the same order as the spectator's cards.

METHOD: Remove the ace through five in spades and clubs. Deal them out exactly as shown in Figure 18. Then have the spectator remove any ace, two, three, four, five. His five cards can end up in any one of these 16 arrangements:

5 2 4 1 3	5 4 1 3 2
3 1 4 2 5	2 3 1 4 5
5 2 4 3 1	5 4 3 1 2
1 3 4 2 5	2 4 3 1 5
5 2 1 3 4	5 1 3 4 2
4 3 1 2 5	2 1 3 4 5
5 2 3 1 4	5 3 1 2 4
4 1 3 2 5	2 4 1 3 5

The spectator may, for example, draw out the five cards shown in Figure 19. After he does, gather his five cards from left to right, one card going on top of the next. Then gather the remaining five cards from left to right, one card going on top of the next. Turn your packet face down and place it alongside the spectator's packet.

Explain that in the game of Replica Poker the cards are compared one at a time. The player with the highest value card wins. You

Fig. 19

further explain that you never lose even though you never win either.

Take the top card of your hand and the top card of the spectator's hand. Place them alongside one another. Turn the face-down card over and show that it has the same value as the face-up card. Repeat with each pair of cards. In each case the cards are the same.

Note that although the spectator can pick his poker hand in any one of 16 different ways, the remaining cards automatically arrange themselves in the same order. This is an example of something called a self-duplicating setup, used here in the context of a reverse or backward riffle shuffle. In other words, when the spectator slides five cards out of the row, he is unshuffling the packet. The setup itself then goes to work to insure that one packet will be in the same order as the other packet.

41 POSI-NEGATIVE CARDS

This is one of the strongest tricks that can be done with a riffle-shuffle setup. The basic effect was developed by several magicians. This handling was suggested by J. W. Sarles.

A spectator is asked to remove a deck of cards from its case, cut the pack a few times, and then give the deck a riffle shuffle. He then deals the deck into two heaps, one face up, one face down. He deals a card at a time off the top, dealing from left to right through the entire deck.

The spectator picks up the face-up packet and sorts it into two heaps according to color. The magician uses the face-down packet and follows the spectator's actions exactly, sorting his cards into two face-down heaps. For example, if the first three cards on the face of the spectator's packet were red, he would deal them into a heap on the left. The magician would deal three cards from the top of his face-down packet, sight unseen, into a heap near the spectator's. If the next five cards on the face of the spectator's packet were black, he would deal them into a separate heap on the right. The magician simultaneously deals the next five cards from the top of his face-down packet into a heap alongside the spectator's black heap.

The magician explains that the spectator has *visibly* separated his cards into reds and blacks. Because of the attraction the cards have for one another, the magician's cards have *invisibly* sorted themselves into reds and blacks. Turning over the face-down packets, the magician reveals that one contains nothing but red cards while the other contains nothing but black cards.

METHOD: Set up the deck so the colors alternate red-black-red-black from top to bottom. The spectator removes the deck from its case, cuts the deck and completes the cut. Then he cuts off about half the deck and riffle shuffles the two halves together.

Take back the deck and spread it face up to show the colors well mixed. Spot two cards of the same color that are adjacent to one another near the center. Cut the deck between these two cards and complete the cut. Then hand the deck back to the spectator.

He separates the deck into two packets, one face up and the other face down, by dealing the top card face down to the left, the next card face up to the right, the next face down to the left, and so on. Using the face-down packet, simply follow the spectator's actions as he sorts his face-up cards into reds and blacks. At the finish you will have two face-down heaps near his face-up heaps. Remark that your colors separated invisibly, then spread each of your heaps face up on the table to reveal all reds in one heap and all blacks in the other.

The fact that the spectator himself shuffled the deck makes this trick appear impossible. There is the further point that, when dealing the cards face up, the spectator sees that reds and blacks are randomly mixed. These two points combine to produce a stunning card effect using ordinary cards.

42 INCORPORATED COLOR CONTROL

The magician removes two cards from the deck, jots down a prediction on each, and then inserts the cards back into the pack. The pack is handed to a spectator for a riffle shuffle.

After he shuffles the cards, the spectator is told to deal pairs of cards face up off the top. Matching red pairs go into one heap, matching blacks into a separate heap, and red-black or non-matching pairs go into a third heap.

When he comes to the pair containing one of the prediction cards, the spectator reads it aloud. It says: "You have just dealt the fourth and last matching pair of blacks. However———"

The prediction is correct. The spectator has *just* dealt the fourth matching pair of black cards. It is not known if this is the last such pair because that can't be verified until the end of the trick, but the rest of the prediction can't be read until the spectator comes to the second half of the prediction.

He continues dealing pairs of cards off the top of the deck, sorting them into the proper heaps as before. Ultimately he comes to the second half of the prediction. It reads: "———you are destined to deal two more matching pairs and both will be red."

The spectator deals pairs of cards until he has dealt through the entire deck. The second prediction is indeed correct. He did deal two more matching pairs and both were red.

METHOD: Stack the deck as follows. The top half is arranged red-black-red-black and so on from top to bottom. The bottom half is arranged five blacks–red–3 blacks–five reds–black–♠2–black–red–black–red–♣2–five reds from top to bottom.

To present the trick, remove the ♠2 from the deck, jot down the first prediction ("You have just dealt the fourth and last matching pair of black cards. However———"), and return the ♠2 to its original position in the pack. Then remove the ♣2; jot down the second prediction ("———you are destined to deal two more matching pairs and both will be red"), and return the ♣2 to its original position in the pack. Split the deck at its midpoint. Let the spectator riffle shuffle the two halves together once. He then deals as already explained.

The outcome is automatic.

43 WHY YOU CAN'T WIN

People are fascinated with demonstrations of cheating. This routine exploits the fact that many people believe that if they shuffle and deal the cards it would be impossible for anyone to cheat. In this demonstration you show conclusively that the game is always under your control even though you don't handle the cards.

For best results you should have three spectators participate, though the trick can be carried out if there are fewer participants. One spectator shuffles and deals, another plays the part of the banker and one spectator will be your partner. As the game progresses it becomes clear that the dealer is going to lose on every round even though he shuffled and dealt the cards.

Before presenting the game, arrange the deck so the colors alternate red-black-red-black from top to bottom. This is the only preparation.

When the spectators are seated around the table, remark that it's possible to cheat even though you never shuffle or deal the cards. As you patter, remove the deck from its case. Cut it at about its midpoint, making sure there is a red card on the face of one half of the deck and a black card on the face of the other. Place the two packets face down on the table in front of the volunteer dealer.

Have him riffle shuffle the two halves of the deck together and square up the pack. Then tell him to deal out four packets of cards. He deals four hands in the conventional way, dealing from right to left in order. He continues the deal until he has gone through the entire deck. There will be four packets on the table, each containing 13 cards. From left to right the packets will be referred to as *A, B, C, D*.

Tell the dealer to take *A* for himself. Turn *B* face up and give it to the banker, explaining that these face-up cards will serve as poker chips or betting markers. Whoever wins a round gets one face-up card. At the end of the game the winner is the one with the most face-up cards.

Take packet *C* for yourself and give packet *D* to your partner. Before proceeding, make it clear that you and your partner are going to win and that the dealer is positively going to lose on every round, even though he shuffled and dealt the cards.

The game is this. On each round each player takes the top card of his packet and places it face up on the table. Two of the three cards must be the same color. The player who holds the odd-color card is the winner. Thus if the dealer turns up a black card and you turn up a red card and your partner turns up a black card, you would win because you have the odd-color card on that round.

On each round the banker gives the winner a card from the face-up packet. If all three players deal a card of the same color, the round is a draw and no one wins. The game appears fair, yet the dealer will not win a single round.

Using giant cards available in magic shops, you can perform this routine from the platform or stage. Give the banker a top hat and give the dealer a green visor. This makes it easier for the audience to follow the action. The game is a graphic example of why you can't win at the other man's game, even if you shuffle and deal the cards.

TWO-DECK CARD TRICKS

The premise of the two-deck trick is that if each of two parties gets a deck of cards and each chooses a card in the same way, then each person will choose the same card.

This simple premise is responsible for the development of some of the most intriguing card routines. In such tricks the presentation is important. Stress that it is possible for two minds to operate on the same wavelength. When the trick is brought to a successful conclusion the spectator can only conclude that it was the result of an amazing coincidence or a demonstration of genuine mind reading.

44 HYPNOTISN'T

In this routine one spectator gets a red-backed deck and the other spectator gets a blue-backed deck. Each chooses two cards in a random way using his own deck. Although neither spectator appears to have been influenced by the other, when the two chosen cards are turned over, it is found that the spectators chose exactly the same two cards.

METHOD: Prior to the performance of the trick, arrange to have the ♠5 on top of each deck and the ♥9 on the bottom of each deck.

To present the routine, patter about the fact that on occasion two minds can operate on the same channel or the same frequency. To illustrate, remove each deck from its case. Each spectator takes a deck and holds it face down in his left hand. Now ask each spectator to lift off about a quarter of his deck, turn it over and place it face up on top of the balance of the deck. Then each spectator lifts up about half of his deck, turns it over and places it on top of the balance of the deck. Finally, each spectator cuts his deck at about the midpoint and completes the cut.

In performing the above actions the spectators should strive to follow one another as closely as possible. This is in keeping with the idea that if they perform the same actions at the same time, they will choose the same cards.

Have each spectator spread his deck on the table. There will be a face-up group of cards in the center of the deck. Tell each spectator to remove the face-down card directly to the left of the face-up group, and the face-down card directly to the right of the face-up group. The result is shown in Figure 20.

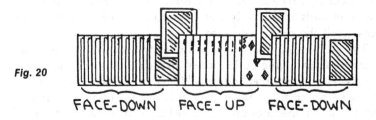

Fig. 20

FACE-DOWN   FACE-UP   FACE-DOWN

Each spectator turns over his two cards. It is seen that both spectators have chosen the same cards.

45 THE JAKS TWO-DECK TRICK

This trick by Stanley Jaks is a classic of contemporary card magic. The routine will be described as Jaks originally presented it, with a third deck used to obtain an additional effect, but you will see that even without the third deck the routine is exceptional.

The performer gives two decks of cards to two spectators. One deck has red backs and the other has blue backs. While these decks are being removed from their cases and shuffled by the spectators, the magician gives a third deck to another member of the audience to hold.

One of the assisting spectators takes one deck for himself and pockets it. The performer takes the other deck and pockets it. Each person reaches into his pocket and removes one card. The selected cards are exchanged and placed into opposite decks. Thus the chosen red-backed card ends up in the blue-backed deck, and the chosen blue-backed card ends up in the red-backed deck.

Both people now remove the decks from their pockets. The odd-backed card in each deck is turned face up. They prove to be the same card!

The magician then turns to the spectator who holds the third deck. He spells the name of the chosen card, dealing a card off the top for each letter. When he gets to the last letter he turns over that card. It matches the two chosen cards!

METHOD: Prior preparation is simple and the trick is foolproof, yet the simple means produces a tremendously effective mental mystery with cards.

Before presenting the trick, remove the ♦5 from each deck and place these two cards in the right jacket pocket. The blue-backed ♦5 should be closest to the body. Return each deck to its case.

In a third deck place the ♦5 in a position fourteenth from the top of the deck. Case this deck and you are ready.

To present the routine, hand the red-backed deck to one spectator, the blue-backed deck to another. Ask each person to shuffle his deck. Hand the cased third deck to another spectator. Tell him to hold onto it for safekeeping until the end of the trick.

Ask one of the spectators to take the red-backed deck and place it in his outside right jacket pocket. You take the blue-backed deck and place it in your right jacket pocket so that the two ♦5's in the pocket will be on the bottom or face of the deck.

Have the spectator remove any card from the red-backed deck. He does not look at this card. You pretend to remove a random card from your deck, but really remove the blue-backed ♦5 and place it face down on the table.

Take the spectator's card from him. Give him your card. Tell him to place your card in the center of his deck. Pretend to place his card in the center of your deck. Actually place it on the bottom of the blue-backed deck. Then place the red-backed ♦5 in the center of the blue-backed deck.

Remove your pack but leave the red-backed indifferent card in the pocket. Have the spectator remove his deck. Each of you spread your pack and outjog the odd-color card. Have them turned over to reveal that you both chose the ♦5.

For the added climax call attention to the spectator holding the third deck. Have him remove the deck from its case and hold it face down in his left hand. Then ask him to spell F-I-V-E-O-F-D-I-A-M-O-N-D-S, dealing a card for each letter. He turns up the last card and it is the ♦5.

J. W. Sarles added several touches to this routine. At the start he would arrange to have keys or coins in the pocket that also contained the two ♦ 5's. As the trick began, he asked the spectator to empty his right jacket pocket. Of course Sarles did the same, removing everything except the two cards. The subtle point here is that in emptying his pocket of keys he implied that the pocket must be otherwise empty.

In the Sarles handling the spectator was given a choice of either deck. This may seem a small point but it adds to the impression of fairness of the handling. After cards were chosen and exchanged, the deck was brought out of the pocket but the indifferent card was on the bottom of the pack. In other words, the indifferent card was not left in the pocket.

After the two odd-backed cards were outjogged, Sarles would take both decks, holding them so that the outjogged odd-backed cards faced the spectator. The spectator removed a card with each hand and then turned both cards face up to reveal that both were the ♦ 5. Finally, Sarles would place his deck on top of the spectator's deck and put both aside. By doing this, the indifferent card at the bottom of the performer's deck was quietly added to the top of the spectator's desk. All could now be left with the audience.

In the Jaks method the preparation does not involve the decks, so either deck may be used for other tricks. At any time in the performance you are ready to do the Jaks two-deck trick.

46   THE DREAM DECK

If you do not have two decks handy to perform the Jaks two-deck trick, there is a subtle variation that uses only one deck. In this trick the spectator picks a card from a packet he holds behind his back. You pick a card from a packet you hold behind your back. When the chosen cards are compared, it turns out they are the black fives. The kicker is that they are the *only* black cards in both packets. All the other cards are red.

METHOD: Take any borrowed, shuffled deck and hold it so you alone can see the faces. Beginning at the face of the deck, upjog the first 13 red cards you come to. Strip them out of the deck without showing their faces and place the packet face down before the spectator.

Upjog any black card near the face of the balance of the deck.

Then upjog all of the remaining red cards as well as the mate of the black card. If the black card is the ♠5, upjog the other black five —the ♣5. Strip this packet out of the deck and place the balance of the deck aside.

Place the two mating black fives on the bottom of your packet. Then place your packet behind your back. Instruct the spectator to place his packet behind his back. When the cards are out of sight, each of you mixes your cards. Actually you do nothing. The spectator is asked to remove any card from his packet. You remove the bottom card.

Exchange cards with the spectator. Tell him to place your card behind his back, turn it face up, and then insert it reversed in his packet. Pretend to do the same with his card, but simply place it on top of your packet. Take the black five from the bottom of the packet, turn it face up, and insert it into the center of the packet.

Each person brings his packet into view. The packets are spread face down to show that each of you chose a black five. Then have the remaining cards turned face up to reveal the even more remarkable fact that both of you chose the only black cards in the packet.

47   THE CLUELESS CARD TRICK

This version of the two-deck trick is a bit different. Here each of two spectators chooses cards from a single deck. The magician then chooses two cards which prove to be the same cards chosen by the spectators. The routine is based on a card problem devised by the British magician E. G. Brown. There is no preparation and no force. The spectators may choose any two cards.

Have a spectator shuffle the deck until he is satisfied that you could not possibly know any card. Then have him divide the deck into three approximately equal piles. We'll call the piles *A*, *B* and *C*.

Have the spectator take pile *A*, shuffle it and take some of the cards for himself. He gives the rest of pile *A* to the second spectator. It does not matter how many cards each person has. Turn your back and have each person silently count the number of cards in his possession. Point out that you could not possibly know how many cards either person holds.

There are still two piles on the table. Pick up pile *B*. Turn to the first spectator and explain that you are going to deal cards one at a time onto the table. He is to note a card at a position corresponding to the number of cards he holds. Thus, for example, if he holds eight cards, he would note the eighth card you deal.

Hold the pile of cards face down in the left hand. Take the top card, call it "One," and show it to the spectator. Then deal it face down onto the table. Take the next card, call it "Two," show it to the spectator and deal it onto the card you just dealt to the table. Continue in this way until all of the cards have been dealt. Remember how many cards are in the pile. Assume there are 17 cards in pile *B*. At the completion of the deal have the spectator place his small packet of cards on top of this pile.

Now pick up pile *C*. Turn to the second spectator. Explain that you are going to deal the cards one at a time. He is to note and remember the card at a position corresponding to the number of cards he holds. If he holds 11 cards, he would silently remember the eleventh card you deal.

Deal the way you did with pile *B*. Remember how many cards are in pile *C*. Say there are 20. Have the second spectator drop his packet on top of pile *C*.

Turn now to the first spectator. Remark that you too have decided on two numbers and that you will choose cards the same way the spectators did. Pick up the group of cards at *B*. Recall that there were originally 17 cards at *B*. Count down to the seventeenth card, remove this card and place it face down on the table near the first spectator.

Pick up the group of cards at *C*. Recall that pile *C* originally contained 20 cards. Count silently to the twentieth card and place it near the second spectator.

Have the spectators name their cards. Then remark that since you chose cards in the same way, it should follow that you chose the same cards. Turn over each of your cards to reveal a perfect match.

48 CRISS CROSS

The ingenious exploitation of an offbeat principle makes this one of the best tricks with two decks of cards. It is suggested for use after a trick like the Jaks Two-Deck Trick (No. 45). This trick is a simplified version of a famous George Sands routine. The effect is something of a novelty in that nothing magical happens to the cards. Rather, something happens to the spectator that makes it impossible for him to carry out a simple procedure.

The nines through aces are removed from a deck. Using just these 24 cards, you show the spectator a simple way to sort the colors. He finds it easy to do, but then you say that it will never work for him again, and with a snap of the fingers you make it impossible for him to succeed.

METHOD: Two decks are used. Both may be borrowed, as there is no preparation. One deck is red-backed and the other deck blue-backed. Hand the red-backed deck to the spectator and instruct him to remove the nines, tens, jacks, queens, kings and aces. While he does this, pick up the blue-backed deck. Fan the cards with the faces to you. Find two adjacent cards that have values of nine or higher. You may find a jack adjacent to an ace, or a nine adjacent to a queen. Cut these two cards to the top of the deck. If you don't find two such cards, simply place two of them on top of the pack.

Beginning at the face of the blue-backed deck, run through the cards and upjog all cards having a value of nine or higher. Do not upjog the top two cards.

Remove these upjogged 22 cards and place them on the table. This packet will be used at the beginning of the demonstration. Place the balance of the blue-backed deck aside.

When the spectator has removed all of the cards having a value of nine or higher from his deck (a total of 24 cards) tell him to place these cards on top of the red-backed deck for the moment.

Explain that you will show him a simple way to sort colors. As you patter, pick up the blue-backed packet and sort the cards according to color, blacks in one heap, reds in the other, as in Figure 21.

Fig. 21

REDS   BLACKS

Remove the face card of each heap and place it above the heap, as in Figure 22. Then remove the next card of each heap, cross the hands and place the cards on opposite color heaps, as in Figure 23.

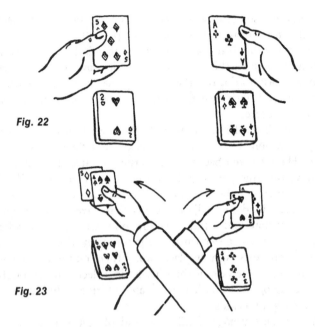

Fig. 22

Fig. 23

The next cards are placed on top of the heap directly above them (referring to Figure 23, the ♥6 would go on the ♠4 and the ♣3 on top of the ♥2). Then the next cards are picked up, the hands crossed and the cards dropped on opposite heaps.

This alternating procedure continues until all cards from the original two heaps have been transferred. The result is two new heaps in which the colors alternate. Turn each packet face down. Then place one packet on top of the other. Finally, deal the combined heap into two packets. Deal alternately as if dealing two hands for a card game. After all cards have been dealt, turn both packets face up and spread the cards. One heap contains all reds and the other heap contains all blacks. This result is not surprising. Indeed, the spectator will have anticipated it.

The spectator is asked if he can duplicate the feat. He tries, following the above procedure, and is successful. He repeats it to be certain he knows the procedure. Then he tries it one more time just to be sure. Each time he mixes the cards as in Figures 22 and 23, deals the mixed cards into two heaps, and successfully separates the colors. Since the procedure is so simple and obvious, he may even wonder why you are doing it at all, and this is exactly what you want him to think.

After the final try, have the spectator pick up the two heaps, shuffle them together, and drop them back onto the top of the blue-backed deck. When he's done this say, "Now I want you to try it with the red-backed cards."

Have him remove the top 24 cards from the red-backed deck. He is to separate them into two heaps, blacks in one heap, reds in the other. After he's done this, say, "The combination of red-backed and blue-backed cards has a curious effect on the mind. Before we started I gave you a subconscious instruction which allowed you to separate the colors. But when we switched to a different deck, the subconscious instruction was destroyed. You will never again separate the colors."

The spectator goes through the procedure of Figures 22 and 23 to mix the colors, he places one packet on top of the other, then he deals them into two heaps. The colors should separate but, oddly enough, they don't. He can try again, but the colors still refuse to separate.

Sooner or later it will occur to him that even if the trick won't work with the red-backed cards, it *must* work with the blue-backed cards. He removes the nines through aces from the top of the blue-backed deck, unaware that he is using the original 22 cards *plus* the two cards you left on top of the deck at the start. He tries to sort the colors using blue-backed cards. The trick should work but, to his amazement, it won't.

49 JUMPBACK

This final routine introduces a paradox to the format of the traditional two-deck trick. If you perform a two-deck trick on some occasion, and on a later occasion are asked to repeat the trick, this is a good routine to do because it seems as if you are doing a standard two-deck trick right up to the last second. Then things take a strange turn. It is the author's solution to a challenging problem.

A spectator choose a card from a red-backed deck and signs his name on the face of the card. Say the card is the ♠4. This card is returned to the red-backed deck. The spectators see it going into the center of the pack, and the red-backed pack is not touched again.

Then another spectator chooses a card from the blue-backed deck. Although he had no idea which card was chosen by the first spectator, he is surprised to find that he too has chosen the ♠4.

The odd point is that although the ♠4 is undeniably blue-backed, although it came from the blue-backed deck, it bears the first spectator's signature! Thus, not only did the second spectator choose the same card, his card turns out to have the same signature.

METHOD: Place the red-backed ♠4 second from the face or bottom of the blue-backed deck. Place the blue-backed ♠4 second from the bottom of the red-backed deck, as in Figure 24. Put each deck in its own case. This completes the preparation.

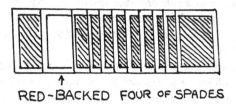

RED-BACKED FOUR OF SPADES

Fig. 24

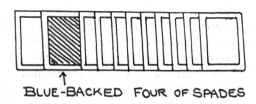

BLUE-BACKED FOUR OF SPADES

When ready to perform, open the blue-backed card case and remove the blue-backed deck. Be careful not to spread the cards accidentally because this might reveal the red-backed card. The easiest way to conceal the presence of the red-backed ♠4 is to remove the deck face up.

Place the blue-backed deck face up on the table to your left, with the card case above it, as in Figure 25. The card just in back of the ♦2 in Figure 25 is the odd-backed ♠4.

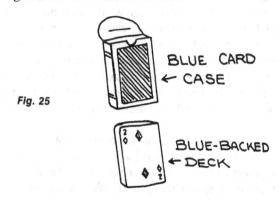

Fig. 25

BLUE CARD
← CASE

BLUE-BACKED
← DECK

Ask one of the volunteer spectators to leave the room, explaining that you will call him back later. When he is gone, remove the red-backed deck from its case. Make sure the deck is face up when you remove it. This insures that no one will spot the blue-backed ♠4 in the deck.

Tell the spectator at the table to give you a number between one and 15. Explain that you will count the number twice, once for him and once for the spectator in the other room.

Say he gives you eight. With the red-backed deck face up in the left hand, deal the face card onto the table, then deal the next card to the right of it. Deal the next card onto the left-hand heap and deal the next card onto the right-hand heap. Continue dealing in this way, a card to each heap alternately, until you have dealt eight cards.

Pick up the leftmost heap and place it on top of the rightmost heap. Place the combined heap back onto the face of the deck. Say, "As I mentioned, we deal once for him and once for you. That deal was for him. This one is for you." Deal eight cards off the face of the deck into a face-up heap. The eighth card you deal will be the ♠4.

Place the ♠4 face up on the table in front of the spectator. Ask him to sign his name in the center of the card. As he does, gather the cards you dealt and replace them on the face of the red-backed deck. Then place the red-backed deck face down on the table.

Take the signed ♠4 from the spectator and drop it face up onto the face of the blue-backed deck. Openly cut the blue-backed deck and complete the cut as you say, "If we were to spread this pack face up for the selection of another card, the person would see your signature on the face."

Turn the blue-backed deck face down and spread it between the hands. A red-backed card will show up in the center of the deck. Say, "If we spread it face down for the selection of a card, he will know your card because it has a different-color back." Cut the deck and complete the cut so the red-backed card is on top.

Remove the red-backed card, taking care not to flash the face. Then insert it face down into the face-down red-backed deck so that about a quarter of it protrudes from one end, as in Figure 26. Say, "The only way to hide your card from him is to return it to its own deck." Lift the red-backed deck with the left hand, as in Figure 27, to show the face of the ♠4. The audience sees just the upper index corner of the ♠4 and is thus unaware that it is not the signed card.

Tap the card square with the deck and place the red-backed deck to one side. The audience is convinced that the signed card has been returned to its own deck.

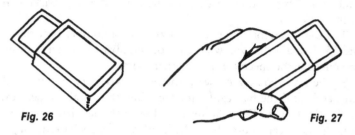

Fig. 26   **Fig. 27**

Ask that the spectator in the next room now return. When he has joined the other guests, ask him for a number between one and 15. At times he will unknowingly choose the same number as the first spectator. If he does, play up the point, remarking that he must be on the same wavelength.

Assume that he chose the number 11. Hold the blue-backed deck face down in the left hand. Deal 11 cards onto the table. Deal the same way you did the first time, alternating a card to each of two packets, dealing from left to right, until you have dealt a total of 11 cards. Then place the leftmost packet on top of the rightmost packet and place the combined packet on top of the deck.

Say, "We deal twice, once for him and once for you. The first deal was for him. This one is for you." Deal 11 cards off the top of the deck. Place the eleventh card aside. Notice that the dealing procedure is the same as for the red-backed deck except that here the deal is done with the cards face down.

Insert the chosen card sideways into the deck and hold it as shown in Figure 28. Slowly turn the deck face up as you say, "You happened to choose the very same card as this fellow."

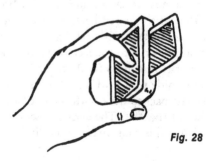

Fig. 28

This appears to be the conclusion of the effect. The audience can see the face of the chosen card. It is the ♠4. But because the card is in the deck, they can't see the initials. Thus they assume the point of the trick is that the second spectator chose the same card as the first spectator, in itself an impressive feat.

Say, "Not only is it the same card . . ." Pause here for dramatic effect. Then add, ". . . it has the same signature."

Remove the ♠4 from the deck to show that it has somehow acquired the first spectator's signature. This is an unexpected ending to a strong coincidence trick.

TOPOLOGICAL CARD TRICKS

The tricks in this chapter use cards that are torn or folded. This may seem a slender premise on which to base a chapter, but topological card tricks represent an offbeat approach that generates surprising and different card effects.

Most topological card tricks require gimmicks or manipulation that lie outside the scope of this book. The tricks in this brief chapter have been chosen because they are easy to perform and provide something of the flavor of this unique area of card magic.

50   THE HOUSE THAT JACK BUILT

The magician makes an impromptu card house out of three playing cards by folding them in half, as in Figure 29, and assembling them on top of the card case. Figures 30 and 31 show how the card house is constructed.

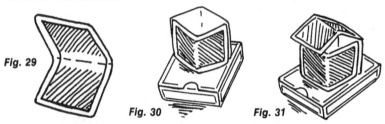

Fig. 29   Fig. 30   Fig. 31

A spectator tries to guess the address of the card house. Whatever number he calls out, this number is used to aid in the selection of a card. His card may be a jack. The jack vanishes from the deck and is found in the card case *under* the card house. For the finish, the house is shown to indeed be the house that Jack built because all of the cards that went into its construction turn out to be jacks.

METHOD: Beforehand arrange to have three jacks on top of the deck and the fourth jack thirteenth from the top. Say this jack is the ♣J. In the card case is a duplicate ♣J from a matching deck.

Remove the top three cards from the deck and fold them in half as in Figure 29. Try not to show the faces of these three cards to the audience. Place two of them together on top of the card case as shown in Figure 30 to form the walls of the card house. Then use the third folded card to form the roof. The finished card house is shown in Figure 31. Point to the card case under the card house and remark that the card case represents the finished basement.

Ask a spectator to guess the address or street number of the card house, adding that the street number is between ten and 20. Whatever number he names, deal that many cards off the top of the deck. Assume the number is 14. After you have dealt 14 cards, say to the spectator, "The number 14 is made up of two digits, a 1 and a 4." Deal one card onto the table to represent the 1 in his number. Then deal four cards onto the table for the 4 in his number. Hand him the last card dealt and ask him to remember this card. It will be the ♣J.

Tell him to put his card onto the top of the deck. Then have him pick up all of the dealt cards and place them on top of his card. Take the deck behind your back and say you will try to find his card. Unknown to the audience, at this point his card will be tenth from the top. Silently deal nine cards from top to bottom, then slip the tenth under your belt in the back. Remove the next card, take it into view but don't show it. Look at this card and say, "Did you pick the jack of clubs?" When the spectator says yes, bring the deck out and insert the supposed ♣J into the center. Say, "That's funny because the address you gave me, the number 14, is the address of the house that jacks built." As you say this, remove the three cards that make up the card house and show that they are all jacks.

"Even more amazing, the other brother, the jack of clubs, lives in the basement." Open the card case and remove the ♣J. The audience can look through the deck but there is nothing to find.

51 MOVING PARTS

The effect briefly is that four cards are torn in half and mixed, yet the halves of each card correctly and instantly find their mating halves.

Preparation is simple. Tear or cut a slit in the ♠A, ♠2, and ♠3, tearing from one side across to the center as shown in Figure 32.

Fig. 32

Slide the cards together as shown in Figure 33 so that the ♠2 and ♠3 slide into the slit in the ♠A. Another view is shown in Figure 34. Square up the packet, turn it end for end and hold it in the left hand, then place the ♠4 face down on top.

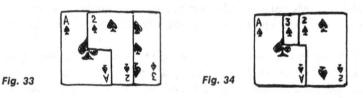

Fig. 33   **Fig. 34**

Hold the packet fairly deep in the left hand so that if you raise the packet for the spectator to see the faces, he can see the ♠A but not the slit in the middle of the packet. A spectator's view is shown in Figure 35.

With the right forefinger, slowly riffle the upper right corners of the cards one at a time, as in Figure 36, so that the spectator gets a clear view of the four cards. This shows him that the cards are in numerical order.

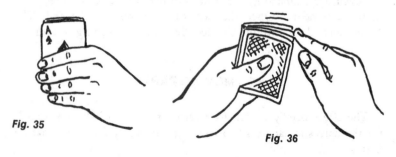

Fig. 35

Fig. 36

Then fold the four-card packet in half, as in Figure 37, straighten it out and tear it across the middle. This gives you a packet of eight half-cards. Hold them together with the left hand as shown in Figure 38. It is important that the packet should not get turned end-for-end during the tearing process. If you look at the faces of the half-card packets, as in the exposed view of Figure 39, the ♠A should be at the top and the ♠2 at the bottom.

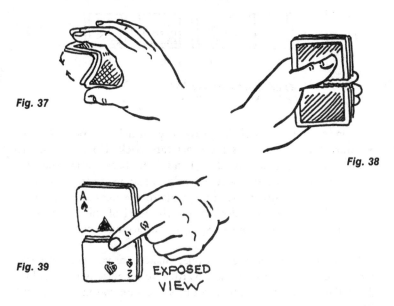

Fig. 37

Fig. 38

Fig. 39   EXPOSED
VIEW

Holding the packets face down as in Figure 38, use the right thumb and first finger to deal the top card of the top (or outer) half-card packet onto the table. Then deal the top card of the bottom (or inner) half-card packet just below it onto the table. These are the two halves of the ♠4.

Deal the top card of the top half-card packet to the right of the first half-card. Then deal the top card of the bottom half-card packet under that. Continue in this way with the remaining half-cards.

Turn up the half-cards in the upper row. The result will look like Figure 40. Note that these half-cards are in correct numerical order, so all appears fair. Exchange A with B, then exchange the half-card at B with the half-card at C. These exchanges are made with the face-down half-cards only. It appears as if all the half-cards are mixed. Snap the fingers, then turn up each of the face-down pieces in place. Matching halves are back in their correct position. You will find this an odd and puzzling trick, unlike almost all other card tricks both in terms of effect and in terms of method.

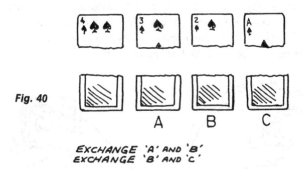

Fig. 40

EXCHANGE 'A' AND 'B'
EXCHANGE 'B' AND 'C'

In presenting this trick it is easy to gimmick the ♠A, ♠2 and ♠3 during the course of some other card trick. Do any trick that requires that you place the deck behind the back. With the deck out of sight it is an easy matter silently to tear a slit across the ♠A, ♠2 and ♠3. Return these three cards to the deck until ready to perform. Then place the deck below the level of the tabletop, remove the ace through four of spades, and arrange them as in Figure 33.

When doing tricks like this one, make sure you use your own cards, and an old deck at that. With rare exceptions people don't like having their own cards torn up, so be sure you use an expendable deck.

52 THE LINKING CARDS

In *Amusements in Mathematics* (Dover 20473-1) H. E. Dudeney describes "The Cardboard Chain," a puzzle in which each cardboard link is solid. In some older books the piece of cardboard is a playing card. The following is the author's version, in which two playing cards magically link together. The cards are solid and there are no gimmicks.

As seen by the audience, you tear the center from each of two cards, Figure 41. The cards are then opened out, as in Figure 42, and placed under a handkerchief. The magician makes a mystic adjustment and then brings the cards into view to show them linked, as in Figure 43.

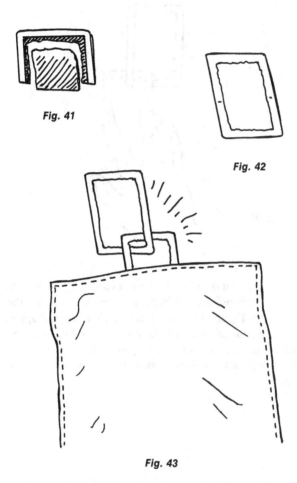

Fig. 41

Fig. 42

Fig. 43

The cards are then unlinked under the handkerchief and handed out for examination. The cards may be borrowed and marked by the spectators. You use only two cards and there is no prior preparation.

METHOD: After the centers of the cards have been cut out and discarded, place the two cards under a large handkerchief or scarf. Secretly fold one of the cards in half across its original fold line or crease. Slide the other card over it so the two cards are "linked," and hold them in place as shown in Figure 44. The card held by the left fingertips is actually the card folded in half across the middle. The fingertips hold the card flat on the table and keep it from unfolding.

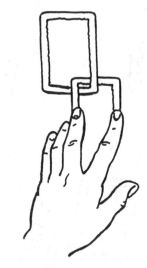

Fig. 44

While the left hand holds the linked cards in position, the right hand draws the handkerchief back far enough to expose the linked condition, as in Figure 43. The cards are then covered again.

Unlink them under the handkerchief, straighten out the folded card, and bring both cards out for examination.

The trick may also be done with borrowed business cards or with play money.

CARD-FORCING SECRETS

Most of the chapters in this book group card routines according to effect. This chapter represents an important exception because here effects are grouped according to method, specifically, techniques used to force a card on the spectator.

In the best forces the spectator seems to have an unlimited choice in selecting his card. Many force methods take place with the deck in the spectator's hands. He thinks he has control over the cards, yet you compel him to choose the card you want him to pick.

Here is a collection of some of the best force methods. Each is tied in with an application so the reader can see how the force is worked into an effect. Other force methods are described throughout this book. These methods are fundamental to an understanding of card magic. Study them and you will have on hand important and powerful techniques.

53 THE X-FORCE

From a borrowed, shuffled deck the magician removes the two red jacks. The spectator then cuts the deck anywhere and removes the card cut to. This card is placed between the jacks. When it is removed, it is seen to have changed into a jack.

The basic method is known as the X-Force because the packets are placed on top of one another at right angles to form an X. Basically you are going to force the top card of the deck by a seemingly fair process. It would be too obvious to force the card and then reveal it, so the conclusion of the trick is delayed, making it seem as if a freely chosen card placed between two jacks is caused to change to a jack.

When you get the deck, turn it face up and begin to look through it for two cards. Glimpse the top card of the deck. Whatever it is, remove two cards of the same value but of opposite color. In our example the top card of the deck is a black jack. Remove the two red jacks from the deck and place them face down on the table.

To force the top card, place the deck face down on the table in front of the spectator. Have him cut off about half. In Figure 45 he has cut off packet A. You then place packet B on top of it, but at right angles, as in Figure 46.

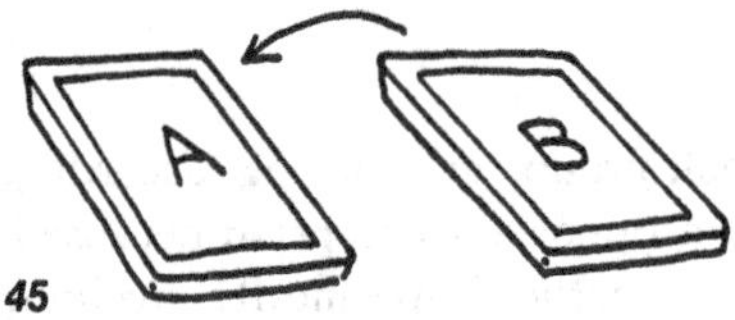

Fig. 45

Fig. 46

It is not wise to have the spectator take a card immediately. Instead, call attention to the two cards you removed from the deck. Turn them face up to show they are the red jacks.

Now have the spectator take the top card of packet A in Figure 46. You can lift packet B away to make it easier for him to take the top card of A. It appears as if he is taking the card he cut to, but really the top card of packet A is the original top card of the deck.

Place his card, sight unseen, between the face-up red jacks. Square up the three-card packet, snap the fingers, then deal out the three cards. Turn up his card to show that it has changed to a jack.

54 HORNSWOGGLED

A packet of cards is removed from the deck. The spectator takes a small group of cards from the top of the packet, shuffles them and secretly counts them. Only he knows the number of cards in the packet.

The magician openly transfers ten cards from the top of the packet to the bottom. Then he has the spectator replace his group of cards on top. Then the magician openly transfers another ten cards from top to bottom.

The spectator looks at the top card of the packet. Then he places it at the same position from the top as the number of cards in the group he cut off originally. If he cut off five cards originally, he would place the chosen card fifth from the top.

The magician does not know how many cards the spectator took originally, so he hasn't a clue as to the present location of the chosen card. Yet without asking a question, the magician deals cards off the top of the packet into a face-up heap and correctly stops on the very card chosen by the spectator.

METHOD: This trick is an example of a means of forcing a card that lies in a particular position in the deck. In this case you are going to force the bottom card of a packet by an underhanded means.

Beforehand secretly note the top card of the deck. Count 21 cards off the top into a heap, thus reversing their order. Proceed with the trick exactly as described. The spectator must arrive at the secretly noted card.

To say it another way, whatever card is on the bottom of the 21-card packet, the spectator will choose this card. All of the mumbo jumbo prior to this merely keeps the trick from looking too simple.

55 COLOROTO

A subtle force devised by Lin Searles is combined here with a previously unpublished method for quickly determining the suit of a chosen card. Preparation consists of placing a club, a heart and a spade, in that order, in your jacket pocket. Then place the four fours on top of the deck.

To present the trick, hold the deck face down in the left hand. Invite a spectator to cut off a packet of any size and turn it face up, as in Figure 47. He then places the face-up packet on top of the face-down cards in your left hand.

Fig. 47

The left hand is palm up at this point. Turn the left hand palm down and spread the cards from left to right on the table, as in Figure 48. There will be a group of face-up cards on the right followed by a group of face-down cards on the left.

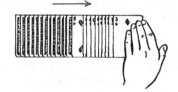

Fig. 48

Say, "We will use the first four face-down cards." Slide the face-up cards away. Let the spectator remove the first four face-down cards on the face-down portion of the deck. That is, going from the right end of the deck toward the left end, he removes the first four face-down cards he comes to. Unknown to him, these are the four fours.

Keeping the four cards face down, he mixes them thoroughly, places one in his pocket and returns the others to the deck. The deck is assembled face down. The spectator then shuffles it and hands it to you.

Drop the deck into the pocket containing the three cards you placed there earlier. While you turn your back, have the spectator look at and remember the card in his pocket. He then returns the card to his pocket so it remains hidden from view.

You know he chose a four, but you don't know which one. By asking just two questions, you will correctly pinpoint the suit of the chosen four. This is the author's method of determining the correct suit and is handled as follows.

Remark that you will use random cards to focus the spectator's mind. Reach into the pocket and remove the club card. Hold it so the spectator can see the face. Turn your head aside so it is clear you cannot see the card. Ask, "Is your chosen card the same color as this card?"

After he answers, return this card to your pocket. Then remove the heart and the spade together. Show them to the spectator, keeping your head turned aside, and ask, "Was your card the same suit as either of these cards?"

After the spectator answers, return these two cards to your pocket. You are now ready to name the chosen card.

The first card you held up was a club and you asked if the spectator's card was the same color as that card. If he said yes, you know he picked a black card. If he said no, he picked a red card. Thus you know the color of his card.

When you bring the heart and the spade out, it looks as if you reached into the deck and brought out two random cards. With your head turned aside ask the spectator if his card is the same suit as either of these cards.

Since you know the color of his card, his answer to this question will tell you the suit. Thus if you know the card is black and he says one of these cards is the same suit as his card, you know he picked a spade. If the card is black and he doesn't see a card of the same suit, you know his card was a club.

If his card is red and he says one of the cards in your hand is the same suit as his card, you know he chose a heart. If his card is red but he says he doesn't see a card of the same suit in your hand, he chose a diamond.

Since the value of his card is four, you then go on to name the value and suit of the chosen card. The deck may then be examined as there is nothing to find.

The key to success here lies in the fact that you apparently do not know which cards you remove from the shuffled deck in your pocket. Note too that the trick can be done with just two cards in the pocket at the start, a club and a heart. Remove the club and ask if it is the same color as the chosen card. Then remove the club and the heart and ask if either of these cards is the same suit as the chosen card. The spectator's answers reveal the identity of his card.

56 CUT DEEPER

This excellent method was devised by Ed Balducci. Beforehand, spot the top card of the deck. This will be the force card. Hand the deck to the spectator and have him hold it face down in his left hand.

Instruct him to cut off about a quarter of the deck, turn it face up and place it on top of the balance of the deck. Then have him cut off about half the deck, turn it over and place it on top of the balance of the deck.

At this point there will be a group of face-up cards on top. Have the spectator remove the face-up cards. then tell him to look at the first face-down card. This will be the top card of the face-down portion in his left hand.

Although the cutting procedure seems fair and beyond your control, the card he arrived at will be the force card. No applications of this force will be given here, but for one routine incorporating the Balducci force, see "The Open Prediction" (No. 7).

57 ON THE LAM

This prediction effect is based on a force idea of Louis Lam. The magician successfully predicts the location of a chosen card. There is an additional surprise in that the chosen card has mysteriously turned itself face up in the deck.

To prepare the trick, place the ♠A on top of the deck. Then place a light pencil dot in the upper left corner of the card that lies thirteenth from the top of the deck. This preparation is done secretly prior to performance. The prepared deck is shown in Figure 49.

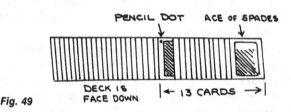

Fig. 49

Hold the deck face down in the left hand. Say, "I'm going to pick a card for myself and write something on it." Turn the top card (♠A) face up on top of the deck.

Pretend to concentrate for a moment, then write the number 13 on the face of the ♠A. Say, "I'll bury my card in the deck."

Leave the ♠A face up on top of the deck. With the left thumb push cards over to the right until you have pushed over the pencil-dotted card. The right hand takes this group of 13 cards as shown in Figure 50. Then the right hand turns palm down and places its packet back onto the deck.

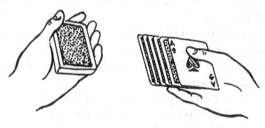

Fig. 50

To check that the procedure has been correctly followed, at this point you should have 12 face-up cards on top of the deck, then the face-down ♠ A, then the rest of the deck face down.

Spread the cards between the hands and have the spectator choose any face-down card. If he chooses the ♠ A, pretend that this was the point of the trick and simply stop at this point because you are never going to top this. In the more likely case he will choose some card other than the ♠ A.

When he has taken the card out of the deck, instruct him to look at the card and remember it. Place the balance of the deck on the table. The 12 face-up cards should still be at the top of the deck.

Tell him to place his chosen card face down on top of the deck. Then have him lift up about half the deck, Figure 51, turn it over and place it back onto the balance of the deck. His card is now buried in the pack at a location that neither of you know.

Fig. 51

Hand him the pack. Ask him to deal cards off the top until he comes to the ♠ A. All of the cards he deals will be face-up cards. When he deals the ♠ A off, remark that it is the last face-up card. Point out that you wrote the number 13 on it.

Have him deal 13 cards off the balance of the deck. These cards are all face down. When he gets to the thirteenth card it will be face up and it will be his card!

58 SPEAK OF THE DEVIL

After signing a pact with the Devil, the unwary victim is frequently offered a chance to double his money. The bet is simple. The Devil removes the 13 spades from the deck. He picks one of these cards for himself. A simple process of elimination is used to discard all of the remaining cards except one. If this card is higher than the Devil's card, the victim wins. Otherwise he loses. The ace is low; the king is high.

"Obviously, if I picked the king," the Devil says, "You couldn't pick a card that beats me. If I picked the seven, you would have an even chance of beating me.

"If I picked the six or the five, then you would have a better than even chance of choosing a card that beat me. But to make it an attractive offer, I'll choose a really low card, the three of spades."

The Devil (ably played by the magician) removes the ♠3 from the packet, leaving the other 12 spades.

"All you have to do is get a card that's higher than ♠3," the Devil says, "And we'll leave the process of elimination in your hands."

The process is this. The remaining 12 spaces are mixed face down. The spectator withdraws any two face-down cards. The magician chooses one of these two cards and discards it. Then the magician picks up any two cards. The spectator chooses one of these and discards it.

The process continues until just one card is left. If it beats the ♠3, the spectator wins. Otherwise he loses.

The bet seems simple, honest and completely aboveboard. When the magician takes two cards from the deck the spectator can freely discard either one. When it is the magician's turn, he must withdraw one of the two cards offered to him by the spectator. Thus on every round the spectator is in complete control.

Needless to say, he loses.

METHOD: This ingenious force was devised by Roy Baker. The only preparation is lightly to pencil-dot or otherwise mark the back of the ♠2. With this card in the pack you can perform other tricks, since the marked ♠2 does not interfere with other stunts you may want to perform. When ready for "Speak of the Devil," proceed as follows.

Remove the 13 spades from the deck. Explain the bet. Then place the ♠3 aside, face up. Remark that the ace is low, the king is high.

The remaining 12 spades are mixed face down. The spectator goes first. He takes any two face-down cards. You choose one and discard it. Always choose a card that is not pencil-dotted. Discard that card. The other card goes back onto the pile.

Then it is your turn. Pick up two unmarked cards. The spectator chooses one of these and discards it. The remaining card goes back onto the pile.

Continue in this way, always following the simple rule. When the spectator offers you a choice of either of his two cards, pick the unmarked card. When you take two cards from the pile and offer the spectator a choice, take two unmarked cards.

At the finish there will be only two cards left. One will be marked. This card is the ♠2. The spectator offers you a choice of either card. Naturally you choose the unmarked card. This leaves him with the ♠2 and he loses.

The trick may be expanded. If there are two force cards, either of which is equally acceptable (two deuces, for example, if you are doing a variation of the above trick) then mark both cards. At the finish there will be two cards left. Give the spectator a choice of discarding either card. Of course he must then be left with one of the force cards.

The approach works just as well with objects other than cards. Put blank pieces of paper in each of 12 envelopes or matchboxes. Put a $5 bill in the remaining envelope or matchbox and secretly mark this container. The spectator mixes the containers. Twelve of them are discarded, leaving just one *for you*. The spectator gets to keep the contents of the other 12. He gets 12 pieces of paper and you get the $5 bill.

59 THE STAPLED CARD

After you become acquainted with different force techniques, you can choose a method that is exactly appropriate to the trick you want to perform. One example will be given here, an application of the X-Force described in the opening pages of this chapter. Although the method is simple, the effect is spectacular.

As seen by the audience, the spectator chooses a card and signs the face. The card is returned to the deck. Then two jokers are shown. They are stapled together and placed on the bottom of the deck.

The magician causes one joker to come free of the staple. This is not a particularly magical effect, but then he causes the signed chosen card to become instantly stapled to the other joker!

METHOD: This is a streamlined handling of an intriguing plot idea suggested by Joseph Prieto. Two different approaches will be described here. You will need four jokers, a stapler and about a minute to set up the trick. Begin by stapling one joker back to back with the ♦3 as shown in Figure 52.

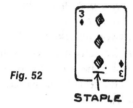

Fig. 52

STAPLE

Then staple one of the other jokers at the bottom and remove the staple. You want staple holes to mark this joker, so that later it will appear that this joker was magically released from the staple; that's why you first staple this joker and then remove the staple.

Hold the deck face up in the left hand. Place the three jokers on the top or back of the deck. The joker with the staple holes is third from the top. Place the ♦3–joker stapled pair at the face of the deck with the ♦3 showing. The setup is shown in Figure 53. This apparatus can be carried in the pocket until ready to perform. The extra cards can be added to the deck in just a few seconds when you are in another room.

Fig. 53

To perform the routine, place the deck face down on the table. Have the spectator cut off half and place this half on the table. Place the other half on top, but crosswise, so that the stapled end of the packet is on top of the other half of the deck. This is the X-Force. Grasp the crossed packets as shown in Figure 54.

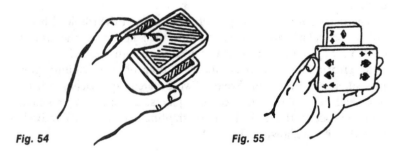

Fig. 54   **Fig. 55**

Turn the left hand palm up, Figure 55, to show the spectator that he cut to the ♦3. With the cards held exactly as shown in Figure 55, have the spectator sign his name on the face of the ♦3. Note that the lower packet hides the staple in the ♦3.

Place the deck face down on the table and square the cards. The signed ♦3 is now buried in the center of the deck. Remove the stapler from the pocket and place it on the table. Pick up the deck and fan it so you can see the faces. Remark that you will need two jokers for this effect. Cut the deck and complete the cut so that the stapled ♦3 is again on the bottom. Without showing the face of the ♦3 to the audience, place the deck face down on the table. Remove the top two cards and turn them face up to show they are jokers.

Place them back to back and staple them at one end. Try to have the staple in the same position on the jokers as it is on the ♦3. When the jokers have been stapled together, hold them in one hand and the deck in the other.

Say, "I could put these stapled jokers into the deck right next to your card without looking." As you say this put both hands behind the back. Immediately tuck the stapled jokers under the belt and leave them there. Take the stapled pair of cards off the bottom of the deck. This pair consists of the ♦3 and a joker. Hold them in the hand so that the joker is uppermost.

Bring the hands out into view again. It appears as if nothing has changed. The deck is in one hand and the two stapled cards are in the other. There is a joker showing at the top or face of the stapled pair, so the audience assumes the hand holds the two stapled jokers (see Figure 56). As you bring the cards back into view, say, "That is more easily said than done. Let me try something else."

Fig. 56

Place the deck on the table. Ask a spectator to hold his right hand palm up. Place the stapled pair of cards onto his palm. Have him cover the cards with his left hand palm down. Remove the top card of the deck. Don't show its face (it is a joker). Slide it between his palms, pause for dramatic effect, then abruptly pull this card out and turn it face up. It is a joker.

"It's easy to pull one joker free of the staple," you say. "The hard part is to cause your signed card to become stapled to the other joker."

The spectator opens his hands and finds that his signed card has somehow become stapled to the joker!

If you have access to double-sided adhesive tape, there is no need for duplicate cards. Any deck may be used. Place the two jokers that normally come with most decks on top. Double-sided tape has the adhesive on both sides, and is available in stationery and hardware stores. Cut a quarter-inch of clear double-sided tape and fasten it to the back of the top card of the deck. This card is a joker and there is a joker directly below it.

This is the only preparation. Hold the deck from above with the right hand. The left hand removes cards one at a time from the bottom until the spectator calls stop. Hand him the stopped-at card and tell him to sign the face. When he's done this, place his card face down on top of the deck. Cut the deck and complete the cut. Press down on the deck to make sure his card adheres to the joker that has the tape on top.

Bring the stapler out as you remark that you're going to use two jokers for the trick. Turn the deck face up, run through the cards and cut the two jokers to the bottom or face of the deck.

Remove them and place them face up in the left hand. Because of the adhesive tape, the chosen card adheres to the backmost joker. Take the face joker with the right hand, turn it face down and place it behind the double card in the left hand. When this joker is back to back with the double card, staple the two jokers together. Turn the stapled packet over so that the double card is at the bottom. Place the deck face down on top of the stapled cards.

Say, "That's how most people staple two cards together. A magician wouldn't bother with that method." Grasp the deck from the above with the right hand. The left hand grasps the bottom card of the deck and pulls it free of the staple. Toss this joker out face up on the table.

"Magicians staple cards together without the stapler." Cut the deck and complete the cut. Snap the fingers and spread the deck to reveal a face-up joker in the center. The spectator removes this card and will be surprised to discover that there is a card stapled back to back with it, and further, that this card is the signed chosen card.

TELEPATHY WITH CARDS

"Tricks dependent on thought foretold or divined are unquestionably the most striking in the whole range of conjuring. In truth, how is it possible to explain how anyone can know what you have chosen to think of, or even what you are going to think of presently?"

The above comment, written by Robert-Houdin a century ago, is as true today as when he practiced magic. Mental magic is almost always accepted as real magic by laymen. Properly presented, feats of mind reading with cards (or other objects) seem to lie beyond rational explanation. This chapter and a later one, "Thought-Card Methods," consider a number of telepathic experiments with cards.

60 THE PREDICTION DECK

The magician opens an envelope and takes out a deck of cards, explaining that the deck was mailed to him by an Oriental. In the deck, he says, is a prediction, fortunately written in English. It involves an event that has not yet taken place.

The pack is placed face down on the table. The spectator is invited to lift off less than half the deck. He can take one card or 25. The choice is entirely his and he is encouraged to try and second-guess the prophet by taking fewer or more cards than might be expected. After he takes some cards, he turns this packet face up and places it on the table.

When he has done this, have him place about half the remainder of the deck face down on top of the tabled face-up portion. The number of cards is not important as long as it contains the prediction slip.

Then have him turn the remainder of the deck face up and place it on top of the rest. At this point you have a face-up portion on top, then a face-down portion, then another face-up portion. No one has any idea of how many face-up cards and face-down cards there are.

Tell the spectator to lift off all the cards above the prediction. Then have him place the prediction aside without looking at the writing. Finally have him take the portion that was above the prediction, turn it over, and shuffle it into the balance of the deck. He can give the deck two or three more shuffles if he likes. The shuffles should be riffle shuffles.

Finally, have him count the number of face-down cards in the deck. He will arrive at a total of 24 face-down cards, exactly matching the prediction.

Note that you never touch the deck, yet the prediction is always correct.

METHOD: On a business card or square of cardboard write, "You will have exactly 24 face-down cards." Place the prediction, writing-side down, between the twenty-eighth and twenty-ninth cards from the top of the deck. Proceed as written above and the prediction will be correct. The routine is based on an idea of Bob Hummer's.

To add an exotic note, write your name and address on an airmail envelope and mail the empty envelope to yourself. Slide out the flap, place the deck with the prediction inside, and seal the flap. It will appear as if the deck was mailed to you. Remark that you have a mystic friend in the Far East who is good at writing predictions. Tear open the envelope, remove the deck and proceed as described above.

61   LAST OCTOBER

A deck of playing cards can act as a time-keeping device. On a slip of paper the magician writes, "October 21," explaining that this is the date of the first and only time he attempted this strange experiment with cards.

"Let me show you," he says. "October has 31 days. Please count 31 cards off the top of the deck." After the spectator does this, he discards the rest of the pack.

"Cut off a small packet of cards, count them and place them in your pocket," the magician says. The spectator secretly removes a small number of cards and pockets them. Say he has six cards. Only he knows this.

"Shuffle the rest of the packet. Then turn the top card face up on the table and sign your name on it." After the spectator has completed these instructions the magician adds, "Turn your signed card face down on the table. However many cards you have in your pocket, deal that many cards from the packet onto your signed card."

In our example the spectator deals six cards onto his signed card. After he has done this, he takes the small group of cards on the table (his signed card plus the six cards on top of it) and places this group on top of the packet in his hand. His chosen card is now buried somewhere in the packet.

"Since you have some cards in your pocket," the magician says, "I can't possibly know how many cards you have in your hand. That's what makes this so strange an experiment."

Turning attention to the date on the slip of paper, he says, "Before we started I wrote this date, October 21st. It happens that October is the tenth month. Count ten cards, moving each from the top to the bottom of your packet."

After the spectator has done this the magician says, "The date is the 21st, so count 21 cards, moving each from the top to the bottom of your packet."

When the spectator has done this, the magician says, "Now we get to the strange part. I wrote that date before we began. It would have been impossible for me to know how many cards you put in your pocket. Please turn over the top card of the packet in your hand."

The spectator does and it is his signed card!

The trick works itself. Just follow the above instructions and the signed card will always end up on the top of the packet.

62 MENTAL RESCUE

This splendid mental effect was originated by L. Vosburgh Lyons. Two spectators are seated opposite each other at a table. Each takes five cards from the deck. Each person shuffles his cards, chooses one, and places it in the other person's packet. The packets are each shuffled again by the spectators.

Picking up a packet, the magician concentrates for a moment, then removes one card. Picking up the other packet, the magician again concentrates and then removes a card. It turns out that these are the actual cards chosen by the two spectators.

METHOD: On top of the deck have five cards that you can easily memorize. The best plan when starting out is to use five digits in order from your telephone number and assign a suit to each. For the purpose of this explanation we'll use the ♣A, ♥4, ♠7, ♦10, ♣K. Note that the values increase by three as you go from card to card. The suits are in club-hearts-spade-diamond rotation, with a final club at the end. Place these five cards in any order on top of the deck.

Place the deck face down on the table. Have a spectator cut off about half and place this half on the table. Pick up the remainder of the deck (the original bottom half) and place it on top, but crosswise in the manner of the X-Force illustrated in Figure 46.

Explain that you would like to perform the first mind-reading experiment devised to allow you to do sleight of hand by telepathy. Lift off the portion of the deck that lies on top and deal the top five cards to one spectator. Put this portion aside. Then deal the top five cards of the other portion to the second spectator. These five cards are the force cards.

Have each spectator mix his cards without looking at them. Then have each choose a card, remember it and place it in the other spectator's packet. When this has been done, have each person mix his five cards.

Take the first spectator's packet, fan it and look for the ♣A, ♥4, ♠7, ♦10 or ♣K. Remove this card and place it face down on the table. Then pick up the second spectator's packet and look for the one card that does not belong with the force cards in that packet. The packet might contain the ♠7, ♥2, ♦10, ♣A and ♣K, in which case the card that doesn't belong to the force group is the ♥2. Remove this card and place it face down on the table.

Have the two chosen cards named. Then turn over the two cards you removed to show that you correctly found the two chosen cards.

Regarding presentation, after the cards have been chosen, exchanged and placed in opposite packets, have the packets shuffled, then ask each spectator to try and guess which card in his packet belongs to the other fellow. The difficulty of the problem becomes immediately apparent because neither spectator has a clue as to which card was chosen by the other spectator.

Another point is this. When you are going to find the chosen cards, take the second spectator's packet. This is the one containing four force cards plus the first spectator's card. Look through this packet, locate the card that doesn't belong to the force group, and place it face down on the table. But then look through the packet again and see which card is missing from the force group. In the above example the ♥4 is missing, and this is the second spectator's card. Thus you know his card *without* going near the other packet.

63 PAST AND FUTURE

The most impressive and memorable tricks are those that involve the spectator in a personal way. In this routine you predict the future by correctly foretelling which card a spectator is going to pick. Then you disclose the past by telling the spectator his date of birth.

The trick is impromptu. It uses no gimmicks or confederates.

METHOD: The basic idea is a routine of Verne Schoneck's. Use any borrowed deck and a paper bag. Take the deck and a pencil. Explain that you are going to write a prediction about an event in the future.

Lower the deck out of sight below the level of the tabletop. When the deck is out of the spectator's view, note the bottom card of the deck. Assume it's the ♠2. Remove the top card. On the face of this card write, "Two of spades." Place this card on the bottom of the deck face to face with the ♠2. Then remove the new top card, reverse it and place it on the bottom. The situation now is that there are two face-up cards on the bottom of the face-down deck. The third card from the bottom is the ♠2.

Remark that you'll put your prediction into the bag for safekeeping. Lower the deck into the bag and pretend to thumb off the prediction card into the bag. All you really do is rattle your hand a bit inside the bag.

Take the deck out of the bag. Remove the top card, toss it out face up and ask the spectator to write the month and day of his birth on the face of the card. Turn your head aside while he does this.

Have him place his card face down on top of the deck. Explain you want him to choose a card in a random way. Hand him the deck behind his back. As you do, secretly turn over the deck. Tell the spectator to take his card, reverse it and insert it into the deck. He follows your instruction, unaware he is actually inserting an indifferent card into the pack. After he has done this, have him cut the deck three times, and then turn it over three times.

He thinks his card is reversed somewhere in the deck. Take back the deck, turn it face up and spread it between your hands until you find the face-down card. Cut the deck and complete the cut so the reversed card is at the face of the deck. Remove this card and the card below it, explaining that the spectator's birthday card has found a card in a completely random way. Place both of these cards into the paper bag. Make it obvious you do not look at the face of the face-down card.

Now say that your first disclosure was a prediction about the future. Your next disclosure is more difficult because it's about the past. Place the deck below the level of the table. Note the writing on the top card. It will be the spectator's date of birth. Copy this date on another card and place this card on top of the face-down deck.

Say you will place your new card in the bag. As soon as the hand holding the deck goes into the bag and is hidden from view, thumb off the top two cards, letting them fall into the bag.

To finish, the spectator dumps out the contents of the bag, four cards in all. Two of the cards will be his, the other two yours. It is found that you successfully predicted the card he would choose, and then you disclosed his exact date of birth.

64 HOUDINI'S SECRET

This is a streamlined handling of a double prediction that appears in the Houdini notebooks. Before performing the trick, place a pencil dot at diagonally opposite corners of the top card of the deck, as in Figure 57. The dots should be large enough for you to spot easily but not so large as to make their presence obvious to the audience.

Fig. 57

The only other preparation is to note and remember the sixth card from the top of the deck. Assume this card is the ♥2. At the start of the trick you will thus have the pencil-dotted card on top of the deck and the ♥2 in position sixth from the top.

Tell the first spectator that you want him to think of a number and to deal that many cards off the top. "For example," you say, "If you thought of five, you would deal five cards like this." As you patter, deal five cards off the top into a heap on the table. Say, "Then look at the top card of the ones you dealt and drop the deck on top to bury your card." As you patter, glance at the top card of the dealt packet, place it back on top of that packet, and drop the balance of the deck on top of all.

Say, "Are you thinking of a number?" The spectator says yes. Lift off about half the deck from above with the right hand and remove the face card of this packet with the left fingers, as in Figure 58. Then replace the cut-off packet on top. Take the card removed with the left fingers, turn it face up and on it write, "Two of hearts." Place this card face down on the table.

Fig. 58

While you turn your back the spectator deals any number of cards between two and 12 onto the table, looks at the last card he dealt, and drops the balance of the deck on top of this card to bury it in the pack.

Face the spectators again. Cut off about two-thirds of the deck and complete the cut. You want to cut slightly fewer than 40 cards because your pencil-dotted key card is somewhere in the bottom 12 cards and you want to leave it undisturbed.

Turn to a second spectator. Say to him, "I want you to do the same thing. Deal cards like this." Here you deal single cards off the top into a tabled heap until you deal the pencil-dotted key card. Deal one more card. Say, "After you have dealt the cards, I want you to look at the last card dealt, like this." Glimpse the face of the last card you dealt. This is important because the card is the one chosen by the first spectator. Assume it is the ♠7.

Drop the deck on top of the dealt packet. Then lift off about half the deck with the right hand and take the face card, as in Figure 58. Glimpse the face of this card, say, "I want a card with more white space to write on," and put this card on top of the right-hand packet. Then take a new card with the left fingers. Drop the right-hand cards on top of the balance of the deck.

On the face of this card write the name of the card chosen by the first spectator. In our example you would write, "Seven of spades," the name of the card you glimpsed. Place the prediction on the table, writing side down.

Turn your back. Have the second spectator deal the same number of cards as the first spectator. He notes the last card dealt (it will be the force card, the ♥2 in our example), and drops the deck on top to bury his card.

Have the two cards named. Then have the predictions read to reveal that you knew all along which cards would be chosen.

This is a clever mental mystery that never fails to impress laymen.

65   HEX SQUARED

Shortly after its appearance in print, this routine was featured in a television show devoted to mental magic and was reprinted in a nationally distributed news weekly. To describe the effect is also to describe the method so we shall proceed immediately into the details. Arrange 16 cards in the color sequence indicated in Figure 59. The actual values and suits are of no consequence so long as the colors agree with the layout. Assuming the deck is red-backed, the card shown in the third column as the ♥A would be blue-backed. If the odd-color ♥A is not handy, draw a large X on the back of the ♥A in the deck you are going to use. Arrange the cards in the layout with the deck face up so that the X on the back of the ♥A is not seen by the audience.

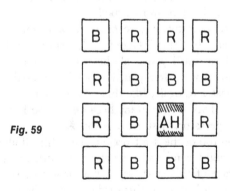

Fig. 59

After the cards are arranged in the face-up array, have the spectator use a ring or a coin as a marker. Caution him that he is not to study the cards or fix his attention on any card in the layout. Stress that he must act entirely on impulse in response to each command you give him.

To begin, tell him to place the ring on any red card in the layout. There are no restrictions. Emphasize that he must not hesitate in his choice. The card must be chosen on impulse.

Next tell him to move the ring either to the left or right to the nearest black card. Again there are no restrictions. He can move either to the left or right as long as he comes to rest on the black card nearest his starting position.

Now tell him to move vertically up or down to the nearest red card. Again stress that the move must be made without hesitation. In some rows he will have a wide degree of movement, in others he won't. In either case he is to move the ring without pause.

For the third move he is to move diagonally to the nearest black card. Again in some cases he is restricted, in others he is not.

There is one final instruction and this one is specific. Tell him to move the ring either down (toward himself) or to the right, in either case to the nearest red card.

All looks fair. The spectator has been given an unlimited choice in the way he may move, yet each move draws him deeper into a trap. If the above instructions are carried out correctly, the ring will now rest on the ♥A. To finish the trick, turn each card face down on the table until all cards in the layout are face down except the chosen card. Emphasize that the spectator had complete freedom of choice on each move, that he could slide the ring any way he chose. Then say that Fate nevertheless exercised a guiding hand. Turn over the ♥A to reveal that it has a different-color back.

In order for the trick to work, the layout of Figure 59 must be as the spectator sees it, not as the magician sees it.

66   THE SQUARE RING

This version of "Hex Squared" uses only three instructions to the spectator. As before, the spectator slides a coin or a ring over an array of cards in response to three directions from the magician. It is then shown that the magician knew all along which card would be chosen. This version was developed by Sam Schwartz and the author.

Because only three instructions are given to the spectator, he will not always end up on the same card. There are in fact two cards he can end up on. They are accounted for by means of two "outs" (alternate endings) used by the magician.

The array is shown in Figure 60. The ♥A has a back colored differently than the other cards.

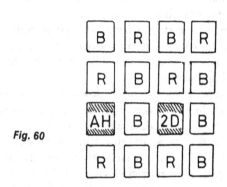

Fig. 60

On a square of cardboard write the following instructions:
1. Slide the coin up or down to the nearest red card.
2. Slide the coin left or right to the nearest black card.
3. Slide the coin diagonally to the nearest red card.

On the back of this card write the words, "You will choose the ♦2." This completes the prior preparation. The entire outfit may be placed in an envelope and carried in the pocket. When ready to perform this routine, remove the cards and the cardboard square, saying that these particular cards seem to exert a psychic influence on certain mental wavelengths.

To present the routine, deal out 16 cards in the array of Figure 60. The cards must be dealt out face up from the face-up deck to conceal the odd-color back of the ♥A.

Place the cardboard square on the table with the instructions up. Do not let the audience see the writing on the back of the cardboard. Have the spectator remove a coin from his pocket. Instruct him to place it on any black card. Emphasize that the cards and the cardboard square are the *only* apparatus you will use.

Have the spectator slide the coin according to the three instructions described above. If the coin ends up on the ♥A, turn over the other 15 cards, then the ♥A to show the odd-color back. If the coin ends up on the ♦2, turn over the cardboard square to show the written prediction. The coin can end up on only one of these two cards, so all possible outcomes have been accounted for.

67 THE UNMATCH GAME

In this game the magician correctly predicts the outcome, then issues a second prediction and is correct once again.

Ten pairs of cards are arranged so that suits match up. A sample arrangement might be a pair of spades, a pair of hearts, a pair of clubs, a pair of spades, a pair of diamonds and so on. On top of these ten pairs of cards place a heart, a spade, a diamond and a club. Place this packet of 24 cards on top of the deck and you are ready to begin.

To present the routine, remove the top 24 cards. Discard the rest of the deck as it will not be used. Give the packet to the spectator and let him shuffle it thoroughly. While the spectator shuffles the cards, you write on a slip of paper, "There will be exactly four cards left over, and there will also be just one of each suit." Fold the paper and place it in plain view on the table.

Have the spectator place the shuffled packet face down on the table. Then ask him to divide it into two *unequal* heaps with any number of cards in each heap. He keeps one heap for himself and gives the other to a second spectator.

The game is to fan the cards out and remove any pair of the same suit. Place the pair face down on the table and keep removing matching-suit pairs until he has no more matching pairs. The second spectator similarly does this with the cards in his packet. Remark, "If for instance you have two Hearts, place them on the table. Then two clubs, two diamonds, and so on."

When they have done this, they will be left with a number of unmatched cards. The prediction is then opened and read aloud. There are indeed just four cards left unmatched, and they are one of each suit.

Offer to repeat the trick. Take the four cards from them and drop them onto the balance of the deck or put them in the pocket since they are not used. Pick up the matching pairs on the table (ten pairs in all) and hand them to one of the spectators. Ask him to shuffle them thoroughly.

While the cards are being shuffled, write, "The first spectator will have exactly the same number of cards remaining as the second spectator. In addition, the suits of the first spectator's remaining cards will be exactly the same as the suits in the second spectator's remaining cards."

Again the spectators remove matching-suit pairs (two hearts, two clubs, etc.) from their respective packets until they can go no further. The remaining cards are compared with the prediction and it is seen that, once again, the prediction is correct.

There is a slight chance that all cards will be perfectly matched up, but the prediction is still correct. The above routine is based on ideas of Roy Walton and the author.

68 THE MASTER MIND

The magician removes a deck from his pocket and deals cards off the face one at a time. The spectator can call stop at any time. There is no force and every card is different. The spectator chooses any card. This card is buried in the deck. No one knows where the card is in the pack. This pack is then returned to the jacket pocket.

Another deck is brought from a different jacket pocket. The magician says, "Before I came here tonight I reversed a card in this deck." He spreads the pack face up and it is seen that one card is face down. This card is pushed out of the deck.

"Your card was the eight of clubs," the magician says. "Wouldn't it be amazing if the card I reversed was also the eight of clubs?" The reversed card is turned over and it is indeed the ♣8!

"Not only that," the magician adds, "But I was so sure you'd pick the ♣8 I put another one in the deck." He spreads the deck to reveal that there is another ♣8 in the pack.

Tapping the ♣8 in the deck, the magician says, "But *this* eight of clubs belongs here." He flips the deck over to show it is blue-backed.

"*Your* eight of clubs doesn't." Now the ♣8 on the table is flipped over. It has a red back. The spectator picked the only red-backed card in the deck!

All may be left with the spectator for examination.

METHOD: This is a streamlined version of an effect whose originator is unknown to me. It can be done with two regular decks but you may find the working a little easier if you use the smaller novelty decks which are half the size of regular playing cards. The small decks are available in novelty and gift shops. In a moment you will see why the smaller decks are more convenient.

Two decks are needed, one red-backed and one blue-backed.

After shuffling the red-backed deck take the top 26 cards. Assume the ♠A is at the face or bottom of this packet.

Remove the same 26 cards from the blue-backed deck, shuffle them and place this packet face down on the table. Place a blue-backed joker face down on top of the packet. Then place a red-backed joker face up on the packet. Finally, place the 26-card red-backed packet face up on top of all. The ♠A will be on top at this point. Snap a rubber band around this deck and place it in your right jacket pocket. The rest of the blue-backed deck is in the left jacket pocket. Place a pencil in the right pocket. You are ready to begin.

Remove the banded deck from the pocket with the ♠A uppermost. Take the rubber band off the deck and place the band in the right jacket pocket. Hold the deck in the left hand. The ♠A shows at the face of the deck.

Deal the cards one at a time onto the table in a face-up heap. Tell the spectator to stop you at any time. Of course he must stop you somewhere in the first 26 cards. When he does, have him remember the card he stopped at. Keep this card face up. Insert it face up into the deck about 13 cards up from the bottom. Thus the card enters the blue-backed portion of the deck.

Gather the dealt cards and replace them face up on top of the deck. Then snap the rubber band around the deck. Keep this face of the deck toward the spectator as you place the deck into your *inside* left jacket pocket with the right hand.

The crucial action takes place at this point. The deck does not go into the pocket. It goes into the left jacket sleeve. The right hand comes out of the jacket so that the spectator can clearly see that the hand is empty. The left hand then goes to the left (side) pocket to remove another deck. Actually the deck just dropped into the sleeve tumbles down the sleeve and into the left hand and it is *this same deck* that is brought out of the left pocket. The deck is brought out with the blue-backed packet uppermost. The deck appears to be face up.

Remark that yesterday you had a sudden thought that someone was going to choose a particular card and that you reversed one card in this deck. Spread the facemost 26 cards between the hands, revealing a face-down card in the middle of the face-up group. Be careful not to spread past the joker.

The right hand removes all of the face-up cards except the joker and spreads them face up on the table. All attention is on that single face-down card in the middle of the spread. Both hands go to the jacket pockets as you remark that you will need a pencil. The left hand drops its packet (a red-backed packet plus two jokers) into the left pocket and comes out with the balance of the blue-backed deck. At the same time the right hand comes out of the right pocket with the pencil. To focus attention on the right hand, look at the pencil as it is being removed from the pocket.

Use the eraser end of the pencil to slide the face-down card out of the spread as you say, "I don't want this card touched by human hands. You might think I switched cards."

Have the spectator turn the card over. It is the same as his freely chosen card. After this has registered with the spectator, use the pencil to point to the duplicate in the face-up spread. Finally, gather the complete deck (tabled cards plus the cards in the left hand) and flip the deck face down, revealing blue backs. The spectator chose the only red-backed card in a blue-backed deck.

It should be obvious that if you use the smaller decks, the cards will slide down the jacket sleeve more easily. Try it with regular cards also. If it works, stick to those cards. Otherwise use the smaller decks.

GAMBLING SECRETS

Almost everyone has played cards, even if only the occasional game of Old Maid or Go Fish, and has probably wished for the ability to deal himself a winning hand. Gambling demonstrations are always popular because they satisfy the dream of being able to control a deck of cards.

If you can deal any hand called for, demonstrate your prowess at a classic swindle like Three-Card Monte or produce the aces, you will have impressed your audience with a demonstration of uncanny skill. These feats and others will be explained in this chapter.

69 FLIM FLAM

In this quick demonstration of skill at Seven-Card Stud Poker you deal a face-down heap of seven black cards and a separate face-down heap of seven red cards. Don't show the audience the faces of the cards as you remove them from the deck. Place one heap on top of the other.

Hold the face-down packet from above in the right hand. The left thumb draws the top card off. Simultaneously the left fingers draw the bottom card off, in Figure 61. Explain that you will draw pairs of cards off like this and that at some point the spectator is to call stop.

Fig. 61

Drop the first pair of cards onto the table. Draw off the next pair. If the spectator doesn't call stop, drop this pair onto the first pair. Continue drawing pairs of cards and dropping them onto the tabled pairs until the spectator calls stop. Whatever pair of cards you are holding in the left hand at this point, turn the two cards over as a unit, remarking that these will be the hole cards in two stud-poker hands. Leave them face up and drop them onto the tabled pairs of cards.

Continue drawing pairs of face-down cards off until all seven pairs have been dropped onto the tabled heap. Square up the cards. Invite the spectator to cut the packet and complete the cut. He can give the packet any number of straight cuts. Just make sure the face-up cards are in the middle of the packet before proceeding.

Deal the cards into two hands of seven-card stud poker. The face-up card in each hand is the hole card.

Say, "I'm not going to switch the hole cards. That would be too easy. Instead I'm going to switch all the other cards in each hand." Snap your fingers over the cards. Then point to the face-up black card, saying, "This card is black, but now all the others are red." Turn over this hand to show that the face-up black card is the only black card in the hand. The other cards are red.

Point to the face-up red card. Say, "This card is red, but now all the other cards in the hand are black." Turn over the hand to show that the face-up red card is the only red card in the hand. All the other cards are black.

70 MONTE MIRACLE

Three-Card Monte is a fair-seeming game that requires sleight-of-hand ability and a quick tongue to demonstrate successfully, but there is a version that uses a puzzling optical illusion to bring about the basic effect. As in the classic trick, you use two black cards and a red ace. The spectator is asked to guess the whereabouts of the ace. Although the ace is prominently placed, the spectator fails to find it.

Use the two black deuces and the ♥A. Place the ace between the deuces, but at right angles, as in Figure 62. Grasp the leftmost two cards with the left hand from above, and the rightmost deuce with the right hand as shown in Figure 63.

Turn the left hand palm up to show that the ♥A is at right angles to the other card. Then slip the two face-up cards under the

Fig. 62

Fig. 63

right thumb, as in Figure 64. The left hand then releases its grip on these two cards and regrips the two face-up cards with the fingers on top, thumb below. The grip is shown in Figure 65A.

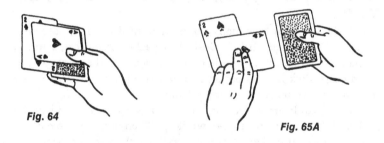

Fig. 64

Fig. 65A

Both hands now turn over simultaneously. The left-hand cards are face down and the right-hand card is face up, as in Figure 65B. As you do this, say, "And here is the other black deuce," calling attention to the black deuce in the right hand.

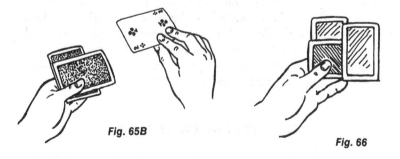

Fig. 65B

Fig. 66

Turn the right hand palm down and place the right-hand card on top of the left-hand cards as shown in Figure 66. There is one card between two others, and this card is at right angles to the other two cards. The audience assumes this is the red ace, but when you turn it over, it is not an ace.

71   WHIZ BANG POKER

One of the most difficult poker deals is to deal any number of hands from two to six, guarantee that each hand is a good hand and, finally, give the dealer the best hand of all. T. Nelson Downs devised an excellent method requiring no skill.

From two to six hands may be dealt. The top part of the deck is stacked. The setup from the top down is as follows: ♠J-♣7-♦8-♦9-♠10-♥6-♥7-♣8-♠9-♦10-♠6-♦7-♥8-♣9-♥10-♦6-♠7-♠8-♥9-♣10-♥J-♦A-♠2-♥4-♥3-♣6-♦Q-♦5-♠4-♥5-♥A.

Ask the spectator how many hands are to be dealt. If he says two, remark, "That's ten cards." Deal off a packet of ten cards into a heap on the table, reversing their order as you deal them into a face-down heap. Pick up this packet and deal two hands. Each hand is a straight, but yours is the winning hand.

If three hands are called for, say, "That's 15 cards," and deal a packet of 15 cards into a face-down heap. Then deal out three hands from the 15-card packet. Again you will get the winning hand.

If four hands are called for, say, "That's 20 cards," deal off 20 cards into a packet, then deal out four hands from this packet. Again all hands will be pat hands and you will have the winning hand.

If five hands are called for, *don't* reverse count the cards. Simply deal out five poker hands. You will get four tens, a winning hand.

Finally, if six hands are called for, bury the top card of the deck on the bottom of the deck, then count 30 cards into a packet, and then deal out six hands from this packet. The players will get straights and flushes but you will get a straight flush, the winning hand. As Downs himself remarked, "Try this—it's a corker!"

72   ANY HAND CALLED FOR

In the T. Nelson Downs poker deal, the magician dealt any number of hands and always came up with the winning hand. Here Michael Zens varies the plot by having the spectator name any kind of hand (royal flush, four of a kind, etc.). The magician deals the cards, turns up the dealer's hand, and it is the very hand named by the spectator. This is an impressive demonstration of skill at the card table.

By means of ingenious thinking, complicated setups are done away with. The Zens stack is ♥10-♥J-♥K-♥Q-♥A— ♠A-♠K-♦A-♣A-♣K, from the top down. Place this packet on top of the deck.

Ask for any poker hand. If the spectator names a straight, a straight flush or a royal flush, proceed directly into the deal described below by dealing out five hands, then gathering the hands one on top of the next, and then dealing out five hands again. The dealer's hand will contain the straight, the straight flush or the royal flush.

If the spectator asks for one pair, take one card from the top of the deck and bury it in the center of the pack. If he calls for two pair, bury the top two cards in the center of the pack. If he asks for three of a kind, bury the top three cards in the center. If he asks for four of a kind, bury the top four cards in the center. Finally, if he asks for a full house, bury the top five cards in the center of the deck.

When this has been done, deal out five face-down poker hands of five cards each. Deal from left to right, a card at a time, until you have five Draw Poker hands. As you deal, say, "This is how the honest gambler deals out poker hands. You don't see too many honest dealers these days." You can even show one or two hands to be worthless.

Gather the hands by placing the hands on top of one another until all five hands have been gathered and placed on top of the deck. Then deal out five hands again as you say, "This is how the card cheat deals poker hands."

Remind the spectator which hand he called out. Then turn over your hand to show that you dealt yourself the very hand called out by the spectator.

Note that in most cases the spectator will ask you to deal a royal flush and that you can proceed immediately into the deal with no adjustment in the cards.

73 THE OMEGA BET

Properly presented, this wager will establish your reputation as master of betting games. It begins as a simple game. When the spectator begins to get suspicious about the procedure you immediately tighten the conditions. When he gets more suspicious you tighten the conditions further. Should he still be suspicious (especially in view of your unbroken winning streak) you make it impossible for cheating to occur, yet you still win.

The game is simple and the cards are handled by the spectator from start to finish. Your only task is to watch the cards and see to it that the simple handling procedure is adhered to. This routine is the author's use of a riffle-shuffle set up in which a single card is "shuffled" into the deck by the spectator.

To establish the setup, arrange the cards so the colors alternate red-black-red-black from top to bottom. This is the only preparation. As the audience sees it, the spectator cuts the deck and completes the cut. Then he deals the top card and the next card face up onto the table. He chooses either card and inserts it face up anywhere in the deck. The spectator then deals the cards off the top in pairs, that is, two at a time. Sooner or later the pair containing the face-up card will show up. You bet whether the card paired with it will be the same color or not.

Since you win on every round, the spectator will eventually suspect that the color of the face-up card has something to do with it. When this proves wrong, he will suspect that you gauge the location of the face-up card in the deck. The real secret is much simpler. When he deals the top two cards onto the table, remember which one he dealt first. If he inserts that card face-up into the deck, it will pair up with a card of the same color, no matter where it goes into the deck. If he inserts the other card into the pack, it will not pair up with a card of matching color. This is *all* there is to it.

Knowing the system, you now proceed as follows with the routine. Tell him to cut the deck and complete the cut. He can give the deck any number of straight cuts. Then tell him to turn the top card face up onto the table. Say this is the ♥A. He then deals the next card face up alongside it. Say this card is the ♠4.

Have him choose either card and place it face up anywhere in the face-down deck. Say he decides to insert the ♥A face up in the deck. Since this is the first card he dealt off the top, it will pair up with a card of the same color. This means that both cards of the pair containing the face-up ♥A will be red.

Don't make the game look too easy. Before you say anything, glance at the ♠4 still on the table. Then glance at the deck. Pretend to make a mental calculation. Then announce that when the spectator deals the pair containing the face-up ♥A, both cards of that pair will be red.

The spectator pushes the top two cards off the deck and transfers them to the bottom. He does the same thing with the next pair and the next, continuing until he comes to the pair containing the face-up ♥A.

The card paired with the ♥A is turned face up. It will be red. You have won the wager.

The handling here is important. When the spectator acknowledges you won, have the ♥A dealt onto the table. The red card paired with the ♥A is then turned face down and returned to the top of the deck. Place the ♥A and the ♠4 aside as they are no longer used.

This same pattern of handling is repeated throughout the remainder of the demonstration. Have the spectator cut the deck and complete the cut, then turn the top two cards up, and so on. You should perform this phase of the Omega Bet several more times until the spectator begins to get suspicious. Sooner or later the spectator will tell you that the color of the face-up card must have something to do with it. He will reason that if you don't know the color of the card he inserts into the deck, you won't win quite as often.

When this happens, have him deal the top two cards face down onto the table so that no one can see the faces of the cards. He takes either card, places it behind his back, turns it face up and inserts it reversed into the face-down deck. Simply note whether he places the first card or the second card into the deck. If it's the first card, the colors will match. If it's the second card, the colors won't match.

Have him bring the deck forward, deal cards from top to bottom two at a time, and stop when he gets to the pair containing the face-up card. As before you will have correctly predicted whether the pair containing the face-up card will or won't contain two cards of the same color.

For the next phase of the routine, write on a slip of paper, "The cards won't match." Toss the paper out, writing-side down. Then have the spectator place the deck behind his back, cut the deck and complete the cut. With the cards still out of sight, he takes either the top card or the bottom card of the face-down deck, turns it face up and inserts it anywhere in the deck. The deck is brought forward.

Then he transfers pairs of cards from top to bottom until he comes to the pair containing the face-up card. This pair will contain one red card and one black card. The colors don't match, so your prediction is correct.

For the final phase, write on a piece of paper, "Each pair will match." Have the spectator put the deck behind his back. Tell him to cut the deck and complete the cut. Have him take the bottom card, turn it face up and insert it into the top half of the deck. Then have him take the top card, turn it face up and insert it face up into the bottom half of the deck.

The spectator brings the deck into view and deals cards off two at a time. Each pair containing a face-up card is placed aside. At the finish, when each of these two pairs is examined, it is seen that the predictions are correct—each pair does contain two cards of the same color.

74 ACES FOR EXPERTS

The production of the four aces is one of the most impressive feats you can perform with a deck of cards. The catch is that if you use a borrowed deck, with no time to set the cards, there is generally a great deal of technical skill called for if you want to produce the aces in a magical manner. The following routine was devised by the author as a streamlined ace production requiring no skill.

Taking a borrowed, shuffled deck, the magician holds the cards face up so that only he can see the faces. He first checks that the aces are evenly distributed throughout the pack. If two or more aces are bunched together, the deck is given a few shuffles to separate them. Then the deck is spread again. Spreading the cards from left to right, when he gets to the first ace he removes the card just to the left of it, turns it around and inserts it in its original position. This reversed card is left upjogged.

The same procedure is repeated with the card just to the left of each of the remaining three aces. The result is the situation shown from the performer's view in Figure 67.

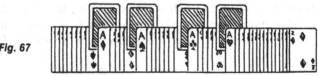

Fig. 67

The deck is squared up. The upjogged cards are carefully squared into the pack. Then the deck is turned over side for side and held in the left hand. All of the cards above the first reversed card are removed and placed on the bottom of the deck.

The topmost face-up card is dealt onto the table. Then all of the cards above the next face-up card are taken and placed on the table below this first face-up card. Then the next face-up card is placed on the table. All of the cards above the next face-up card in the deck are placed on the table in a group below the second face-up card on the table.

The third face-up card is placed on the table. All of the face-down cards above the last face-up card in the deck are placed on the table in a group below the third face-up card. Finally, the fourth face-up card, which is now on top of the remainder of the deck, is dealt onto the table. The remaining face-down cards are placed on the table just below this card. The result looks like Figure 68.

Fig. 68

The four face-up cards are handed to the spectator with the re-mark that his gambling expertise is about to be tested. He is to mix the four cards and place each face-up card next to a face-down packet.

In the example of Figure 68 he may place the ♥5 next to the first packet on the left. Pick up this packet, spell "five," dealing a card for each letter into a heap and place the balance of the packet on top of the dealt cards. He might have placed the ♥4 next to the next packet. Pick up this packet, spell "four," dealing a card for each letter into a face-down heap, and drop the balance of the packet on top of the dealt cards.

Proceed in like manner for the remaining packets, using the deal-spell indicated by the value of the face-up card in front of the packet.

For the finish, turn over the packets to reveal the four aces at the face of the packets.

75 FACE-UP POKER

This chapter closes with a poker bet that is little known outside a small circle. The details of this ingenious bet have surfaced in various publications, but this is believed to be the first complete description of all angles on the proposition. The game assumes that the players have a knowledge of the way poker hands are ordered. From highest to lowest, the hands are rated as follows:

1. Royal flush	6. Straight
2. Straight flush	7. Three of a kind
3. Four of a kind	8. Two pair
4. Full house	9. One pair
5. Flush	10. High card

The game is this. The deck is shuffled and spread face up on the table. You are going to play two rounds. In the first round the spectator is allowed to go first. He may draw any five-card Draw Poker hand he likes. Everyone sees his cards. After he has drawn a hand, the magician draws a five-card hand.

Knowing what the magician has, the spectator has the option of keeping his hand or of discarding any part of it. He can discard one card or even all five cards, in which case he may draw a completely new hand. Once the spectator has exercised his option, the magician likewise can discard any part or all of his own hand and draw new cards.

Neither player can draw from the discard pile, and all suits rate equally. Although the player goes first and can draw any hand he likes, the magician bets that he can equal or better the spectator's hand. This means that the magician will either tie or beat the spectator on this round.

After the first round has been played, the second round goes like this. The magician goes first and can draw any five cards he likes. The spectator knows what the magician has and can draw any five cards he likes.

The magician then has the option of keeping his hand or of discarding up to five cards and drawing new cards from the balance of the deck. After he does this, the spectator has the option of discarding up to five cards from his hand and drawing new cards from the balance of the deck.

The difference in this round is that the magician goes first. But on this round he bets that he will positively beat the spectator. After the hands have been drawn it is seen that although the spectator knows how the magician has played on the first round and can utilize a similar strategy, the magician does indeed win on the second round.

We'll consider first-round play in detail. Almost always the spectator will draw a royal flush the first time. If he does this, you draw a royal flush too. The round ends in a tie.

Don't go on to the second round yet. Instead, point out that the game is more interesting if neither you nor the spectator draw a royal flush. Tell the spectator that by drawing some other hand, he will get a chance to see the strategy you use, and he can borrow from that strategy on the second round of play.

If the spectator agrees to this, chances are he will draw four aces and a king. This is the next highest hand after a straight flush, so it is to be expected that the spectator will draw this hand.

Should he draw four of a kind, you want to prevent him from improving the hand but at the same time you don't want to expose the strategy you intend to use on the second round. The approach you use is to draw three tens plus two more cards in the suit not included among the tens. The two cards can be any of these pairs: A-9, K-9, Q-9, J-9, K-8, Q-8, J-8, Q-7, J-7, J-6. This approach was suggested by Charles Foster and Christine Peipers.

For example, say the spectator draws the four aces plus the ♥K. You then draw the ♠10-♦10-♣10 plus the ♥Q and ♥9. The spectator now has a chance to improve his hand but has trouble because you have blocked him from getting anything above a nine-high straight flush. If he draws, say, a nine-high straight flush in diamonds, you easily win with a ten-high straight flush in spades. You do this by discarding all but the ♠10, then draw the ♠9, ♠8, ♠7 and ♠6.

Second-round play is even easier. This time you draw *four* tens and any king. The best the spectator can do is settle for a nine-high straight flush. You easily beat him with a ten-high straight flush.

To summarize, on the first round you draw three tens plus two more cards. On the second round you draw four tens plus any king. The only way the spectator can beat you is if he knows the system.

There are two unpublished variations that the reader may want to consider. In the first, each player takes a turn and draws a single card out of the deck. Players alternate until each has five cards. The player with the highest hand wins.

A discussion of this game lies outside the scope of this book, but the reader may be interested in an amusing variation of the original bet, called Revenge Poker. Here the magician draws five cards, then the spectator draws five cards. Then the magician may discard and draw up to five new cards, and then the spectator may discard and draw up to five new cards. The difference is that each person draws cards for the *other* player. In other words, the magician draws the spectator's hand and the spectator draws the magician's hand.

The game gets its name from the fact that the spectator here can exercise revenge and give the magician the worst possible hand. If the magician ends up with a poker hand more awful than the spectator's hand, the magician loses.

The magician goes first. He draws four deuces and any other card. The spectator might just as well quit at this point, but since the cards drawn by the magician are for the spectator's poker hand, it appears as if the magician made a mistake since four of a kind represents an excellent hand.

The spectator will probably draw a three, four, five, six, eight, in mixed suits for the magician. This is a hand that contains an eight-high and nothing else. It is assumed that aces are higher than kings, in which case the hand drawn by the spectator for the magician represents the worst possible hand he can give the magician under the circumstances.

The magician holds onto one deuce, discards the rest of his hand, and then draws a three, four, five, seven. This hand becomes the spectator's hand. It is a truly awful hand and must lose for the spectator, no matter what cards he gives the magician. To say it another way, the worst the magician can get from the spectator is a hand with an eight as the highest possible card. The worst the magician can give the spectator is a seven-high hand. Since the spectator gets the lower hand, he loses.

CONJUROR'S QUARTET

This is a series of four quick tricks which use a variety of props that can be carried in the pocket, and require nothing special in the way of setting-up procedure. The props consist of a deck of cards, a die and two rubber bands. The other prop is an invisible confederate who helps out with one of the tricks.

The reader should find it easy to choose four or five tricks from the material presented in this book to make up his own personal card routine. The tricks in the present chapter might be used as a guideline. They are easy to perform, clear in plot and varied in both the type of effect and the props that are used.

76 INVISIBLE CON MAN

In this trick you require one visible spectator and one invisible spectator. A prediction is written and placed aside. You have a card noted by the throw of a die. The die then locates the chosen card, and for a kicker it locates a card that the invisible spectator would have chosen had he been present.

Before beginning the trick, note the top card of the deck. Say it is the ♠A. This small bit of preparation is done secretly. To perform the trick, remark that you wanted to include a friend of yours in the trick, a well-known con artist who frequently acts as your confederate, but he couldn't make it. "He did tell me, though, that he'd call as soon as he got out of jail." You further explain that he said that he'd pick a card anyway. The name of this card (the ♠A) is then jotted down on a slip of paper, which is placed aside.

Have the spectator deal two heaps of seven cards each. The heap which contains the ♠A at the bottom will be called A. The other heap will be called B. After he has dealt the two heaps, have him roll a die and note the top number. Whatever the number, he deals that many cards off the top of *B*, notes the face or bottom card of this dealt packet, and places the dealt packet on top of *A*. Then he places the combined packets at *A* on top of heap *B* and squares up the cards.

Have him deal seven cards into a heap on the table and place the balance of the cards aside. Turn the die over. Whatever number is up, deal that many cards off the top of the dealt packet. Turn up the next card and it will be his card. This completes the first part of the trick; the die has found his card.

Turn the die over again, bringing the original number uppermost. Deal that many cards off the top of the other packet and turn up the last card dealt. It will be the ♠A. Say, "Not only did the die find your card, it found the card my friend would have chosen had he been a free man." Have the spectator open the slip of paper and verify that the die did indeed locate a card chosen by the phantom spectator.

77 THE CALCULATOR CARD TRICK

This version of a classic swindle was proposed by J. W. Sarles. Explain that you have a deck of cards which has been programmed to act like a pocket calculator. It has the advantage that it requires no batteries and will never wear out.

Place the deck on your fingers. Have the spectator cut off about half and place the cut portion on your palm, Figure 69. In the drawing he would have cut off packet *A* and placed it on your palm. Turn up the top card of *B*. It might be an eight-spot.

Fig. 69

Say, "If I had 15 dollars and gave you eight [point to the eight-spot when you say this], how much money would I have left?"

The spectator answers, "Seven." Congratulate him on his being right. Then turn up the top card of packet *B* and it is a seven-spot!

The trick is immediately repeated and the calculator is once again correct.

METHOD: The only preparation is to note and remember the top card of the deck. In the above example this card is a seven-spot. Have the spectator cut off a packet of cards onto your palm. Then turn up the top card of packet B. Whatever its value, mentally add this to the card you memorized. In our example the top card of B is an eight, so you would silently add eight and seven, getting 15. Say to the spectator, "Suppose I had 15 dollars [here you name the total of the two numbers] and gave you eight [here you point to the eight-spot he cut to]. How much would I have left?" When he says, "Seven," simply turn up the top card of A to show it is a seven.

The trick is over so quickly that the spectator will ask you to do it again. J. W. Sarles devised this ending. Beforehand you note both the top card and the bottom card of the deck. Assume the bottom card is a three-spot.

Do the first part of the trick as described above. Then put packet A back on top of packet B. Say, "It works with other problems too. Here, cut the deck again." Once more the deck is placed on the fingers. The spectator cuts off a packet onto the left palm. Call this packet A.

Turn over packet A, bringing the face card of this packet into view. Whatever its value, add it to the value of the bottom card. If the face card of A is a nine, mentally add it to three, getting 12. Say, "Suppose I had 12 gallons of gas and I used nine gallons to get home. How much would I have left?"

The spectator answers three. Turn over the other packet, showing the three-spot at the face. Then put the deck aside, saying you don't want to burden the calculator with overuse.

78 BANDIT ACES

The four aces are removed from the deck and dealt out in a face-down row on the table. A rubber band is snapped around the rest of the deck for safekeeping. The spectator then names any ace. The four aces are placed on top of the banded deck. On command the named ace penetrates the deck.

METHOD: Remove the four aces from the deck and place them in a face-down row on the table in an order known to you. Assume they are from left to right, the ♣A, ♥A, ♠A, ♦A.

Snap a rubber band around the middle of the deck. The rubber band should fit snugly and it should be untangled.

Have any ace called out. Say the spectator names the ♥A. Drop the banded deck on top of the ♥A, as in Figure 70. Then pick up the deck plus the ♥A and place them on top of another ace. Pick up the deck plus the two aces and drop them on top of another ace. Finally drop the deck plus the three aces on top of the last ace. It makes no difference in which order the aces are picked up under the banded deck so long as the named ace is picked up first.

Fig. 70

The deck is on the table. The right hand grasps the deck from above, bears down on it and slides it to the right as in Figure 71. Three of the aces may spread a bit but the important point is that the ♥A will be secretly stolen under the deck.

Fig. 71

Square the packet of three aces and place them on top of the banded deck. The audience thinks this packet still contains the four aces. Grasp the deck from above with the right hand, using the same grip depicted in Figure 71. Command the named ace to penetrate the deck. Lift the deck with the right hand. There is now a face-down card on the table. When it is turned over it proves to be the named ace.

79 HOUDINI CARD

This clever card mystery was invented by Jack Avis. As the audience sees it, a card is chosen, initialed and returned to the deck.

A rubber band is then placed widthwise around the pack. Another rubber band is placed lengthwise around the pack. The chosen card is still in the deck and the deck is sealed on all sides by the rubber bands.

Nevertheless, when the deck is covered with a handkerchief, the chosen card instantly comes free of the doubly banded deck.

METHOD: Before proceeding, secretly mark the back of the top card of the deck. This card will act as a key card. Spread the pack and have any card chosen. Ask the spectator to sign his name on the face of the card. He then places his card on top of the deck, cuts the deck and completes the cut. Tell him to give the deck several straight cuts to lose his card further in the pack. Take the deck from him and locate the key card. Cut it to the top of the deck. The spectator's card is now on the bottom. The key card may be marked on the back as in the example of Figure 57 (page 94) so that it is easily spotted when you spread the deck face down. It is then a simple matter to cut it to the top of the pack.

You are now going to snap two rubber bands around the deck. Place one band widthwise around the deck, from C to D in Figure 72. A second rubber band is then snapped around the deck from A to B as shown in Figure 73. It is important to place the first band on widthwise and the second band lengthwise. Do not flash the face of the bottom card of the deck when the bands are snapped around the pack.

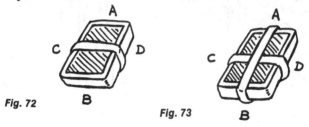

Fig. 72

Fig. 73

To remove the face card without disturbing the rubber bands, you will use a clever bit of handling that seems honest but is really the key to the method. Hold the deck in the left hand from above, as in Figure 74. The right forefinger moves to a position below the deck, presses against the face of the bottom card (the chosen card) and draws this card to the right, Figure 75A. As far as the audience is concerned, you are simply demonstrating the impossibility of withdrawing a card from the side of the pack. The right fingers tug on the card. As the card moves to the right the right thumb comes down on top of the card and helps pull it against the tension of the rubber band. As the card is drawn to the right, the rubber band will stretch. Release the bottom card and let it snap back square with the pack.

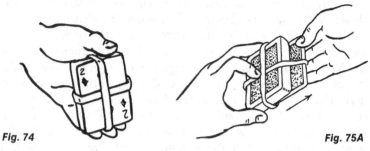

Fig. 74   **Fig. 75A**

Now grip the deck in the left hand as shown in Figure 75B. This time the right first finger takes the bottom card and pulls it forward a little over half its length. This action is shown in Figure 75B. The important point is that the lower end of this card will slip out from under the rubber band. When you allow the card to return, it will be *on top* of this band, as in an exposed view shown in Figure 76.

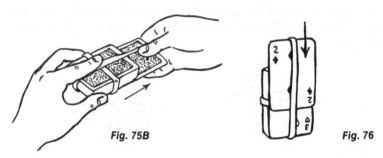

Fig. 75B   **Fig. 76**

Release this card, allowing it to snap back square with the deck. Then drop the deck face down on the table as you remove a handkerchief from your pocket. Cover the deck with the handkerchief. Then have a spectator hold the deck through the handkerchief. He holds the deck by the ends. Reach under the handkerchief, grasp the chosen card, then slide it out of the side of the deck and bring it out from under the handkerchief.

Ask for the name of the chosen card. Then turn over the card in hand to show that the signed card has somehow freed itself from the banded deck. All may be left with the spectator at this point.

THOUGHT-CARD METHODS

One of the most impressive tricks you can do with a deck of cards is to reveal a card merely thought of by the spectator. It is also one of the most difficult in a technical sense, requiring either special cards or sleight-of-hand ability. Still, there are a number of strictly self-working methods, and this chapter represents a survey of some of the best such approaches.

80 PSYCHORAMA

This ingenious trick was devised by Gene Grant and Sam Schwartz. The spectator is given a packet of five cards and is asked to think of one. By means of an elimination process the thought-of card is quickly discovered.

The five cards are chosen so that when the mentalist questions the spectator, he can expect to get not more than one "no" answer. By getting a series of "yes" answers, the mentalist makes it seem that he knows positively from the start which card was thought of.

The cards are the ♥9, ♦A, ♥K, ♣7 and ♥6. Remove them from the deck, mix them and hand them to the spectator. Turn your back and ask him to think of any one of the five cards.

When he has a card in mind, say, "A red card?" If he says no, the card is the ♣7. If he says yes, ask, "A Heart?" If he says no, the card must be the ♦A.

If he says yes, ask, "A spot card, wasn't it?" If he says no, it was the ♥K. If he says yes, ask, "Odd-valued, right?" If he says no, it was the ♥9. Otherwise it was the ♥6.

Note that as soon as you get a no answer, you positively know the thought-of card, and can name it immediately.

81   THOT-CARD MONTE

This is an offbeat method of revealing a thought-of card. The effect will vary from one performance to the next, so we shall detail the effect and method together.

Secretly place the ♠A on top of the deck, the ♠3 on the bottom and the ♠5 under your belt at the back of your trousers. Any three easily memorized cards may be used, but we will assume here that the above cards are employed in the trick.

Spread the deck face down on the table. Ask the spectator to remove the top card, a card from the middle, and the bottom card of the deck. Of course he will assume you know the top and bottom cards, but you don't know the card he takes from the middle. It can be any card.

Turn your back. Ask him to peek at one of these three cards and remember it. When he has done this, turn around and face him again. Place the ace on top of the middle card and place both of these on top of the ♠3. Remark that even if you know one or two of the cards, or even all three, you still don't know which card he chose.

Place the packet behind your back, saying that you will reverse one card. When the cards are out of sight remove the ♠5 from under the belt and place it on top of the packet. Then place the bottom card (♠3) under the belt.

Finally, turn the bottom card face up. You won't know which card this is because it came from the middle of the pack. Bring the packet into view and spread the cards to show the face-up card.

Say, "You didn't choose this card, did you?" If the spectator chose that card, the trick is over. Generally he will telegraph this fact by smiling or exclaiming when you spread the cards.

In the more likely case he will say no. Nod and say, "I thought so. And you didn't pick this card either. Turn the ♠5 face up. Of course the spectator could not have chosen this card because it was under your belt when he selected a card.

At this point the situation is as shown in Figure 77. The spectator assumes that the center card is his card but this is not necessarily true. He could have chosen the card behind your back. The ambiguity is cleared up in a subtle way.

Say, "Was your card a low spade?" If the spectator chose the ♠3 he will immediately say yes. You then name the ♠3 as his card. But if the spectator chose the ♠A, he will hesitate, because aces are

Fig. 77

considered both low and high. If you spot any hesitation, smile and say, "Aces are low." Then go on to name the ♠A as his card.

Turn all three cards face down and return them to the center of the deck.

82 HYPNODECK

In this routine the spectator can think of any card in the deck. The magician never knows the name of the card, yet he places the deck behind his back and instantly produces the thought-of card. The routine was devised by Howard Adams.

This is one of the few tricks in this book that require a full-deck setup, but the effect is worth the effort. After the pack has been made up, it can be reserved for use just on those occasions when you want to present this routine. Arrange the deck as follows: ♣A-♥A-♠A-♦A, then ♣2-♥2-♠2-♦2, then ♣3-♥3-♠3-♦3 and so on. The four cards of the same value are grouped together, and the suits always are in club-heart-spade-diamond order. The various four-card blocks are arranged in order, aces at the top of the deck, kings at the bottom.

With the pack thus arranged, have the spectator think of any card. Tell him to jot it down on a slip of paper. This insures against the possibility that he may forget the name of the card or that he might change his mind midway through the trick.

Deal the entire deck into two heaps, dealing from left to right. Turn your head away so you can't see the cards. Say to the spectator, "If your thought-of card is black, place the left-hand packet on my hand. Otherwise place the right-hand packet on my hand." By left-hand packet, you refer to the packet on *your* left. You can even point to it as you speak to make clear which packet you refer to.

After the spectator places the proper packet on your outstretched left hand, have him place the other packet on top of all. Square up the complete deck and face the spectator again.

Deal the deck into two heaps, dealing from left to right as before. Turn your head aside and say, "If your card was a club or a heart, place the left-hand packet on my hand. Otherwise place the right-hand packet on my hand."

After the spectator places the proper packet on your hand, have him place the remaining packet on top of all. Square the deck and place it face down in front of the spectator. Keep your head turned aside.

"I want you to deal on the table a number of cards equal to the value of your card. If you thought of the six of diamonds, for example, you would deal six cards."

After the spectator has dealt the proper number of cards, one at a time into a packet, have him place the dealt packet on top of the deck and hand you the deck behind your back.

"What was your card?" you ask. The spectator names his card. Immediately you produce the card from behind your back. It is done simply. If the above instructions were carried out correctly, the chosen card will be on top of the deck. Remove it and bring it into view.

83 RITUAL OF THE KINGS

Sometimes a simple but offbeat trick will be remembered long after more complex mysteries are forgotten. This is a strange effect, in which the spectator himself locates any card he himself names. Since there is a bit of ritual involved, the trick gains in dramatic effects if performed late at night in a dimly lit room.

To prepare, have 20 indifferent cards on top of the deck, then the four jacks, then the four kings, then the four queens and finally the balance of the deck.

Hand the spectator a piece of paper and a pencil. Ask him to think of any card in the deck. Then have him jot down the name of this card on the paper. Before he writes anything, explain that you are going to enact a ritual once associated with royalty and now carried out with picture cards.

When the spectator writes a card, make sure you see what it is. After he has done so, tell him to crumple the paper and drop it into a glass. Then place the deck in front of him. Tell him to cut the deck at about the center and complete the cut. Then have him place the card he cut to (the top card of the deck) face down on the table. Then have him cut the deck again and complete the cut.

Take the deck from him. Due to the stack in the center, the spectator must have cut to either a king, a queen or a jack. Spread the deck, locate your stack and find out which card he took. Most often, if he cut the deck at or near the center to pick a card, he will have chosen a king. Assume this is the case here. Say, "Remember, before we began I said I was going to enact a ritual with the kings. Let's use the four kings." Actually you spoke of "royalty" and "picture cards," but the spectators will think you did say kings.

Remove the three kings still in the deck plus the spectator's chosen card. Mix these four cards, glance at them, rearrange them a bit, then place the spectator's card second from the top of the packet.

Drop the supposed king packet on top of the card that the spectator placed on the table earlier. Place the rest of the deck aside. Then pick up the packet and hold it face down in the left hand.

Say, "Here is the ritual." Deal the top card to position 1 in Figure 78. Place the next card under the packet and deal the next card to position 2. Put the next card under the packet and deal the next card to position 3. Put the next card under the packet and deal the new top card to position 4. Place the remaining card in position 5 in the layout.

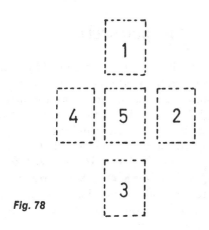

Fig. 78

Exchange cards 1 and 2, then exchange cards 3 and 4, as if it mattered to the outcome. The situation now is as shown in Figure 79. Turn up each of the cards in positions 1, 2, 3, 4, showing the four kings.

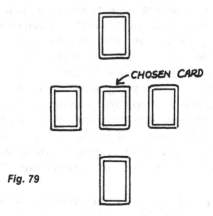

Fig. 79

Say, "Recall that you cut the deck randomly and removed a card. It could have been any card. Wouldn't it be interesting if the card you removed from the deck turned out to be the same as the card you wrote on that piece of paper?"

Pause and then turn up the card in the center of the layout. It is indeed the very card decided on by the spectator before the trick began!

84 DUO SPELL

By means of the remarkable principle proposed by Paul Swinford, each of two spectators locates a card mentally chosen by the other. It is worthwhile noting that at no time does the magician know either of the thought-of cards. In terms of thought-card methods this represents the apotheosis of clever thinking.

Begin by stacking 16 cards on top of the deck in the following order from the top down: ♥Q-♣6-♥2-♠J-♠8-♦K-♦3-♣4-♦J-♣10-♥A-♣Q-♠7-♦5-♦8-♠3. When ready to begin the routine, cut these 16 cards off the top. Place the top eight cards in front of the spectator on the right. Place the bottom eight cards in front of the spectator on the left.

Fan the left packet with the faces toward the spectator and ask him to think of a card. He can think of any card except the top or bottom card because, you explain, "This is to remove any suspicion that I might have you think of an obvious card." Close the fan and hold the packet face down in the left hand.

Follow the same procedure with the spectator on the right, using the other eight-card packet. After he has thought of a card, drop his packet on top of the other packet.

You are now going to perform an action known as a reverse faro. Beginning with the top card, jog every other card down. This means that you will downjog the first card, the third card, the fifth, the seventh, and so on. When you have done this, strip out the down-jogged cards and fan them before each spectator. Ask each person if he sees his card.

If both spectators answer the same (both say yes or both say no), put this packet *on top of* the other packet. If one spectator says yes and the other says no, place this packet *under* the other packet.

Explain that it takes two or three mental impressions before a clear mental picture emerges. Repeat the reverse faro described above. Remove the downjogged packet and show it to both specta-tors. As before, if both answer the same, put this packet on top of the other. If the spectators answer differently, put this packet under the other.

Repeat the above procedure one more time. Perform the reverse faro, then strip out the downjogged packet and show it to both persons. If they both see their card, put the packet on top of the other packet. Otherwise put it below the other packet.

You are now ready to conclude the effect. Downjog every other card, beginning with the top card. Strip out the downjogged packet and hand it to the spectator on the left. Give the remaining eight cards to the spectator on the right.

Ask each person to spell his card mentally, transferring a card for each letter from top to bottom. On the last letter, they place the card on the table. Each spectator includes the word "of" in the spelling. Thus if one spectator thought of the ♥ 2, he would spell T-W-O-O-F-H-E-A-R-T-S.

Each spectator now names his card. Turn over both of the tabled cards to show that each spectator located the *other* person's card! It is a stunning conclusion.

MIRACLES WITH ACES

In the first chapter of this book, mention was made of the importance of the opening trick in a series of card routines. Of no less importance is the closing trick. It is the last routine the audience sees and will be the one most likely to be remembered. Therefore it should be your strongest card routine.

All of the card routines in this final chapter were collected with this idea in mind. Each is suitable as a closing routine. Note that each involves the four aces because the aces impress the audience whenever they are produced or vanished. Learn the routines in this chapter and you will always finish to a round of applause.

85 FOUR-STAR ACES

Generally, the most difficult moves to perform consistently well are the second deal, the middle deal and the bottom deal. They are put to good use in this routine. The four kings are shown and dealt onto the table. On command they show up in another location. The tabled cards are turned over and prove to be the four aces.

METHOD: This fine routine was invented by Lin Searles. Secretly place the aces on top of the deck. That is the only preparation. To present the routine, run through the cards and remove the four kings. Place them in a face-up row on the table as you remove them from the deck.

Turn each king face down in place. You now have a row of four face-down kings on the table. From here on the trick proceeds at a fairly rapid pace as you say you will demonstrate middle deals and bottom deals.

Deal four cards from the top of the deck onto the leftmost king. Pick up this packet, place it on top of the deck, then deal the top card to the right, away from the king row, into a heap we'll call *A*.

Remove the top four cards of the deck without reversing their order. Place them on top of the next king. Pick up this packet and place it on top of the deck. Deal the top card off to the right on top of the first card you dealt, in heap A. The situation at this point is shown in Figure 80. There are two face-down kings left on the table. Two cards have been dealt off to the right in heap A.

Fig. 80   KINGS

Remove the top four cards of the deck without reversing their order. Drop them on top of the next tabled king. Pick up this packet and place it on top of the deck. Deal the top card of the deck onto heap A.

Finally, place the top four cards of the deck on top of the last king. Pick up this packet and drop it on top of the deck. Deal the topmost card of the deck onto heap A.

Say, "Where are the kings?" The spectators, thinking you used the bottom deal, will point to heap A. Say, "No, they're over here." Deal the top four cards of the deck into a face-up heap on the table to the left, revealing the four kings.

Point to the four cards in heap A and say, "I used the bottom deal, not for the kings but for the aces." Turn up the cards in heap A to show the aces. Done quickly, it is a routine that is both surprising and baffling.

86 ACE TRIUMPH

Some of the strongest card tricks substitute clever handling for sleight of hand. Once the handling is learned well enough for it to be performed without hesitation, the magic just seems to happen. In this routine face-up cards are mixed with face-down cards. The magician snaps his fingers and all the cards turn face down. The kicker is that four of the cards remain face up, but they are the four aces!

METHOD: Beforehand secretly reverse the four aces on the bottom of the deck. Thus the deck will be face down with the four aces face up on the bottom.

To perform the trick place the deck face down on the table. The long sides of the cards are parallel to the near edge of the table. Cut off the top half of the deck with the left hand, turn it face up and place it to the left of the other half of the deck. Then grasp both packets from above, as in Figure 81.

Fig. 81

Push both halves of the deck toward the center of the table. This will allow you enough room to cut the packets back toward you. Lift off about two-thirds of each half. Cross the hands and place the cut-off packets on the table as shown in Figure 82. The hands then cut off about half of these packets, the arms uncross, and the packets are placed on the table as shown in Figure 83. Note that face-up and face-down packets alternate in two rows on the table.

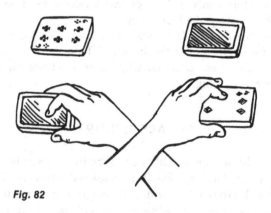

Fig. 82

Without letting go of the packets held in the hands at this point, draw them back to the near edge of the table, get the thumbs under the packets and lever them over. Place them on top of the next packets in line, as in Figure 84. The arrows in Figure 84 indicate that the packets in the hands are flipped over onto the next packets.

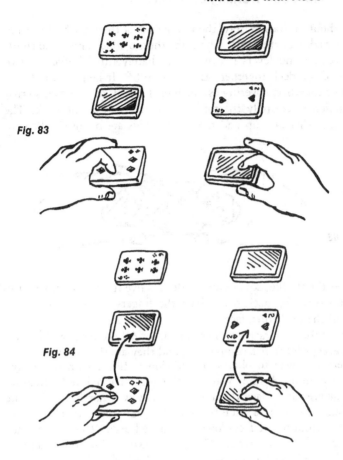

Fig. 83

Fig. 84

Slide these packets back to the near edge of the table. Get the thumbs under these packets and lever them over. Place them on top of the remaining packets, as in Figure 85. You now have just the two halves of the deck on the table. But when you do this smoothly and quickly, it appears as if face-up and face-down cards have been hopelessly mixed.

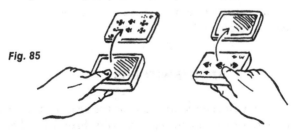

Fig. 85

Without hesitation draw the two halves of the deck back toward the near edge of the table. The right thumb slides under the right-hand packet and levers it over. Immediately riffle shuffle the two halves of the deck together, as in Figure 86. It helps if the hands are close together, covering as much of the cards as possible, so that the audience sees only the top card of each half of the deck. The illusion is that face-up and face-down cards are being shuffled together.

Fig. 86

After the shuffle, square up the deck. Give it a cut, complete the cut and turn the deck over. Snap the fingers and say, "Just like that, all the cards turn face down."

Spread the deck face down on the table. All the cards will be face down except for four face-up cards, and they are the four aces.

There is a way to obtain an additional climax with no change in the handling. Assume you are using a red-backed deck. Remove the four aces and place them aside as they will not be used. Take the four aces from a blue-backed deck and place them face up on the bottom of the face-down red-backed deck. Then on the face of a red-backed joker write, "They're marked!" Turn the joker face up and place it on the bottom of the red-backed deck.

This completes the preparation. From the top down you have the red-backed deck, then four face-up blue-backed aces, then a face-up joker on the bottom with "They're marked!" written on the face.

Perform the routine exactly as described. At the finish you will have a face-down deck with five face-up cards in the middle. Remove the joker and have the spectator read aloud the writing. Act puzzled for a moment, then turn the aces over to show that they are indeed marked, with blue ink!

87 EYEWITNESS

It is well known that the eye witnesses at the scene of a story can give conflicting testimony as to what actually happened. This is strikingly demonstrated in the following routine.

The bottom card of the deck is shown to a spectator and then dealt onto the table. This is repeated with three other spectators. When each party is asked to name his card, each names the same card. Then when the four tabled cards are turned over, none of them is the card seen by the spectators. Instead they are the four aces.

For the finish the deck is spread to show that the card they all thought they saw is reversed in the center of the pack.

METHOD: A half-card is used. As shown in Figure 87, it is half of a ♥2. Put the real ♥2 reversed in the center of the deck. Since the back of the half ♥2 is never seen, it can come from any pack. Less than a minute is needed to make up the gimmick, and the time is well spent in view of the effect that is achieved.

The half-♥2 is placed on the bottom of the deck. The four aces are placed above it. A rubber band is then snapped around the deck as shown in Figure 88.

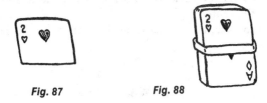

Fig. 87   **Fig. 88**

Hold the deck in the left hand so the fingers hide the ace. Display the face card to the first spectator as shown in Figure 89. Note that the fingers cover the ace that is behind the half-♥2. Lower the deck. The right fingers slide out the supposed bottom card, as in Figure 90, but instead of taking the ♥2, they take the first ace. Place this card face down on the table.

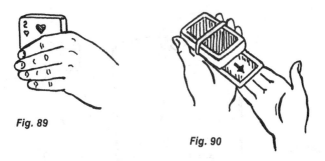

Fig. 89

Fig. 90

Put the deck behind the back, saying you are going to make a small adjustment. In fact, do nothing. Bring the deck out again and show the face card to the second spectator. He too will see the ♥2. Lower the deck, remove the bottom card (really the ace behind the half-card) and place it face down on the table. Then put the deck behind your back, saying you are going to make a small adjustment. In fact, do nothing.

Repeat the above handling with the third spectator, and repeat it again with the fourth spectator. After the fourth card has been placed face down on the table, put the deck behind the back again. Slide the half-card out from under the rubber band and quickly tuck it under the belt. Then bring the deck into view again.

Ask each person to name the card he saw on the bottom of the deck. Each will name the same card, the ♥2. It is an amusing situation because it is clear they could not possibly all have seen exactly the same card. Remove the rubber band from around the deck and spread the deck face down on the table to show the ♥2 face up in the center.

Then turn over the four cards on the table to reveal that they are the four aces.

88 WILD ACES

This is Martin Gardner's method of causing four aces to vanish from under a handkerchief and appear reversed in the center of the deck. It is one of the best tricks you can do with four aces and it requires no preparation or gimmicks.

Remove the aces from the deck and hold them in the right hand as shown in Figure 91. The left thumb and forefinger hold the deck. The other fingers grip the handkerchief as indicated in Figure 91.

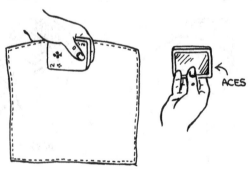

Fig. 91

The left hand remains stationary. The right hand is brought behind the handkerchief. As soon as it is hidden from the audience's view, curl the right third and fourth fingers in, bringing the aces back toward the palm, as in Figure 92.

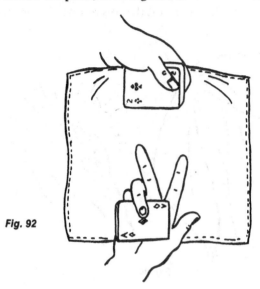

Fig. 92

The right hand moves forward under the handkerchief as if to place the aces under the cloth (see Figure 93). As the right hand moves up under the handkerchief, the aces will naturally move under the deck. It is a matter of a few minutes' practice to learn to slip the left thumb under the aces and add them onto the deck. The sequence should be smooth and rapid. It should look as if you merely placed the aces under the handkerchief.

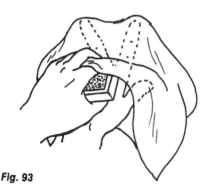

Fig. 93

Place the deck (with the aces on the bottom) face down on the table. Cut the deck and complete the cut. Announce that you will cause the aces to vanish. Snap the handkerchief away, as in Figure 94, to show that the aces are gone. Show the right hand on both sides. Then spread the deck to reveal the aces reversed in the center.

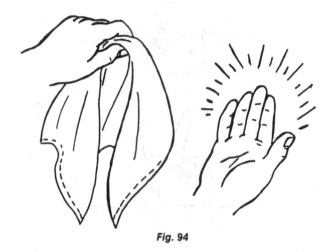

Fig. 94